THE BUSINESS OF BENEVOLENCE

THE BUSINESS
OF BENEVOLENCE

Industrial Paternalism in Progressive America

ANDREA TONE

CORNELL UNIVERSITY PRESS ITHACA AND LONDON

First published 1997 by Cornell University Press.

Printed in the United States of America.

Cornell University Press strives to utilize environmentally responsible suppliers and
materials to the fullest extent possible in the publishing of its books. Such materials
include vegetable-based, low-VOC inks and acid-free papers that are also either
recycled, totally chlorine-free, or partly composed of nonwood fibers.

Library in Congress Cataloging-in-Publication Data

Tone, Andrea, 1964–
The business of benevolence : industrial paternalism in
progressive America / Andrea Tone.
        p.   cm.
Includes index.
ISBN 0-8014-3028-3 (alk. paper)
1. Industrial welfare—United States—History—20th century.
I. Title.
HD7654.T66   1997
361.973—DC21   97-16814

Cloth printing   10 9 8 7 6 5 4 3 2 1

TO MY FAMILY, WITH LOVE

Contents

Preface

I was born in Massachusetts, grew up in British Columbia, spent my college years in Ontario, and completed graduate work in Georgia. For family, for school, and for love, I have spent most of my life straddling two countries and two cultures. To a degree, this book grew out of my experience of national differences and my interest in divining the origins of one of the most recognizable: the comparative absence of government provisions for workers and citizens in the United States.

One of the virtues of comparative history is that, by drawing attention to alternative paths taken, it reminds us that things might have turned out differently. Studying United States history with the Canadian model as a point of departure, I became wary of interpretations that seek to explain differences—be they local, regional, or national—as the natural outcome of a destiny-driven past. By this rendering, the present is as it is simply because it could not have been otherwise. One of the arguments of this book is that the highly privatized American welfare system, in which employers finance and control the distribution of provisions that workers in other countries (including Canada) receive from the public sector, was not foreordained by a mythic American "character." Rather, it must be understood as a historical creation that has been politically, economically, and socially constructed and maintained. In this book I focus on the Progressive period, an era of particular political fluidity, when hundreds of individuals and groups demanded changes in the way the social welfare landscape was configured. One of my objectives is to illuminate why, in the end, an only marginally modified status quo prevailed.

Eschewing explanations of historical inevitability enables us to take seriously human agency, the power of individuals to modify their environment. To acknowledge agency, however, is not to say that everyone has been given an equal voice in historical outcomes. The fiction of perfect pluralism—what we get fairly reflects our diverse, often competing interests—denies the reality of inequalities in power that have worked to silence and immobilize the wishes of many people; so-called consensus views are frequently forged by those best positioned to articulate and defend them. In the realm of labor, historians have exposed the weaknesses of the pluralist model by drawing attention to the power of state-sanctioned violence to curb and contain workers' resistance. This book extends this critique by looking at how, ironically, business benevolence toward workers in the Progressive period, as expressed in the welfare work movement, served similarly conservative ends.

When I began my research, I envisioned this project as a social history of business, part of the new institutionalist labor history that recognizes the importance of both the vitality of worker culture and the structural constraints that affect workers' lives. My research soon pushed me in new directions, compelling me to recognize the interconnectedness of the workplace, politics, and the law, and to acknowledge that each of these constructs, in important ways, was gendered. Taking my cue from those who have called for a return to historical synthesis, I have tried to weave together labor, gender, business, social, and legal history, elucidating the political meanings of the integrated narrative we end up with when we do.

The historiographical orientation of this book has profited immeasurably from historians' studies of women, gender, and the state. Acknowledging that political history includes but goes beyond electoral politics, I have analyzed the ways in which such things as the provision of pensions, the way workers are photographed, and the treatment of female wage earners on the baseball field were politicized. Seemingly apolitical incidents such as a male employee's refusal to drink a cup of coffee "freely provided" to him by his employer and a group of female store clerks' use of a company-sponsored noon-hour dance as an "opportunity" to dance their way through the afternoon shift reveal how issues of authority, dependency, and control—issues of power—were asserted and contested in various domains. In the same spirit, I have looked at how gender—the construction of masculine and feminine identities—shaped "high" politics. When businessmen in the Progressive era condemned social provisions sponsored by the government as enervating and unmanly, they invoked masculine appeals to support the desirability of a private sector welfare system. The inseparability of public and private, gender and politics, the workplace and the legislature, provides the theoretical framework within which I analyze the dynamics of labor reform at the turn of the century.

My vast intellectual debts will be obvious on every page; my personal debts, no less profound, are more easily specified. Grants from Emory University's Department of History and the Graduate School of Arts and Sciences, Queen's University, Simon Fraser University, the Hagley Museum and Library in Wilmington, Delaware, and the Rockefeller Archive Center in North Tarrytown, New York, enabled me to complete research for this book. Along the way, archivists and librarians at the Baker and Littauer libraries at Harvard University, the State Historical Society of Wisconsin, the Hagley Museum and Library, the Rockefeller Archives, the New York Public Library, Wright State University, Yale University, Cornell University, Georgia Institute of Technology, and especially Emory University graciously assisted me, sharing in my excitement and fueling it further.

When I was an undergraduate at Queen's University, the late George Rawlyk first taught me the joy and value of studying history; for saving me from the clutches of law school, I owe him a special debt. For their support at Emory, I thank Dan Carter, Dan Costello, Andy Doyle, Margot Finn, Michelle Kilbourne, James Melton, Mary Odem, Jim Roark, John Rodrigue, Ed Shoemaker, Susan Socolow, Steve White, Jeff Young, and especially Sharon Strocchia.

As I researched and wrote this book, I benefited greatly from the insights of Mary Odem, Alex Keyssar, Michael Bellesiles, and Jonathan Prude, each of whom enriched my understanding of social and industrial history. Michael Bellesiles's inexhaustible energy and intellectual vitality were an inspiration; he has always been there for me, and he has not only my sincere thanks but also my profound respect and deepest admiration. My greatest academic debt is to Jonathan Prude, whose critical acumen, wisdom, and friendship I cherish.

At Simon Fraser University, Candace Dias, Hannah Gay, Mary Lynn Stewart, and especially Joy Parr gave welcomed support; Dennis Pilon and students in my Progressive era classes challenged me to rethink assumptions; Mark Leier provided stimulating conversations on comparative labor history and free IWW office concerts; and Michael Fellman, always the iconoclast, offered his playfully combative spirit and shared fascination with the American past.

At Georgia Tech, Greg Nobles, Jon Schneer, and Steven Vallas have been the best of colleagues; Joan Sokolovsky, who has stood by me through thick and thin, has been a great friend. For past and present support I am also grateful to Jack Brown, Kate Dornhuber, Robyn Fivush, Mary Frank Fox, Gus Giebelhaus, Paul Gilmore, Haven Hawley, Karen Hegtvedt, Bob McMath, Barbara Patterson, Sandra Thornton, and Steve Usselman.

Portions of this book were presented to the Atlanta Roundtable in the Comparative History of Labor, Industrialization, Technology, and Society, and to the Hagley Museum and Library. I have profited from the helpful suggestions I received on each of these occasions. Carl Becker of Wright State University kindly offered his own findings on the National Cash Register Company, material that proved critical to this investigation. At Cornell University Press, Peter Agree has been a perfect editor: enthusiastic, supportive, and fully committed to this project from beginning to end; Barbara H. Salazar and Trudie Calvert's attention to detail ironed out inconsistencies. Careful review and detailed suggestions by three anonymous readers supplied an invaluable road map for revisions; my deepest thanks to all of them for helping to make this a better book. Thanks, too, to Alan Dawley for last-minute comments on several chapters.

My husband, John, a historian of modern Spain, read this book from cover to cover, offering encouragement, love, humor, and a shared passion to get the story right.

Finally, my family, in all its configurations, has given me faith, love, and understanding. This book is dedicated to them.

ANDREA TONE

Atlanta, Georgia

THE BUSINESS OF BENEVOLENCE

Introduction

Industrial paternalism has enjoyed a long reign in American history. From the Sunday schools of early New England mill towns to the benefit packages of present-day corporate America, employers have consciously and consistently supplemented pecuniary remuneration with "something beyond wages." Industrial capitalism, predicated on the use of workers for profit, seems inimical to sympathetic relations between employer and employed. Yet despite the oppositional relationship embedded in capitalism, employers have been compelled to treat workers as more than disposable commodities. Employers, confronted with economic and political variables that render the notion of a perfect market meaningless and aware that wage earners sell their potential and not a finished product, have sought to maximize productivity, eradicate labor unrest, and curry public approval by furnishing special provisions to workers. In theory, the cash nexus has constituted the cornerstone of capitalist relations. In practice, remunerating labor has often entailed more.

While capitalism and paternalism have matured in tandem, significantly, not all manifestations of industrial paternalism have been alike. Anchored in the reality of employer provision and the expectation of employee deference, guided by a familial metaphor accentuating reciprocity, mutuality, and obligation, industrial paternalism, notwithstand-

1

ing its distinguishing features, has assumed multiple guises. As its form and expanse have varied by time and place, so, too, has its agenda. As Philip Scranton and Steven Vallas have argued, historical precision requires that we contextualize paternalism, identifying the specific settings and meanings that have bounded its existence. What follows is an exploration of one chapter of paternalism's variegated past.[1]

This book examines the origins, development, and legacy of American welfare work. In keeping with the premise that not all paternalisms are alike, its temporal boundaries are specific. Welfare work, known since the 1930s as welfare capitalism, is discussed here as an outgrowth of the Progressive period, the years from 1900 to 1920, whose practice, in turn, established the foundation for modern personnel management. Reformers coined the term "welfare work" in the early 1900s to denote a movement to promote nonlegislative workplace reforms in factories, stores, and shops across the country. In an era characterized by unprecedented industrial strife and violence, welfare work seemed to herald the advance of a new age in labor relations, one that would be guided by the gentle hand of management rather than the big stick. For employers who established it and for the hundreds of thousands of working men and women who experienced it, welfare work took many forms, ranging from company-sponsored leisure activities such as gun clubs and cricket creases to more pecuniary benefits such as profit sharing and pensions. Not every company made welfare benefits an integral part of its labor management, but many did. By World War I, at least 2,500 of the largest firms in the United States had crafted labor policies based on ostensible beneficence.[2]

In past decades, the purpose and significance of these disparate programs have evoked lively debate. Historians have disagreed chiefly about employers' motives and workers' responses. Irving Bernstein's *Lean Years* (1960), a pioneering history of American labor in the 1920s

1. Philip Scranton, "Varieties of Paternalism: Industrial Structures and the Social Relations of Production in American Textiles," *American Quarterly* 36 (Summer 1984): 235–57; Steven Peter Vallas, "Paternalism and Modern Industry: Factory Regimes at Ford and Bell," paper presented at the annual meeting of the American Sociological Association, Cincinnati, August 1991; and Vallas, *Power in the Workplace: The Politics of Production at AT&T* (Albany: SUNY Press, 1993).

2. U.S. Bureau of Labor Statistics, *Welfare Work for Employees in Industrial Establishments in the United States,* Bulletin 250 (Washington, D.C.: Government Printing Office, 1919), pp. 3–8; Arthur J. Todd, "The Organization and Promotion of Industrial Welfare through Voluntary Efforts," *Annals of the American Academy of Political and Social Science* 105 (January 1923): 77; Sanford Jacoby, *Employing Bureaucracy: Managers, Unions, and the Transformation of Work in American Industry, 1900–1945* (New York: Columbia University Press, 1985), p. 54.

and 1930s, offered the first serious treatment of welfare capitalism. For Bernstein, the motives behind welfare work were crudely transparent: employers adopted eleemosynary measures to forestall or eliminate unionization. Setting aside their guns, employers strove to crush labor through kindness. For Bernstein and the many historians who have echoed his refrain, welfare work was simply a "padded glove over an iron fist"; violence and benevolence were merely different sides of the same capitalist coin.[3]

This argument explains the motives of some employers but leaves certain issues unresolved. It cannot, for instance, explain why many welfare employers accepted unionism in principle and in practice. Nor does it account for the fierce political animosity and ideological chasm separating welfare leaders and anti-union, anti–welfare work organizations such as the National Association of Manufacturers. The thesis that welfare work was an anti-union ploy also fails to explain why women workers, who as a group were the least likely and least able to unionize or strike, were the primary targets of welfare programs.[4]

3. Irving Bernstein, *The Lean Years: A History of the American Worker* (Boston: Houghton Mifflin, 1960), pp. 145–89. The quotation is from Lizabeth Cohen's otherwise carefully nuanced characterization of welfare work in *Making a New Deal: Industrial Workers in Chicago, 1919–1939* (New York: Cambridge University Press, 1990), p. 160. Similar interpretations of the employer's vision include Robert Ozanne, *A Century of Labor-Management Relations at McCormick and International Harvester* (Madison: University of Wisconsin Press, 1967); Milton Derber, *The American Idea of Industrial Democracy* (Urbana: University of Illinois Press, 1970); Alice Kessler-Harris, *Out to Work: A History of Wage-Earning Women in the United States* (New York: Oxford University Press, 1982).

4. Comparatively lower unionization rates for wage-earning women are not, of course, evidence of the absence of female radicalism. For a discussion of social, ideological, and institutional obstacles hampering female unionization, see Alice Kessler-Harris, "Where Are the Organized Women Workers?" *Feminist Studies* 3 (Fall 1975) : 92–110; Sharon Hartman Strom, "Challenging 'Woman's Place': Feminism, the Left, and Industrial Unionism in the 1930s," *Feminist Studies* 9 (Summer 1983) : 359–86; Martha May, "Bread before Roses: American Workingmen, Labor Unions, and the Family Wage," in *Women, Work, and Protest: A Century of U.S. Women's Labor History*, ed. Ruth Milkman (Boston: Routledge & Kegan Paul, 1985), pp. 1–21; Patricia A. Cooper, *Once a Cigar Maker: Men, Women, and Work Culture in American Cigar Factories, 1900–1919* (Urbana: University of Illinois Press, 1987); Susan Levine, *Labor's True Woman: Carpet Weavers, Industrialization, and Labor Reform in the Gilded Age* (Philadelphia: Temple University Press, 1984).

In opposition to historians who have cast welfare work as an anti-union ploy, others, particularly business revisionists, have displayed greater faith in the American employer, describing welfare capitalism as a sincere attempt to humanize industry. Employers invested profits in workplace reforms because such actions were ethical, not only because they expected something from labor in return. This interpretation also has serious limitations. It does not explain why thousands of businessmen became sentimental at once, or why employers such as John D. Rockefeller Jr. supported policies of armed surveillance and welfare work concurrently. Nor does it account for those businessmen who candidly admitted that welfare work was primarily a paying investment. This perspective is perhaps

More recent studies of American welfare capitalism, including those by Stephen Meyer, Gerald Zahavi, and Lizabeth Cohen, have revised and expanded Bernstein's formulation. These studies reflect renewed interest in the means by which power is exercised in the workplace. Rejecting Harry Braverman's thesis that the technological features of monopoly capitalism degraded and disempowered workers, they have explored more subtle and covert systems of labor domination. At the same time, they have illuminated the ways in which workers manipulated oppressive circumstances to their own, albeit limited, advantage.[5]

Labor historians, the chief architects of this burgeoning scholarship, have tended to agree that welfare capitalism was a form of labor control that permitted modification by workers. Equating welfare capitalism with labor control, they have defined "control" broadly, subsuming many employers' ambitions—for labor efficiency, social and moral uplift, the prevention and dispersion of labor radicalism, to name a few—under a single banner. A strikingly consistent representation has emerged from this scholarship: whether viewed as an unfruitful attempt to destroy workers' ethnic subcultures or as a potent anti-union stratagem whose triumphant sweep was halted only by the Great Depression, welfare capitalism was a business response to a labor "problem," its

---

best articulated in Allan Nevins and Frank Ernest Hill, *Ford: Expansion and Challenge, 1914–1933* (New York: Scribner's, 1957).

5. Contributions to the literature on welfare capitalism include Gerald Zahavi, *Workers, Managers, and Welfare Capitalism: The Shoeworkers and Tanners of Endicott Johnson, 1890–1950* (Urbana: University of Illinois Press, 1988); Stephen Meyer III, *The Five Dollar Day: Labor Management and Social Control in the Ford Motor Company, 1908–21* (Albany: SUNY Press, 1981); and Rick Halpern, "The Iron Fist and the Velvet Glove: Welfare Capitalism in Chicago's Packinghouses, 1921–1933," *Journal of American Studies* 26 (August 1992): 159–83, which looks at the coexistence of coercive and cooperative styles of labor management in Chicago packinghouses. Other studies that examine welfare capitalism more peripherally but employ a similar approach are Stanley Buder, *Pullman: An Experiment in Industrial Order and Community Planning, 1880–1930* (New York: Oxford University Press, 1967); Tamara Hareven, *Family Time and Industrial Time: The Relationship between the Family and Work in a New England Industrial Community* (New York: Cambridge University Press, 1982); Francis G. Couvares, *The Remaking of Pittsburgh: Class and Culture in an Industrializing City, 1877–1919* (Albany: SUNY Press, 1984); and Cohen, *Making a New Deal.* In his provocative reinterpretation of the origins of the New Deal, Colin Gordon looks at the relationship between welfare capitalism in the 1920s and welfare statism in the 1930s, arguing that federal social security legislation stemmed, in part, from business's desire to "even out the competitive disparities" created by welfare capitalism. See Gordon, *New Deals: Business, Labor, and Politics in America, 1920–1935* (New York: Cambridge University Press, 1994).

See also Harry Braverman, *Labor and Monopoly Capital: The Degradation of Work in the Twentieth Century* (New York: Monthly Review Press, 1974); Richard C. Edwards, *Contested Terrain: The Transformation of the Workplace in the Twentieth Century* (New York: Basic Books, 1979); and Michael Burawoy, *Manufacturing Consent: Changes in the Labor Process under Monopoly Capitalism* (Chicago: University of Chicago Press, 1979).

history the rise and demise of yet another form of subjugation of labor in America's past.[6]

Ironically, the labor control model, employed in some of the most exciting studies to emerge from the so-called new labor history, has limited the ways in which we have understood welfare work. Its inclusivity has encouraged historians to draw parallels between welfare capitalism and earlier instances of labor subjugation that ignore important chronological distinctions in the organization of work and labor relations. Applied to conjoin a wide array of employment activities practiced in the last two hundred years, welfare capitalism has become a remarkably protean concept in the historian's lexicon, indistinguishable from, rather than a variant of, paternalism itself. The universalization of welfare capitalism has prompted its decontextualization. If welfare capitalism has been a ubiquitous feature of American industry, the political, social, and economic settings in which employers and laborers have made decisions ultimately have had little bearing on decisions made.

The methodology of recent research has reinforced this perspective. Since the publication of Stuart Brandes's pioneering *American Welfare Capitalism* in 1976, a comprehensive cataloging of welfare benefits that studiously eschews the historiographical quagmire, no national study of welfare capitalism has been published. Rather, welfare work has been examined by labor historians as a feature of the history of individual companies or industries or as a catalyst of class consciousness in a single

---

6. Accepting and working within the labor control model, these historians have often disagreed about other characteristics of welfare capitalism, particularly the nature of labor's responses and the meaning and timing of the movement's decline. See, for instance, David Brody, "The Rise and Decline of Welfare Capitalism," in *Change and Continuity in Twentieth-Century America: The 1920s,* ed. John Braeman et al. (Columbus: Ohio State University Press, 1968), pp. 147–78. Brody argues that welfare capitalism endured in the 1920s because of employees' acceptance, the "evident satisfaction of the American workingman with the status quo." Others, notably Stuart D. Brandes, have noted workers' disapproval throughout the 1920s, including the growing incidence of strikes at welfare firms. See Brandes, *American Welfare Capitalism, 1880–1940* (Chicago: University of Chicago Press, 1976), pp. 135–37. Brody and Brandes agree, however, that the Depression terminated welfare capitalism. Other historians have emphasized an earlier decline, noting the subsumption of welfare activities under personnel management in the 1920s. See Daniel Nelson, *Managers and Workers: Origins of the New Factory System in the United States, 1880–1920* (Madison: University of Wisconsin Press, 1975), pp. 153–62, and " 'A Newly Appreciated Art': The Development of Personnel Work at Leeds & Northrup, 1915–1923," *Business History Review* 44 (Winter 1970): 520; and Jacoby, *Employing Bureaucracy,* pp. 3–6. More recently, Howard Gitelman has discussed the futility of a "rise and demise" framework, arguing that welfare capitalism has been a constant feature of American capitalism: "Welfare Capitalism Reconsidered," *Labor History* 33 (Winter 1992).

city. These studies have enriched our understanding of how welfare work functioned at a microscopic level, but they have left its history incomplete. Exploring welfare work under a specialized rubric, mapping its course within narrow geographic parameters, this scholarship has highlighted the movement's industrial component while discounting the larger social and political issues it forcefully and simultaneously engaged.[7]

In this book I seek to expand the theoretical and geographical boundaries within which welfare work has most frequently been examined. While retaining a focus on labor and business, I am equally attentive to Progressive politics, gender dynamics, and social reform. I examine welfare work not simply as it flourished in a single town, company, or industry, but as a national movement—the goals and experiences of employees, welfare workers, and employers that transcended the peculiarities of place. At one level, welfare work did represent employers' inveterate attempt to subordinate labor. At the same time, the spread of private welfare provisions signaled a larger national debate among labor, capital, and the state at the turn of the century. At stake was not only the issue of how capital could best control labor, but the obligations of the state to its citizens, the gendered meanings of welfare and reform, and the rights and autonomy of wage earners themselves.

While extending the analytical scope of previous investigations of welfare work, I simultaneously attempt to tighten their chronological moorings. That welfare capitalism can properly be viewed as belonging to a long history of industrial paternalisms should not blind us to the meanings associated with its particular formulation. Welfare work is discussed here as a moment and a movement in its own right, a distinct juncture in the evolution of labor management in the United States. Employers used welfare work to reorganize long-standing patterns of labor control to meet political and social exigencies of the day; recast-

7. Brandes, *American Welfare Capitalism;* Zahavi, *Workers, Managers, and Welfare Capitalism;* Meyer, *Five Dollar Day;* and Ronald W. Schatz, *The Electrical Workers: A History of Labor at General Electric and Westinghouse, 1923–60* (Urbana: University of Illinois Press, 1983), study welfare capitalism in individual firms. Susan Porter Benson, *Counter Cultures: Saleswomen, Managers, and Customers in American Department Stores, 1890–1940* (Urbana: University of Illinois Press, 1986); Jacquelyn Dowd Hall et al., *Like a Family: The Making of a Southern Cotton Mill World* (Chapel Hill: University of North Carolina Press, 1987); and Angel Kwolek-Folland, *Engendering Business: Men and Women in the Corporate Office, 1870–1930* (Baltimore: Johns Hopkins University Press, 1994), examine its development in specific industries. Lizabeth Cohen has assessed the significance of welfare work to industrial workers in Chicago in the interwar era in *Making a New Deal,* as has Rick Halpern in "Iron Fist and the Velvet Glove."

ing older traditions, they created a style of labor management that was recognizably new. What distinguished welfare work from other forms of business benevolence and made it chronologically inseparable from Progressivism was its scope, substance, and ambitious political agenda. I explore the chronological distinctiveness of welfare capitalism through an examination of three interconnected themes: the antistatist politics of welfare work; the gendering of workplace reforms; and the responses of labor, both organized and rank and file. I conclude with an analysis of how the triumph of the private sector model in the Progressive era worked to stymie the growth of the welfare state in subsequent decades.

Subtle but omnipresent, politics is central to the welfare work story. Employers watched closely the steady advance of the welfare state at the turn of the century. The Progressive era witnessed an expanded role for all levels of government as political authority was increasingly enlisted to regulate the social and economic order. In a period of labor history whose signature was discontent—evidenced in increased unionization, strikes, work stoppages, sabotage, and soldiering—the workplace became a priority for reform. Without abandoning its practice of forcibly suppressing labor unrest, government began to search for ways to prevent its fruition. The establishment of government commissions to unmask the source of workers' frustrations suggested an acceptance of what only half a century earlier would have been unthinkable to most Americans: the possibility that business bore direct responsibility for industrial discord. As commission findings were parlayed into legislation, the view that laborers needed and deserved state protection was institutionalized. The number and scope of laws mandating workers' compensation, maximum work hours, and restrictions on night work for women increased during the Progressive era, collectively circumscribing employers' authority.

Employers eager to check and repel the tide of government regulation proffered welfare capitalism as an alternative to welfare statism. Intending to persuade critics that the employment relationship could be moral as well as contractual, businessmen publicized their benevolence, making speeches, circulating pamphlets, even opening factory doors so that the world could witness "happy workers" at work and play. They extolled the efficiency of private benefits, repudiated the need for public provisions, and launched an effective offensive against widening government management of industrial affairs. Benefiting from the reform label they so proudly sported, welfare employers nevertheless distinguished themselves from other "labor" reformers by insisting that improvements in working conditions be made voluntarily rather than in compliance with law.

I seek to add a new tier to our understanding of the politics of Progressivism by examining the antistatist impulse of business benevolence. Characterizations of Progressive reform have varied, ranging from the consensus historian Richard Hofstadter's "status anxiety" thesis to Robert Wiebe's emphasis on the bureaucratic and professional underpinnings of reform to Gabriel Kolko's analysis of the "triumph of conservatism" through business-initiated regulation. Historians have disagreed on fundamental points, including who the reformers were, the ideologies to which they subscribed, and the short-and long-term impact of regulations that were enacted. In this book I focus on the labor reforms of the business elite and what their response to the "labor question" reveals about their social and political views. Disaggregating the term "Progressive regulation" so as to identify its constituent parts and proponents, I argue that although businessmen may have been divided in their support of acts establishing the Federal Trade Commission, the Federal Reserve System, and more comprehensive meat inspection, they stood united, almost without exception, in their animosity toward social welfare and labor legislation. But the character of business opposition varied. While independent industrialists in small and medium-sized establishments often endorsed the National Association of Manufacturers' antilabor extremism, big business was able to express its antipathy to state-sponsored social provisions through the extension and promotion of private provisions. Working to achieve their own "triumph of conservatism," employers used voluntary reforms to thwart the enactment of more stringent provisions.[8]

8. Richard Hofstadter disputes the existence of a humanitarian-based reform tradition in *The Age of Reform: From Bryan to F.D.R.* (New York: Random House, 1955). Robert Wiebe's argument is best developed in *The Search for Order, 1877–1920* (New York: Hill & Wang, 1967), Gabriel Kolko's in *The Triumph of Conservatism: A Reinterpretation of American History, 1900–1916* (New York: Free Press, 1963).

For modified support of Wiebe's organizational modernization thesis, see Samuel P. Hays, *The Response to Industrialism, 1885–1914* (Chicago: University of Chicago Press, 1957); John F. McClymer, *War and Welfare: Social Engineering in America, 1890–1925* (Westport, Conn.: Greenwood Press, 1980); Alfred D. Chandler Jr., *Strategy and Structure: Chapters in the History of American Industrial Enterprise* (Cambridge: MIT Press, 1969) and *The Visible Hand: The Managerial Revolution in American Business* (Cambridge.: Harvard University Press, 1977); Richard M. Abrams, *The Burdens of Progress, 1900–1929* (Glenview, Ill.: Scott, Foresman, 1978); Louis Galambos, "The Emerging Organizational Synthesis in Modern American History," *Business History Review* 44 (1970): 279–90, and "Technology, Political Economy, and Professionalization: Central Themes of the Organizational Synthesis," *Business History Review* 57 (1983): 471–93.

For corporate liberalism arguments more closely aligned with those of Kolko, see Hace

Welfare capitalist ideologues often worked behind the scenes to influence the outcome of specific legislative battles on such protections as workers' compensation and sickness insurance. My emphasis here, however, is less on those battles than on the ways in which employers created a public culture that lent support to their antistatist views. This focus has resulted in an in-depth analysis of corporate publicity and the political meanings embedded, for instance, in company advertising, visual appeals, and gendered rhetoric. My objective throughout is not to discount the importance of electoral and legislative politics, but rather to color in more fully the political picture by investigating the myriad ways—from photographs to linguistic metaphors—institutional power is established and preserved.

Integrally yoked with the politics of welfare capitalism and welfare statism were issues of gender. Theda Skocpol, Kathryn Kish Sklar, Robyn Muncy, Linda Gordon, Gwendolyn Mink, and Sonya Michel have identified the importance of gender to reform politics and social welfare in Progressive America. Reformers emphasized a "natural" link between women's maternal experience and political reform to endow domestic roles with a public objective. Affirming an ideology of gender difference that stressed women's ability to influence and uplift through moral suasion, female reformers insisted that women be given a greater political role in cleaning up the dislocations wrought by America's transition to an urban industrial order. Through the politicization of traditional female roles, women would become, as Jane Addams put it, the "housekeepers of the nation."[9]

Sorel Tishler, *Self-Reliance and Social Security, 1870–1917* (Port Washington, N.Y.: Kennikat Press, 1971); Martin J. Sklar, *The Corporate Reconstruction of American Capitalism, 1890–1916* (New York: Cambridge University Press, 1988), which argues for cross-class support of corporate liberalism; Roy Lubove, *The Struggle for Social Security, 1900–1935* (Cambridge: Harvard University Press, 1968); and James Weinstein, *The Corporate Ideal in the Liberal State, 1900–1918* (Boston: Beacon Press, 1968). Though sympathetic to Weinstein's characterization of what Progressivism preserved—corporate power—I disagree with his larger argument that the business elite sought to contain political radicalism through the passage of social legislation. His political characterization is also disputed by Hace Tishler in *Self-Reliance and Social Security*.

For a useful introduction to literature on Progressivism, see Daniel T. Rodgers, "In Search of Progressivism," *Reviews in American History* 10 (December 1982): 113–32; and Joseph F. Tripp, "Law and Social Control: Historians' Views of Progressive Era Labor Legislation," *Labor History* 28 (Fall 1987): 447–83.

9. On women, maternalist politics, and the creation of the welfare state, see Theda Skocpol, *Protecting Soldiers and Mothers: The Political Origins of Social Policy in the United States* (Cambridge: Harvard University Press, 1992); Kathryn Kish Sklar, "Explaining the Power of Women's Political Culture in the Creation of the American Welfare State, 1890–1930," and Sonya Michel, "The Limits of Maternalism: Policies toward American Wage-Earning

Maternalism, legitimating women's expanded political activism, was also encoded in state policy. Paradoxically, the growing number of middle-class women who demanded the right to reform also spearheaded a successful campaign to pass state statutes that reinforced the conventional family ideal of an independent male breadwinner in the marketplace and a dependent female homemaker in the home. Mothers' pensions, provided by thirty-nine states by 1919, paid single mothers to stay out of the waged workplace and in the home. The Sheppard-Towner Infancy and Maternity Protection Act of 1921 also made maternalism a matter of public policy by establishing a network of federally subsidized health clinics offering pre-and postnatal care.

The gendered web of these provisions, woven by the coupling of state provisions with women's implied need for guardianship, was reinforced by judicial review. Court decisions on freedom of contract in the Progressive era designated women as freely contracting individuals only when wage work did not interfere with their "primary" maternal roles. In contrast, courts upheld men's contractual rights as economic individuals and family providers. Linking masculinity to autonomous breadwinning, judicial rulings ensured that the connection between men and state welfare, already culturally strained, would be harder to forge institutionally as well.[10]

As Eileen Boris has noted, a flood of work on welfare and Progressive reform, while identifying the gendered dimensions of state welfare programs, has largely obscured the gendering of policies affecting workers'

Mothers during the Progressive Era," both in *Mothers of a New World: Maternalist Politics and the Origins of Welfare States*, ed. Seth Koven and Sonya Michel (New York: Routledge, 1993); Kathryn Kish Sklar, *Florence Kelley and the Nation's Work: The Rise of Women's Political Culture, 1830–1900* (New Haven: Yale University Press, 1995); Robyn Muncy, *Creating a Female Dominion in American Reform, 1890–1935* (New York: Oxford University Press, 1991); Paula Baker, "The Domestication of Politics: Women and American Political Society, 1780–1920," *American Historical Review* 89 (June 1984); Linda Gordon, ed., *Women, the State, and Welfare* (Madison: University of Wisconsin Press, 1990), Introduction. Also see Gwendolyn Mink, "The Lady and the Tramp: Gender, Race, and the Origins of the American Welfare State," in the same volume; Linda Gordon, *Pitied but Not Entitled: Single Mothers and the History of Welfare, 1890–1935* (New York: Free Press, 1994); Mimi Abramovitz, *Regulating the Lives of Women: Social Welfare Policy from Colonial Times to the Present* (Boston: South End Press, 1988).

The quotation is from Jane Addams, "Why Women Should Vote," *Ladies' Home Journal,* January 1910, pp. 21–22.

10. Alice Kessler-Harris, "Law and a Living: The Gendered Content of 'Free Labor,'" and Eileen Boris, "Reconstructing the 'Family': Women, Progressive Reform, and the Problem of Social Control," both in *Gender, Class, Race, and Reform in the Progressive Era,* ed. Noralee Frankel and Nancy S. Dye (Lexington: University Press of Kentucky, 1991); Abramovitz, *Regulating the Lives of Women,* p. 2.

everyday experiences on the job. It is almost as if in "bringing the state back in," we have downplayed the impact welfarist politics had on the relationship between employers and laborers, discounting how the same conceptions of gender and welfare that shaped government policy simultaneously structured the workplace. I hope to bridge this gap by showing how Progressive era debates over welfare, manhood, and womanhood shaped the fabric of private sector welfare provisions in ways that profoundly affected the lives of working men and women.[11]

Although gender has been central to histories of British and Canadian welfare capitalism, its significance to the American experience has traditionally been overlooked. Expounding on its economic inequalities, historians of welfare capitalism have paid considerably less attention to how its gender hierarchies simultaneously shaped the workplace. Yet, the spirited public debate on the dangers of wage work on women's maternal health, combined with the predisposition to view welfare in gendered, specifically feminized terms, ensured that the majority of private welfare benefits founded in the Progressive period were established for women. The widespread entrance of women into the external, paid labor force at the turn of the century amplified concerns that women's femininity was being sacrificed on the altar of "masculine" industrial capitalism, giving broader pleas for state regulation for women a pointed urgency. Welfare capitalists presented an alternate version of working women's femininity, one that exalted the social value of industrial labor. According to employers, the workplace could

---

11. Eileen Boris, "What about the Working of the Working Mother?" *Journal of Women's History* 5 (Fall 1993): 104. Two important exceptions are Kwolek-Folland, *Engendering Business*, and Sharon Hartman Strom, *Beyond the Typewriter: Gender, Class, and the Origins of Modern American Office Work, 1900–1930* (Urbana: University of Illinois Press, 1992). My point is that labor historians have discounted the degree to which the maternalist politics that gave rise to a gendered welfare state simultaneously encouraged the development of gendered workplace policies, not that they have ignored the importance of gender. Indeed, the inclusion of gender has generated an exciting body of literature on labor history in the last decade. See, for example, Kathy Peiss, *Cheap Amusements: Working Women and Leisure in Turn-of-the-Century New York* (Philadelphia: Temple University Press, 1986); Christine Stansell, *City of Women: Sex and Class in New York City, 1789–1860* (New York: Knopf, 1987); Cooper, *Once a Cigar Maker*; Alice Kessler-Harris, *A Woman's Wage: Historical Meanings and Social Consequences* (Lexington: University Press of Kentucky Press, 1990); Ava Baron, ed., *Work Engendered: Toward a New History of American Labor* (Ithaca: Cornell University Press, 1991); Mary H. Blewett, *Men, Women, and Work: Class, Gender, and Protest in the New England Shoe Industry, 1780–1910* (Urbana: University of Illinois Press, 1988); Elizabeth Faue, *Community of Suffering and Struggle: Women, Men, and the Labor Movement in Mineapolis, 1915–1945* (Chapel Hill: University of North Carolina Press, 1991); and Dana Frank, *Purchasing Power: Consumer Organizing, Gender, and the Seattle Labor Movement, 1919–1929* (New York: Cambridge University Press, 1994).

be refashioned into an agent of female uplift and feminine reform. Company cooking and nursing classes, sewing circles, and calisthenic breaks, welfare capitalists argued, would transform today's wage earner into tomorrow's better wife and mother. Challenging contemporaries' cry that industrial capitalism was destroying the sanctity of the family, proponents of welfare work nevertheless upheld conventional gender roles by reinforcing the notion that women who worked for wages should also be good mothers. By the same token, welfare firms urged male workers to flex their "masculine might" through participation in gun clubs and hiking groups and by acquiring pensions to sustain their role as family providers. For both sexes, welfare employers reified the "new and improved" workplace as the best site for the affirmation of traditional gender roles.[12]

That both male and female employees frequently rejected company-prescribed roles—indeed, that some rejected welfare programs altogether—speaks to a final dimension of the welfare work story: its indubitable legacy. Although the welfare work movement proved short-lived, its impact on the twentieth-century workplace has been profound. In fact, welfare capitalism did not die so much as it was transfigured. Benefits that many American workers today consider routine originated in turn-of-the-century welfare work. Through its institutionalization and modification in the 1920s, welfare work defined the terrain of modern personnel management and, by extension, mapped the boundaries of corporate responsibility toward labor in modern America.

Labor played an important role in determining this outcome. Indeed, the enduring legacy of welfare work suggests that its florescence in the period from 1900 to 1920 was not an open-and-shut case of insidious employers imposing an anti-union plot on passive employees but part of a protracted negotiation between capital and labor. Gerald Zahavi's discussion of "negotiated loyalties" at the Endicott Johnson

12. Lisa Fine, " 'Our Big Factory Family': Masculinity and Paternalism at the Reo Motor Car Company of Lansing, Michigan," *Labor History* 34 (Spring–Summer 1993): 277. Also see Kwolek-Folland, *Engendering Business*, and Strom, *Beyond the Typewriter*.

For British studies see Angela Woollacott, *On Her Their Lives Depend: Munitions Workers in the Great War* (Berkeley: University of California Press, 1994), and Judy Lown, "Not So Much a Factory, More a Form of Patriarchy: Gender and Class during Industrialisation," in *Gender, Class and Work*, ed. Eva Gamarnikow, David Morgan, June Purvis, and Daphne Taylorson (London: Heinemann, 1983). For Canadian studies see Joy Parr, *The Gender of Breadwinners: Women, Men, and Change in Two Industrial Towns, 1880–1950* (Toronto: University of Toronto Press, 1990); and Joan Sangster, "The Softball Solution: Female Workers, Male Managers and the Operation of Paternalism at Westclox, 1923–60," *Labour/Le Travail* 32 (Fall 1993): 167–98.

Shoe Company and Lizabeth Cohen's analysis of the "contested loyalties" of industrial workers in Chicago remind us that placing workers into polarized categories belies the nuances of their experiences; those encountering the fruits of welfare capitalism were neither fully supplicant nor universally resistant. Welfare capitalism created an arena of negotiation—not just co-option—where workers made their voices heard.[13]

Labor associations and unions formulated specific policies on welfare work that revealed both the centrality of welfare programs to workers' experiences and the strategic differences dividing labor organizations over the issue of industrial reform. Informed by the politics of organized labor, rank-and-file workers evaluated welfare work according to their own criteria. Workers' responses revealed the interstices and bridges between survival and conviction. Their complex patterns of participation and resistance reflected economic pragmatism but also deeply felt beliefs about the extent to which employers owed them "something beyond wages" and what form this "something" should take. Unweaving this tapestry of acceptance, modification, and resistance, we encounter a workers' world replete with suspicion and mistrust of employers' actions, a world in which the desirability of individual financial benefits superseded company picnics and contractual guarantees—rights—were preferable to the arbitrariness of employers' embellishments. The many changes to welfare work after World War I, particularly the shift in focus from social programs to individual financial benefits, reflected both employers' awareness of workers' critique of welfare work and their attempt to tailor benefits to labor's liking.

But workers' agency in modifying the shape and extent of private provisions stopped short of giving workers everything they wanted. Calvin Coolidge's proclamation that "the business of America is business" enunciated well the political spirit of the 1920s. If welfare programs failed to transform workers into abject minions, they also helped ensure that labor would be required to wage its cause with little state support. The duplicity of the federal government in the Progressive era—on the

13. Gerald Zahavi, "Negotiated Loyalty: Welfare Capitalism and the Shoeworkers of Endicott Johnson, 1920–1940," *Journal of American History* 70 (1983): 602–20 ; Cohen, *Making a New Deal*, chap. 4. Also see Fine, " 'Our Big Factory Family,' " pp. 275–76.

On the importance of looking at marginalized groups' resistance to institutional control, see Mary Odem, *Delinquent Daughters: Protecting and Policing Adolescent Female Sexuality in the United States, 1885–1920* (Chapel Hill: University of North Carolina Press, 1995); Eric C. Schneider, *In the Web of Class; Delinquents and Reformers in Boston, 1810s–1930s* (New York: New York University Press, 1992); Linda Gordon, *Heroes of Their Own Lives: The Politics and History of Family Violence* (New York: Viking, 1988).

one hand suppressing labor unrest, on the other seeking ways to pre-vents its eruption—had made state welfarism in industrial affairs a vi-able possibility. Wartime exigencies made this possibility almost a reality. Frantic to meet production schedules, the government regu-lated industrial output and mandated reforms to recruit and retain workers, maximize their efficiency, and minimize costly labor disputes. When the "normalcy" of peace returned, however, it was accompanied by more wage earners, a contracting economy with fewer jobs, the re-moval of many wartime concessions, and renewed frustrations among laborers. As workers' dissatisfaction escalated into national strikes, a new industrial crisis emerged. A state that years earlier had revealed a compassionate side toward labor now rescinded promises of sympathy. Less leverage for labor was accompanied by the belief that laborers in America deserved less.

By 1920, moreover, the question whether workplace reforms should be encoded in law or left to employers' discretion has lost its urgency. Thousands of firms had preempted the need for protracted debate by establishing reforms voluntarily. On balance, welfare capitalism sur-passed welfare statism. Despite the lukewarm successes of lobby groups such as the American Association for Labor Legislation and the Na-tional Consumers' League, measures improving workers' welfare rep-resented only a minority of Progressive legislative reforms. After two decades of welfare work, the state left business to manage labor by itself. A welfare state advancing labor's interests might have been the path taken in American politics during the Progressive era, as it was in other industrial nations. In part because of welfare work, it was not.

In the end, the political capital employers acquired from publicized benevolence is explicable precisely because welfare work came to mean so many things to so many Americans. To wage earners, workplace benefits often meant conditions and provisions better than those the next employer was offering. To consumers, welfare work suggested purer, superior products made by clean hands and attentive minds. To an expanding class of social scientists, it affirmed the importance of efficiency as the foundation for societal reform. To reformers worried about sexual improprieties fostered in integrated public spaces, it of-fered institutional protections for women. To many advocates of work-place reform, it was better than no reforms at all. To employers themselves, welfare work was not only an antistatist gesture but also a way to deal concretely with numerous labor concerns such as recruit-ment, retention, lethargy, and accidents. In short, welfare work claimed multiple beneficiaries, not all of whom supported it chiefly for political reasons. This book analyzes the movement's multivalences in their own right, mindful of contemporaries' ability to support welfare work without overtly endorsing its political message. In the final analysis, however, it suggests that it was precisely welfare work's elasticity—an antistatist reform movement that doubled as so much more—that contributed to the normalization of its larger political message.

The Politics of Labor Reform

On the morning of July 6, 1892, industrial warfare erupted on the banks of the Monongahela River in Homestead, Pennsylvania. That January, Henry Clay Frick, the obdurate anti-union manager of the largest employer in the area, the Carnegie Steel Company, had announced that the wages of members of the Amalgamated Association of Iron, Steel, and Tin Workers would be slashed by 18 percent. Frick refused to accept union representatives' requests to discuss the cut. Instead, he responded to their complaints by instituting a plant-wide lockout on July 2, laying off more than 3,800 union and nonunion men. Four days later, in the early hours of the morning, armed Pinkerton detectives, traveling on barges from Pittsburgh to Homestead, tried to assume control of the plant grounds. While poised to alight, they were stopped by an angry crowd of armed Homestead men and their families who had anticipated the amphibious landing. The ensuing exchange was long and violent. From four in the morning until five in the afternoon, each side attempted to vanquish the other with a battery of rifles, shotguns, pistols, revolvers, and nailed clubs. By day's end, the rampage had exacted a deadly toll: nine strikers and seven Pinkertons had died and more than three hundred men, mostly Pinkertons, had been wounded.[1]

1. On the Homestead strike, see Paul Krause, *The Battle for Homestead, 1880–1892:*

Although exceptional in the extent and acuity of its violence, the Homestead affair was nevertheless symptomatic of the industrial strife that gripped the United States in the late nineteenth century. For contemporaries, the horror of Homestead lay as much in the typicality of industrial confrontation as in the visceral response to the images of fire and mayhem that blanketed newspapers in the strike's wake. Tales of capital brutality, labor intransigence, and military confrontation were legion in the Gilded Age. Collectively they fueled the fear that premeditated violence had become management's standard anodyne for labor unrest and paved the way for wider government regulation of industrial affairs.

The industrial policy that federal and state governments crafted, a curious hybrid of sympathy and repression, set the political stage for the efflorescence of welfare work programs in the Progressive era. As labor regulations became a permanent fixture of the economic landscape, many employers made welfare capitalism their best defense against welfare statism. Never just a strategy for improving labor efficiency, welfare work was, at its inception, also a political movement propelled by employers' desire to halt the advance of the welfare state.

The Politics of Labor Reform

Labor issues had been politicized long before the Progressive era began. Perspectives on the character and value of work had framed understandings of citizenship and republicanism since the United States's founding, linking economic independence and manual labor to political virtue. In the nineteenth century, workers themselves had placed politics at the core of their critique of emergent industrial capitalism, a critique articulated in labor organizations, workplace activities, social clubs, electoral participation, and on the street. Drawing upon a political culture that had traditionally celebrated the laborer's role as producer-citizen, workers invoked republican ideology to protest changes to the character and organization of work.[2]

Politics, Culture, and Steel (Pittsburgh: University of Pittsburgh Press, 1992); Arthur G. Burgoyne, *The Homestead Strike of 1892* (1893; Pittsburgh: University of Pittsburgh Press, 1979); Jeremy Brecher, *Strike!* (Boston: South End Press, 1972), pp. 53–68; Foster Rhea Dulles and Melvyn Dubofsky, *Labor in America: A History,* 4th ed. (Arlington Heights, Ill.: Harlan Davidson, 1984), pp. 157–61.

2. On labor and republicanism, see Drew McCoy, *The Elusive Republic: Political Economy in Jeffersonian America* (Chapel Hill: University of North Carolina Press, 1980); Joyce Ap-

But although work and working conditions had long prompted political comment, it was not until the 1870s that the federal government became actively involved in the management of labor affairs. Before the 1870s bipartisan political support for market, rather than government, coordination of the terms and conditions of employment had impeded federal government intervention. This support stemmed, in part, from the constitutional arrangement of federalism, which assigned powers of economic supervision to the states unless the matter involved interstate commerce—a caveat that, given the local and regional organization of the economy, was of limited significance before the Civil War. Widespread faith among political leaders in the reality of a free labor market promising unrestricted economic mobility to the deserving also buoyed the dominant disposition toward laissez faire. With the "natural" laws of the market presumably affording ample and equal opportunities, government economic intervention was viewed as an impediment to, rather than a guarantor of, upward mobility.[3]

Against this backdrop, the events surrounding the 1877 railroad strike marked a turning point in the laissez-faire course of American industrial relations. Responding to a succession of wage cuts and in-

pleby, *Capitalism and a New Social Order: The Republican Vision of the 1790s* (New York: New York University Press, 1984); Howard B. Rock, *Artisans of the New Republic: The Tradesmen of New York City in the Age of Jefferson* (New York: New York University Press, 1979); Charles G. Steffen, *The Mechanics of Baltimore: Workers and Politics in the Age of Revolution, 1763–1812* (Urbana: University of Illinois Press, 1984); and Eric Foner, *Tom Paine and Revolutionary America* (New York: Oxford University Press, 1976).

On the politicization of antebellum labor protest, see Sean Wilentz, *Chants Democratic: New York City and the Rise of the American Working Class, 1788–1850* (New York: Oxford University Press, 1984); Christine Stansell, *City of Women: Sex and Class in New York, 1789–1860* (Urbana: University of Illinois Press, 1986); Alan Dawley, *Class and Community: The Industrial Revolution in Lynn* (Cambridge: Harvard University Press, 1976); and Mary H. Blewett, *Men, Women, and Work: Class, Gender, and Protest in the New England Shoe Industry, 1780–1910* (Urbana: University of Illinois Press, 1988).

For the persistence of artisan republicanism in the postbellum period, see Leon Fink, *Workingmen's Democracy: The Knights of Labor and American Politics* (Urbana: University of Illinois Press, 1983); Gregory Kealey and Bryan Palmer, *Dreaming of What Might Be* (New York: Cambridge University Press, 1982); and Blewett, *Men, Women, and Work*. On the political dimensions of worker culture, see Leon Fink, *In Search of the Working Class: Essays in American Labor History and Political Culture* (Urbana: University of Illinois Press, 1994); Herbert G. Gutman, *Power and Culture: Essays on the American Working Class*, ed. Ira Berlin (New York: Pantheon, 1987); and David Montgomery, *Beyond Equality: Labor and the Radical Republicans, 1862–1872* (1967; Urbana: University of Illinois Press, 1981).

3. On the federal government and labor regulation in the nineteenth century, see Melvyn Dubofsky, *The State and Labor in Modern America* (Chapel Hill: University of North Carolina Press, 1994), pp. 4–8; and Eric Foner, *Free Soil, Free Labor, Free Men: The Ideology of the Republican Party before the Civil War* (New York: Oxford University Press, 1970), chap. 1.

creased workloads, men working for the Baltimore and Ohio Railroad in West Virginia struck on July 16, soon halting rail transportation from Baltimore to the Midwest. The strikers were joined by railway employees and sympathetic workers in Baltimore, Pittsburgh, St. Louis, Chicago, and San Francisco, and their campaign ground to a halt only after Rutherford Hayes dispatched U.S. soldiers to "restore law and order." Two weeks after it began, the country's first national strike was won for capital by federal troops.[4]

Hayes's intervention marked more than a momentary retreat from a long-standing policy of federal noninterference. To be sure, Hayes's decision reflected his fear of an orchestrated labor revolution. More important, however, it signaled the degree to which monumental changes in the postbellum economy had transformed the industrial landscape, escalated the stakes of labor unrest, and encouraged the federal government to become a key player in the management of labor-capital relations.[5]

This economic reordering resulted from a combination of circumstances. The consolidation of a national, integrated economy created a climate of interdependence in which eastern manufacturers relied on western resources and urban consumers on both coasts depended on railroads for supplies. Expansion was propelled by the rise of big business, characterized by the displacement of specialized, local firms by giant horizontally and vertically integrated organizations with interregional markets. The appearance of monopoly and oligopoly capitalism rendered notions of an economic order internally regulated by "natural" laws of supply and demand increasingly anachronistic; there could be no democracy of opportunity for individual competitors when a combination of firms dictated the rules of the market. The payrolls of these enterprises were so prodigious and their markets so vast, moreover, that the economic health of a single corporation could affect the fate of thousands of people. What on a financial ledger appeared as a single industrial establishment incorporated in one city could, in fact, involve dozens of subsidiaries scattered across the country controlled by individuals who owned but never set foot on company property, what contemporaries disparagingly called "absentee capitalism." One independently owned firm might determine the fate of a town and one

4. Dubofsky, *State and Labor in Modern America*, pp. 1–10, 39.

5. Modern labor theory, rejecting laissez-faire explanations of wage levels and labor markets, also emerged in the 1880s as a response to the labor question. See Clarence E. Wunderlin Jr., *Visions of a New Industrial Order: Social Science and Labor Theory in America's Progressive Era* (New York: Columbia University Press, 1992).

corporation the destiny of an industry, the economic welfare of a work-force numbering in the thousands, and the future of firms and individuals dependent on that corporation for supplies.[6]

The scale and scope of these new economic alignments worsened workers' burdens. As the spread of big business eclipsed the small, proprietorial firm, so too the ascent of full-time wage earning as a permanent condition of life diminished opportunities for self-employment and economic independence. Between 1860 and 1880, the size of the manufacturing labor force more than doubled, growing from 1.3 million wage earners to just over 2.7 million; between 1880 and 1900, it almost doubled again. The rapid expansion of the industrial wage-earning class outpaced the growth in the quantity of industrial establishments, increasing the concentration of workers under the same roof. In the 1870s there were only a few large factories, most of them in the textile industry. By 1900, over 1,500 factories had more than 500 employees on their payrolls. Although firms with large labor forces represented only a minority of establishments in the Progressive era, their arrival profoundly altered wage earners' work environment. By 1909, 62.2 percent of wage earners worked in firms with at least 100 employees, 28 percent in establishments with a labor force exceeding 500.[7]

As more employees became concentrated in a single establishment, growing numbers found themselves locked into the same occupational stratum. While aggregate real wages increased between 1870 and 1880, decisive vertical mobility declined. The crystallization of a permanent wage-earning class proceeded unevenly, but as early as the 1870s, in the words of one historian, "the full-time, dependent wage earner had become more characteristic of the economy than the self-employed artisan." The concomitant hardening of class divisions turned the free labor ideology and its claims to equal opportunity into a myth for most workers. In addition, by encouraging wage earners to recognize the

6. See Alfred D. Chandler Jr., *The Visible Hand: The Managerial Revolution in American Business* (Cambridge: Harvard University Press, 1977).

7. U.S. Census Office, *Abstract of the Twelfth Census of the United States, 1900* (Washington, D.C.: Government Printing Office, 1902), pp. 300–301, 320–25; U.S. Census Office, *Twelfth Census of the United States* (Washington, D.C.: Government Printing Office, 1902), p. lxxii; U.S. Bureau of the Census, *The Integration of Industrial Operation* (Washington, D.C.: Government Printing Office, 1924), and *Thirteenth Census of the United States* (Washington, D.C.: Government Printing Office, 1913), 8:185; Daniel Nelson, *Managers and Workers: Origins of the New Factory System in the United States, 1880–1920* (Madison: University of Wisconsin Press, 1975), p. 4.

structural similarities of their situation, the "permanence of dependence" hastened the development of labor organizations and lubricated the wheels of class protest.[8]

The effects of this yet unfinished industrial revolution—economic centralization, the rise of big business, and dwindling vertical mobility—were evident by the 1870s. It was an economic transformation, but its reverberations were never purely economic. Spawned by a permissive political climate, the new industrial order, enmeshed in an interconnected web linking businessmen, financiers, producers, and consumers, politicized labor unrest by endowing workers with the ability to sever the seams of economic unity, disrupting the flow of goods and services. In the postbellum world, the public consequences of private sector conflicts invited government management of industrial relations on an unprecedented scale.

The events of 1877 attest to the altered relationship between government and labor. Hayes's decision to overwhelm strikers through state-sponsored force certainly spoke volumes about the president's partisanship. But even more fundamentally, the presidential coordination of the anti-strike campaign indexed a deepening political investment in the means by which local wage cuts had unexpectedly imperiled the transportation network of a nation.

By the 1890s the labor question was at the forefront of national debate. In 1895 the American Humane Education Society sponsored a prize for what it deemed one of the "most important questions of the day": a "plan of peacefully settling the difficulties between capital and labor." Indeed, the years since 1877 had witnessed the escalation of labor unrest rather than its eradication. In response to continued outbursts of industrial violence, contemporaries began to characterize the labor problem as a political and social crisis. The apocalyptic imagery evoked by University of Chicago industrial sociologist and reformer Charles Henderson typified the tone of turn-of-the-century jeremiads. Henderson insisted that industrial warfare was destroying not only work relations but the very fabric of American society. "The waste and loss of social friction are enormous," Henderson wrote, "political stability is in peril from class conflicts; there is a recrudescence of savagery in 'sabotage'; victory of either side after a strike is purchased at awful cost

8. Dubofsky, *State and Labor in Modern America*, p. 6. Also see David Montgomery, *The Fall of the House of Labor: The Workplace, the State, and American Labor Activism, 1865–1925* (New York: Cambridge University Press, 1987), chap. 1.

no matter who wins or loses. . . ." If the United States were to withstand this latest challenge to its solidity, "some kind of harmony and adjustment" would have to be found.[9]

Although in hindsight it may be tempting to dismiss Henderson's remarks as rhetorical hyperbole, circumstances supported his and contemporaries' forebodings. Employers' boasts of private armories, detectives, and industrial espionage teams augmented fears that military combat had become the normative method for handling workplace tensions. Time and time again, capital demonstrated that private military reserves and hired spies were intended for use, not deterrence; Homestead proved the point. In the 1890s the Pinkerton National Detective Agency, only one of dozens of agencies specializing in the supply of spies and armed forces to employers, had more active agents and reserves in its ranks than the standing army of the United States.[10]

Employers justified their "big-stick policy"—so named because professional strikebreakers often toted a foot-long lead pipe in addition to sidearms—as a necessary counterpoise to heightened labor initiative. They pointed to escalating labor resistance, spontaneous and planned, as justification for becoming armed and ready. They complained bitterly in contemporary management journals about workers' mounting tardiness, absenteeism, drunkenness, sabotage, and systematic soldiering. By employers' accounting, wage earners had created a workplace grounded in chaos, not order.[11]

Employers found equally menacing the growing number of examples of collective worker action, especially unionization, boycotts, and strikes. The country's largest union association, the American Federation of Labor (AFL), was also its fastest growing. Founded in 1886, the AFL survived the depression of 1893 and thrived in its aftermath. Be-

9. American Humane Education Society, *A Bad Way of Settling Difficulties between Capital and Labor* (Boston, 1896), p. 4; Charles Henderson, *Citizens in Industry* (New York: D. Appleton, 1915), p. 5. Also see Nelson Lichtenstein and Howell John Harris, "Introduction: A Century of Industrial Democracy in America," in *Industrial Democracy in America: The Ambiguous Promise*, ed. Lichtenstein and Harris (New York: Cambridge University Press, 1993), pp. 1–2.

10. Brecher, *Strike!* pp. 9, 55. On the history of labor violence, see H. M. Gitelman, "Perspectives on American Industrial Violence," *Business History Review* 47 (Spring 1973): 1–23; and Philip Taft and Philip Ross, "American Labor Violence: Its Causes, Character, and Outcome," in *The History of Violence in America: Historical and Comparative Perspectives*, ed. Hugh Davis Graham and Ted Robert Gurr (New York: Praeger, 1969).

11. Stuart D. Brandes, *American Welfare Capitalism, 1880–1940* (Chicago: University of Chicago Press, 1976), pp. 2–3; David Montgomery, *Workers' Control in America: Studies in the History of Work, Technology, and Labor Struggles* (New York: Cambridge University Press, 1979), pp. 4–15.

tween 1899 and 1904 AFL membership skyrocketed from 375,000 to 1.7 million. Demanding the right to bargain collectively for higher wages and lower hours, the AFL relied on strikes to win concessions. The AFL's willingness to use the strike as a negotiating tool was evidenced by the unprecedented wave of strikes that rocked the country. Between 1890 and 1900 nearly twenty-three thousand strikes affecting over eighty thousand establishments immobilized close to 4 million workers; 75 percent of these were union-ordered. The economic blow to businesses was acute: targeted companies alone lost $75,562,479. But not only employers suffered. As one contemporary explained in a revealing commentary on the far-reaching impact of labor conflict, strikes could "no longer be regarded merely in the light of conflicts between capital and labor. . . . Because of the tremendous costs they are imposing on the public, [they] are of vital public concern." For employers who considered unions and strikes anathema to company interests and for the many Americans who viewed them as a disruption rather than an understandable response to the spiraling commodification of labor, the late nineteenth century was indeed a time of crisis.[12]

The widening scope and changing character of state intervention enveloped this growing urgency. To be sure, the expansion of government authority was animated by a belief that silencing labor through force was the best way to restore stability. In this sense, the president's call to arms in 1877 marked the beginning of a legacy in which the railway strikes of 1886, Homestead in 1892, and Pullman in 1894, figured as token examples of the violent lengths the combined forces of capital and state would go to suppress labor in the Gilded Age. Increased worker insurgence was usually matched by the state's growing resolve to restrain it. As William Forbath has argued, strikes in the Gilded Age and Progressive era created an environment of semi-outlawry in which workers clashed with conservative courts and recalcitrant police eager to enforce court injunctions. Though not the usual method of resolving strikes, state-sanctioned force was hardly an aberration. Between 1877 and 1903, federal or state troops were deployed in over five hundred labor disputes.[13]

---

12. U.S. Bureau of Labor Statistics, *Strikes and Lockouts in the States*, Bulletin 54 (September 1904), pp. 1098–1101; William E. Forbath, *Law and the Shaping of the American Labor Movement* (Cambridge: Harvard University Press, 1991), p. 98. Strikes were defined by the Department of Labor as any "refusal by the employee of an establishment to work unless the employer complies with some demand made by the former or withdraws some obnoxious demand made by himself."

13. Forbath, *Law and the Shaping of the American Labor Movement*, p. 118. The frequent

Yet even while they quashed worker revolts, state and federal governments sought ways to mitigate the conditions that engendered them. Legislators acknowledged that the shifting economic environment had made labor relations a matter of social welfare. With an ever-growing number of lives dependent on the actions of a concentrated few, minimalist government regulation of capital-labor relations increasingly came to be viewed as a necessity of the modern industrial age. As one proponent of government intervention explained, "It is becoming quite clear that the delivery of coal in a great city is one of the legitimate functions for the interference of the government. So it is with the case of milk. These are things on which the lives and welfare of the population depend. Any government is justified in interfering in any case where the lives of the people are in danger. This is simply the doctrine of common sense."[14]

Lawmakers turned to legislation to minimize the causes and costs of labor strife. The rise of an embryonic welfare state at the turn of the century has been well documented by historians. Its receptivity to working-class interests, however, has often been downplayed or ignored. And yet, both state and federal legislators in the late nineteenth century, attentive to the political impact of labor protest, established agencies and commissions to discover and enumerate the causes of workers' discontent. Based on these findings, lawmakers passed measures that circumscribed employers' liberties and mandated workplace reform. By 1900, as the Progressive impulse quickened, they had already sketched the outlines of a program that was, at least by employers' calculations, discernibly pro-labor.[15]

---

use of violence to contain and crush labor resistance is vital to our understanding of how American exceptionalism—the relative conservatism of the American labor movement— was forged. As several historians have noted, what seems truly exceptional in American history is not workers' radical shortcomings but the freedom managers have had to wield power in the workplace unfettered by government restraints. A discussion of the politics of welfare work enhances this perspective by looking at the ways in which corporate benevolence has functioned to protect business prerogatives. In addition to Forbath, see Robin D. G. Kelley, *Hammer and Hoe: Alabama Communists during the Great Depression* (Chapel Hill: University of North Carolina Press, 1990); Sanford Jacoby, "American Exceptionalism Revisited: The Importance of Management," in *Masters to Managers: Historical and Comparative Perspectives on American Employers*, ed. Jacoby (New York: Columbia University Press, 1991); and Kim Voss, *The Making of American Exceptionalism: The Knights of Labor and Class Formation in the Nineteenth Century* (Ithaca: Cornell University Press, 1993).

14. John Burton Phillips, "Organization of Employers and Employees," *University of Colorado Studies* 3 (February 1905): 171–72.

15. Important exceptions are Dubofsky, *State and Labor in Modern America*; Mary O. Furner, "Knowing Capitalism: Public Investigation and the Labor Question in the Long Progressive Era," in *The State and Economic Knowledge: The American and British Experiences*,

Government regulation of workplace reform in the late nineteenth century took different shapes. Accordant with constitutional divisions of power, much activity took place at the state level. In 1869 Massachusetts, the front runner in legislative labor reform, became the first state to establish a labor bureau; by 1903 thirty-four others had followed suit. Although operating under the guidelines formulated by their respective legislatures, the bureaus shared a common purpose, as Elizabeth Brandeis put it, "to secure reliable information as to wages, hours, and other conditions as a basis for promoting more regulation." Resultant legislation was extensive. Starting with Massachusetts in 1877 and ending with Rhode Island in 1894, every northern industrial state except Illinois passed a general factory act mandating sanitation and safety features. Although the specific requirements of these acts varied by state, there were striking similarities. All required the provision of factory ventilation and a minimum standard of cleanliness and the guarding of machinery, elevators, and hoist openings to protect employees; all but two mandated the reporting of serious accidents (Table 1). To enforce regulations, legislatures established factory inspection bureaus whose itinerant investigators confirmed compliance with state codes and initiated prosecution of violators. In 1897, when the Department of Labor first reported on factory inspection, fourteen states had instituted inspection procedures.[16]

Safety and sanitation measures were supplemented by statutes regulating the employment of children and women. The primary goals of child labor laws were to establish both a minimum age of hire and a maximum number of hours of wage work per day. By 1899 twenty-eight states had established regulations along these lines. Work codes affecting women minimized what lawmakers believed to be the adverse consequences of industrial wage labor on women's health and morals.

---

ed. Furner and Barry Supple (New York: Cambridge University Press, 1990); and Wunderlin, *Visions of a New Industrial Order*. The studies by Furner and Wunderlin focus less on legislative measures than on the ideology that gave rise to institutional mechanisms for investigating the "labor question."

Of course, what employers saw as pro-labor was not always viewed by workers in the same way. State agencies and workers frequently clashed over the determination of suitable hours and wages. See, for example, Alice Kessler-Harris, *A Woman's Wage: Historical Meanings and Social Consequences* (Lexington: University Press of Kentucky, 1990), chap. 1.

16. Elizabeth Brandeis, "Labor Legislation," in John R. Commons, et al. *History of Labor in the United States*, 4 vols. (1918–35; New York: Augustus M. Kelley, 1966), 3:628, 630–31; Nelson, *Managers and Workers*, pp. 122–24; U.S. Bureau of Labor Statistics, *The Inspection of Factories and Workshops in the United States*, Bulletin 12 (Washington D.C.: Government Printing Office, 1897), p. 55. Illinois legislators, contending with some of the nation's best-organized employers, passed comparable legislation only in 1909.

Table 1. Workplace legislation relating to factories, workshops, and mercantile establishments, 1904

Legislation	U.S.	Ala.	Alaska	Ariz.	Ark.	Cal.	Colo.	Conn.	Del.	D.C.	Fla.	Ga.	Hawaii	Idaho	Ill.	Ind.	Iowa	Kans.	Ky.	La.	Me.	Md.	Mass.	Mich.	Minn.	Miss.	Mo.	Mont.	Nebr.	Nev.	N.H.	N.J.	N.Mex.	N.Y.	N.C.	N.Dak.	Ohio	Okla.	Oreg.	Pa.	P.R.	R.I.	S.C.	S.Dak.	Tenn.	Tex.	Utah	Vt.	Va.	Wash.	W.Va.	Wis.	Wyo.
Regulation of labor in—																																																					
Factories and workshops		♦			♦	♦	♦	♦	♦	♦	♦	♦			♦	♦	♦	♦	♦			♦	♦	♦	♦		♦		♦		♦	♦		♦		♦	♦		♦	♦	♦	♦	♦	♦			♦		♦	♦	♦	♦	♦
Mercantile establishments		♦				♦		♦	♦	♦	♦	♦			♦	♦	♦	♦				♦	♦	♦	♦		♦		♦		♦	♦		♦		♦	♦		♦	♦	♦	♦	♦	♦			♦		♦	♦	♦	♦	♦
Sweat shops						♦		♦							♦	♦						♦	♦	♦	♦		♦				♦	♦		♦			♦			♦												♦	
Bakeries																♦																								♦												♦	
Laundries					♦			♦					♦			♦							♦									♦		♦					♦	♦												♦	
Building construction work						♦										♦						♦					♦					♦		♦			♦			♦												♦	
Protection of health of employees:																																																					
Rooms to be properly ventilated						♦		♦								♦	♦	♦				♦	♦									♦		♦					♦	♦		♦										♦	
Rooms to be sufficiently lighted								♦								♦	♦	♦																♦						♦		♦										♦	
Rooms to be sufficiently heated																	♦	♦																♦								♦										♦	
Walls to be lime-washed or painted															♦	♦							♦											♦					♦	♦												♦	
Overcrowding prohibited																♦																																				♦	
Exhaust fans, blowers, etc., required								♦								♦	♦						♦	♦	♦		♦					♦		♦			♦			♦												♦	
Seats for females required						♦	♦	♦								♦	♦						♦	♦	♦		♦		♦			♦		♦						♦		♦									♦	♦	
Separate toilet facilities for each sex required		♦																					♦							♦							♦		♦	♦		♦	♦									♦	♦
Prevention of accidents:																																																					
Cleaning machinery by women or children prohibited																♦																																					
Guards to be placed on machinery						♦		♦								♦	♦	♦				♦	♦	♦	♦		♦		♦			♦		♦		♦	♦			♦		♦										♦	
Mechanical belt and gearing shifters required																		♦						♦	♦									♦			♦			♦		♦										♦	
Means of communication with engine room required																		♦																♦																		♦	
Precautions required in handling explosives																																		♦																			
Guards to be placed on elevators and hoistways						♦		♦				♦			♦	♦	♦					♦	♦	♦	♦		♦					♦		♦			♦			♦		♦		♦							♦	♦	
Stairs to have hand rails								♦		♦						♦	♦					♦	♦				♦					♦		♦						♦		♦										♦	
Doors to swing outward and remain unlocked						♦		♦							♦							♦	♦				♦		♦			♦		♦		♦				♦		♦			♦						♦	♦	
Fire escapes to be provided		♦				♦		♦	♦	♦					♦	♦	♦					♦	♦	♦	♦		♦		♦			♦		♦			♦			♦		♦									♦	♦	♦
Working time of women:																																																					
Hours of labor limited							♦	♦								♦					♦	♦	♦								♦	♦		♦			♦		♦	♦		♦								♦		♦	
Night work prohibited or restricted																♦							♦									♦		♦																		♦	
Working time of children:																																																					
Hours of labor limited		♦			♦	♦	♦	♦		♦		♦			♦	♦					♦	♦	♦	♦	♦		♦		♦		♦	♦		♦			♦		♦	♦		♦			♦				♦		♦	♦	
Night work prohibited or restricted							♦									♦							♦									♦		♦			♦			♦												♦	
Inspection of establishments:																																																					
Inspection service provided for		♦			♦	♦	♦	♦		♦		♦			♦	♦			♦			♦	♦	♦	♦		♦		♦			♦		♦			♦		♦	♦										♦	♦	♦	
Accidents to be reported		♦														♦						♦	♦	♦	♦		♦		♦			♦		♦			♦		♦	♦										♦	♦	♦	

Source: U.S. Bureau of Labor Statistics, Labor Legislation in the United States, Bulletin 54 (Washington, D.C.: Government Printing Office, 1904), p. 1423.

Generally these laws were intended to make work less physically taxing by mandating certain meliorations and restricting the number of hours a woman could work. By 1901, for instance, most northern industrial states required special rest rooms, changing areas, toilet facilities, and seats for women, and sixteen states had imposed daily and weekly limits on women's work hours. Although these "protective" measures were, at least from some female employees' viewpoint, less pro-labor than other regulations—economic exigencies forced many women to view even the most exploitive wage work as a necessity of survival, not a luxury to be legislated away—their passage characterized the dominant trend: a willingness to suspend employers' individual freedoms to promote labor reforms that upheld a general, albeit gendered, public interest.[17]

Federal activity loosely paralleled state initiatives. In 1883 the U.S. Senate initiated a formal investigation of the "relations between labor and capital," and in 1884 Congress established the Bureau of Labor within the Department of Interior and created a new post, commissioner of labor, to head it. Four years later the Bureau was incorporated into the newly organized Department of Labor, whose task was "to acquire and diffuse among the people of the United States useful information on subjects connected with labor . . . especially upon its relation to capital . . . hours of labor, the earnings of laboring men and women, and the means of promoting [workers'] material, social, intellectual, and moral prosperity." In 1893 the new department demonstrated its support of statutory reforms by publishing a favorable study of the German system, *Compulsory Insurance in Germany* by John Graham Brooks (who later became president of the one of the most active legislative lobbying groups, the National Consumers' League). But it was not only what these federal agencies said or did that mattered. Their very founding created new institutional mechanisms for addressing labor issues and, in so doing, conferred a measure of political legitimacy to workers' demands for fair and equitable treatment.[18]

Passage of the Erdman Act and the Industrial Commission Act in 1898 cemented the federal government's sympathetic stance toward

17. U.S. Bureau of Labor Statistics, *Labor Legislation in the United States*, Bulletin 54 (1904); Brandeis, "Labor Legislation," pp. 404, 466; Nelson, *Managers and Workers*, pp. 123, 137. For a more detailed discussion of protective labor legislation, see Chapter 4.

18. U.S. Bureau of Labor Statistics, *The Working of the United States Bureau of Labor*, Bulletin 9 (1904), p. 974; Mimi Abramovitz, *Regulating the Lives of Women: Social Welfare Policy from Colonial Times to the Present* (Boston: South End Press, 1988), p. 231.

workers. The Erdman Act, drafted in response to the Pullman strike, passed by a wide majority in both houses of Congress in May 1898. Its provisions included government recognition of trade unions on interstate railroads and a ban on yellow-dog contracts (requiring workers to promise not to join unions as a precondition of employment). The Industrial Commission Act, signed by President William McKinley in June 1898, authorized Congress to appoint a federal commission to "investigate questions pertaining to immigration, to labor, to agriculture, to manufacturing, and to business, and to report to Congress and to suggest such legislation as it may deem best . . . in order to harmonize conflicting interests." The commission's findings were delivered in nineteen volumes in 1901 and 1902. Its recommendations included the standardization of state labor laws, the federal regulation of the hours, wages, and conditions of railroad work, and the extension of legislated reforms.[19]

By 1900 federal and state initiatives had left their mark. Without abdicating the right to repress labor through force, the myriad tiers of government had successfully managed to institutionalize and legislate a politics of sympathy. The shift in the government's position sent a clear message to employers: traditional prerogatives of labor management were under attack.

Employers fought back. To challenge existing regulations and to campaign against future ones, hundreds joined employer associations: municipal leagues and chambers of commerce, state trade associations, and national business organizations. Although employer associations were often founded for the purpose of strikebreaking, labor regulations also became a focus of their energies. Indeed, the most vocal and powerful employer association, the National Association of Manufacturers (NAM), founded in 1895, ranked the threat of regulation second in importance only to the union "menace." The NAM assailed regulation as prohibitively costly and unjust for small manufacturers and fought tirelessly for deregulation and regulatory containment. It directed antilabor legislation efforts in Washington, sending its officers to Congress

19. U.S. House of Representatives, *Report of the Industrial Commission on the Relations and Conditions of Capital and Labor Employed in Manufactures and General Business*, 57th Cong., 1st sess. (Washington, D.C.: Government Printing Office, 1901), 19:vii; Dubofsky, *State and Labor in Modern America*, p. 33. On the establishment and deliberations of the U.S. Industrial Commission, see Wunderlin, *Visions of a New Industrial Order*, pp. 27–71. On the importance of the standardization of labor law to Progressive reform, see William Graebner, "Federalism in the Progressive Era: A Structural Interpretation of Reform," *Journal of American History* 64 (September 1977): 331–57.

to oppose the establishment of the eight-hour day in firms with federal contracts and to limit the impact of antilabor court injunctions, bills under frequent consideration after 1902. In 1903, the NAM's president, David M. Parry, established the national Citizens' Industrial Association, partly for the purposes of repelling the apparent surge of labor "legislation of a socialistic nature."[20]

Nor was the NAM isolated in its views or activities. The spread of workers' compensation statutes shifted the focus of employer associations from fighting strikes to opposing labor legislation. By 1910, as Robert Wiebe has argued, "every employer association had placed politics first on its agenda." Employers' eagerness to derail legislative initiatives was widely noted. In 1913 the Department of Labor expressed alarm at employers' zealousness to neglect "recognition of [their] obligations to society" by "opposing the passage of laws which tend to secure these benefits for all workingmen." A 1910 editorial in *World's Work* accurately gauged the contemporary business mood, observing that "industrial magnates will tell you that business conditions would be sound and satisfactory if our law-makers would be quiet for a time. 'We have too many laws already.' Stop for a while. Give business a chance."[21]

The business backlash merely fortified the resolve of those who supported legislated reforms, energizing efforts to expand the scope of labor laws and make those already on the books more comprehensive. Ongoing industrial violence coupled with organized employers' intransigence and vitriolic campaigning merely confirmed reformers' belief that, left to their own devices, employers would do their utmost to unravel the still incomplete tapestry of labor legislation. In response, reformers demanded the passage of new labor laws that, in addition to improving the workplace as earlier legislation had done, would provide workers with direct social entitlements such as accident and health insurance.

In addition to coordinated opposition from employers, other incentives furthered the drive for government reform. Most significant, momentum seemed to be on the side of reformers. Not only was an extensive domestic legislative record already in place by the early 1900s,

20. Nelson, *Managers and Workers*, p. 127; Robert Wiebe, *Businessmen and Reform: A Study of the Progressive Movement* (1962; Chicago: Ivan R. Dee, 1989), pp. 170–77; Parry quoted in Marguerite Green, *The National Civic Federation and the American Labor Movement, 1900–1925* (Washington, D.C.: Catholic University Press, 1956), p. 101n.

21. Wiebe, *Businessmen and Reform*, pp. 170–73; U.S. Bureau of Labor Statistics, *Employers' Welfare Work*, Bulletin 123 (1913), pp. 75–76; " 'Big Business' and the People,' " *World's Work* 20 (September 1910):13357.

Table 2. Core social provisions enacted in six countries by 1914, by year of enactment

Country	Sickness insurance	Old-age pensions or insurance	Workers' compensation
Australia	None	1908	1900–1914[a]
Britain	1911	1908	1906
Germany	1883	1889	1884
New Zealand	None	1898	1900
Sweden	1891	1913	1901
United States	None	None	1911–1914[b]

[a]All states.

[b]Twenty-two states. Unlike European compensation laws, the vast majority of those in the United States were elective.

Sources: Peter Flora and Arnold J. Heidenheimer, eds., *The Development of Welfare States in Europe and America* (New Brunswick, N.J.: Transaction Books, 1981), table 2.4, p. 59; Theda Skocpol, *Protecting Soldiers and Mothers: The Political Origins of Social Policy in the United States* (Cambridge: Harvard University Press, 1992), table 1, p. 9; U.S. Department of Labor, *Growth of Labor Law in the United States* (Washington, D.C.: Government Printing Office, 1967), pp. 141–43; U.S. Bureau of Labor Statistics, *Comparison of Workmen's Compensation Laws of the United States*, Bulletin 340 (Washington, D.C.: Government Printing Office, 1918), p. 12.

but reformers could point to impressive developments worthy of emulation in Europe, Australia, and New Zealand: statutory sickness benefits and pensions in Germany, workers' compensation in Britain, and old-age insurance and workers' compensation in Australia and New Zealand (Table 2). Increased attention to the European system was evinced in the growing number of articles, books, and public discussions devoted to the topic; in 1901 the National Conference of Charities and Correction established a three-year commission to investigate social insurance systems abroad. Many organizations, including the American Association for Labor Legislation (AALL), sent representatives across the Atlantic to study European models firsthand. Such investigations inevitably led to comparisons between American "backwardness" and European "progress" that rallied support for reformers' ambitions. Urging congressional backing for the Federal Employer's Liability Bill of 1908, for instance, Theodore Roosevelt made the shame of American exceptionalism the basis for his appeal, noting with condescension that "even" Turkey and China had more progressive welfare measures than the United States. "It is a reproach to us as a nation," Roosevelt lamented in his special address, "that in both Federal and State legislation we have afforded less protection to public and private employees than any other industrial country in the world." Congress enacted the bill, increasing worker safety protections by weakening railroad companies' traditional legal protections against worker-initiated negligence suits.[22]

Comments and outcomes such as these raised the hopes of legislation-minded reformers. As Lee Frankel of the AALL observed in 1908, "the possibilities of adapting European methods to the United States seems to me to be unlimited." As the Progressive era advanced, advocates of labor legislation remained sanguine about their ability to parlay circumstance into statutory entitlements for workers.[23]

Voluntary vs. Statutory Reform

By the end of the Progressive era, however, their hopes had been dashed. To be sure, amplified support for state provisions, set against the larger pro-regulation politics of the period, had, by 1900, created an environment ripe for discussion, argumentation, and experimentation. Throughout the Progressive era, the labor question continued to inspire lively debate. But the discussion was joined by a new set of organized adversaries: welfare capitalists. Although welfare statists and welfare capitalists openly endorsed the principle of workplace reform, each presented competing proposals as to its scope, substance, and sponsorship. The battle over private and public reform raged throughout the Progressive era, but by the time it had played itself out in full, welfare capitalism had won. Industrial strife may have been perceived by many to be the greatest problem of the day, but a welfare state advancing workers' needs never became the solution of choice. Indeed, compared with regulations instituted in other industrialized countries during the Progressive era, laws in the United States bettering the conditions of workers were conspicuously few in number and limited in scope by 1920. In contrast, the provision of private welfare programs flourished, evoking an international encomium unprecedented since the early years of Lowell.[24]

The triumph of private labor reform, the lasting legacy of welfare

22. *Congressional Record*, 60th Cong., 1st sess. (1908), 42:3853. This debate is discussed in Hace Sorel Tishler, *Self-Reliance and Social Security, 1870–1917* (Port Washington, N.Y.: Kennikat Press, 1971), pp. 87–140.

23. Frankel quoted in Tishler, *Self-Reliance and Social Security*, p. 87.

24. On Lowell, see John F. Kasson, *Civilizing the Machine: Technology and Republican Values in America, 1776–1900* (New York: Penguin, 1976), chap. 2. Alan Dawley discusses the American-European contrast in *Struggles for Justice: Social Responsibility and the Liberal State* (Cambridge: Harvard University Press, 1991), p. 104.

capitalism, was not a reflection of statists' inertia. Legislative advocates pushed hard for the establishment of unemployment insurance, industrial health provisions, stringent safety and compensation measures, and protective labor laws covering female *and* male workers. Many published book-length proposals. The coordinated lobbying of the American Association for Labor Legislation, founded in 1906 as the American division of the International Association for Labor Legislation, spearheaded the legislative campaign. Its program, favoring at different stages safety and compensation measures, sickness coverage, and unemployment insurance, received widespread support from civic leaders, journalists, academics, social workers, labor bureau officials, and reform groups such as the National Consumers' League (NCL) and the National Child Labor Committee (NCLC).[25]

By the 1920s these reformers had made significant gains. Beginning with New York in 1910, forty-two states passed workers' compensation laws, abrogating employers' traditional protections under the fellow-servant, assumption of risk, and contributory negligence rules. At the federal level, Congress passed the Adamson Act, establishing an eight-hour day for interstate railway employees; the La Follette Seamen's Act, improving work conditions on merchant vessels; and the Keating-Owens Act (later declared unconstitutional), outlawing child labor. Solidifying an inchoate union-Democratic alliance, Woodrow Wilson made two discernibly pro-labor appointments: William B. Wilson, former secretary of the United Mine Workers, to the position of secretary of labor, and Frank Walsh, a left-leaning Democrat and labor sympathizer, to the chair of the new Commission on Industrial Relations.[26]

25. See, for example, William Willoughby, *Workingmen's Insurance* (New York: Thomas Y. Crowell, 1898); Charles Henderson, *Industrial Insurance in the United States* (Chicago: University of Chicago Press, 1909); Frank Lewis, *State Insurance: A Social and Industrial Need* (Boston: Houghton Mifflin, 1909); Henry Seager, *Social Insurance: A Program of Reform* (New York: Macmillan, 1910); Isaac Rubinow, *Social Insurance; with Special Reference to American Conditions* (New York: Henry Holt, 1913). Also see Howell John Harris, "Industrial Democracy and Liberal Capitalism, 1890–1925," in Lichtenstein and Harris, *Industrial Democracy in America*, p. 51.

26. U.S. Bureau of Labor Statistics, *Comparison of Workmen's Compensation Laws of the United States*, Bulletin 340 (1918), pp. 6, 9–14; Theda Skocpol, *Protecting Soldiers and Mothers: The Political Origins of Social Policy in the United States* (Cambridge: Harvard University Press, 1992), p. 8; Nelson, *Managers and Workers*, pp. 124–25; Stephen Presser and Jamil Zainaldin, *Law and American History* (St. Paul, Minn: West, 1980), p. 649; John S. Smith, "Organized Labor and Government in the Wilson Era, 1913–21: Some Conclusions," *Labor History* 3 (Fall 1962): 265–86; Graham Adams Jr., *Age of Industrial Violence, 1910–1915* (New York: Columbia University Press, 1966), pp. xi, 2, 32, 50; Dubofsky, *State and Labor in Modern America*, p. 55.

Under the fellow-servant rule, employers were not considered liable for injuries to

Notwithstanding reformers' accomplishments, most striking about the balance sheet of Progressive reform was the paucity of public provisions by the era's end. By 1920 compensation statutes were the only significant new body of workplace legislation. The scope of the statutes was modest, however: employees could recover only 50 to 66 percent of former wages; entire occupations, including those in agriculture and domestic service, where women and persons of color were concentrated, were exempt; jobs categorized as casual employment were excluded; and, owing to a New York Court of Appeals decision in 1911, only a handful of compensation statutes were compulsory.[27]

In contrast to legislative advocates' limited successes, welfare capitalists' program for reform triumphed. By 1920 comprehensive private reforms could be found in many of the largest, most prominent industrial and mercantile establishments in the country (Table 3). Hoping to win support by demonstrating that they were riding the same reform wave that was driving the passage of labor legislation, welfare employers introduced measures the magnitude of which easily dwarfed statutory meliorations. Where laws required safety seats and a ten-hour day for women, welfare employers provided these and more: at the National Cash Register Company in Dayton, "rejuvenating" calisthenic breaks thrice daily; at the Metropolitan Life Insurance Company in New York, a "free" hot lunch; at the Curtis Publishing Company in Philadelphia, a rest area decorated "in soft, lazy tones, with lounging chairs, plants, and fresh cut flowers more nearly [resembling] a hotel deluxe lobby than a place for working girls." Responding to proposals for legislated health insurance and pensions, welfare capitalists beat lawmakers to the punch. American Telephone and Telegraph Company's $10 million fund for employee pensions, sick benefits, and life insurance, established in 1913, and U.S. Steel Corporation's $5 million annual invest-

---

employees caused by co-workers. Under the doctrine of assumption of risk, workers were viewed as automatically assuming the risks of the job when they accepted employment. Contributory negligence held that if an injured worker contributed to his or her injury, the employer was not liable. These rules favored capital over labor in compensation disputes.

27. U.S. Bureau of Labor Statistics, *Comparison of Workmen's Compensation Laws,* pp. 16–19; Lawrence M. Friedman and Jack Ladinsky, "Social Change and the Law of Industrial Accidents," *Columbia Law Review* 67 (1967): 59–79. For a useful discussion of gender and the legal rights of employees in the Progressive era, see Alice Kessler-Harris, "Law and a Living: The Gendered Content of 'Free Labor,' " in *Gender, Class, Race, and Reform in the Progressive Era,* ed. Noralee Frankel and Nancy S. Dye (Lexington: University Press of Kentucky, 1991), pp. 87–109.

In Ives v. South Buffalo Railway Company, 201 N.Y. 271 (1911), the New York Court of Appeals ruled that the state's workers' compensation statute was unconstitutional.

Table 3. Selected firms with comprehensive welfare programs, 1913

Atchison, Topeka & Santa Fe (railway), various locations
Bloomingdale's (department store), New York City
Celluloid Co. (novelties), Newark, N.J.
Chicago Telephone (communications), Chicago
Cleveland Hardware (iron and steel), Cleveland
Cleveland Twist Drill (machinery), Cleveland
Curtis Publishing (printing and publishing), Philadelphia
Eastman Kodak (machinery), Rochester, N.Y.
Elgin Watch Company (machinery), Chicago
Filene's (department store), Boston
Firestone Tire & Rubber (rubber), Akron, Ohio
Forbes Lithograph (printing and publishing), Boston
General Electric (machinery), various plants
Gimbel Brothers (department store), Philadelphia
Goodyear Tire & Rubber (rubber), Akron, Ohio
Gorham Mfg. (jewelry), Providence, R.I.
Greenhut-Siegel-Cooper Company (department store), New York City
Hershey's (food), Hershey, Pa.
H. J. Heinz (food), Pittsburgh, Pa.
International Harvester (machinery), Chicago
J. B. Stetson (hats), Philadelphia
Joseph & Feiss (clothing), Cleveland
Joseph Bancroft (textiles), Wilmington, Del.
Marshall Field & Company (department store), Chicago
Metropolitan Life Insurance (life insurance), New York City
National Cash Register (machinery), Dayton, Ohio
Natural Food (food), Niagara Falls, N.Y.
New England Telephone & Telegraph (communications), Boston
New York Telephone Company (communications), New York City
Parke, Davis & Company (chemicals), Detroit
Plymouth Cordage (rope), Plymouth, Mass.
Procter & Gamble (soap) Cincinnati
Remington Typewriter (machinery), Ilion, N.Y.
Scovill (metals), Waterbury, Conn.
Sherwin-Williams (paint), Cleveland
Solvay Process (chemicals), Solvay, N.Y.
Thomas G. Plant (shoes), Boston
United Shoe Machinery (machinery), Beverly, Mass.
U.S. Steel (iron and steel), various plants
Waltham Watch (machinery), Waltham, Mass.
Wanamaker's (department store), New York City
Weston Electric (machinery), Newark, N.J.

Sources: Boston Chamber of Commerce Collection, Case 48, Folder 332–19, Baker Library Archives of the Harvard Graduate School of Business; U.S. Bureau of Labor Statistics, *Employers' Welfare Work,* Bulletin 123 (Washington, D.C.: Government Printing Office, 1913); Daniel Nelson, *Managers and Workers: Origins of the New Factory System in the United States, 1880–1920* (Madison: University of Wisconsin Press), chap. 6.

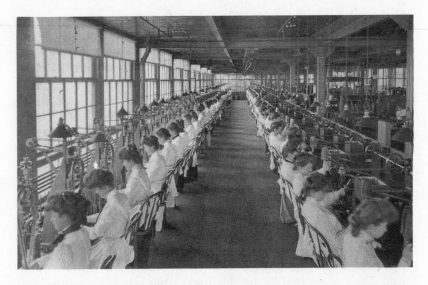

The National Cash Register Company of Dayton, Ohio, was one of many firms that show-cased its "freely" provided benefits and services for workers in the Progressive era. (*Cassier's Magazine*, September 1905.)

ment in employee pensions, health, and occupational safety repeatedly made front-page news. When International Harvester established an employee death, disability, and sickness plan in 1908, Harvester's finance committee chair, George W. Perkins, explained that the plan had been established "with a view to anticipating any legislation that might be enacted in this country."[28]

The "generosity" of welfare capitalists encouraged most contemporaries to view them as more progressive on social welfare matters than other employers. Conservative groups such as the NAM sometimes encouraged this identification. Charles W. Post, NAM member and former president of the Citizens' Industrial Association, likened private welfare to public charity and denounced them both. "I am not a warm

28. U.S. Bureau of Labor Statistics, *Employers' Welfare Work*, pp. 41, 46, 66; Edward Marshall, "Welfare Work May Conquer Great Labor Problems," *New York Times*, November 17, 1912; Arthur J. Todd, "The Organization and Promotion of Industrial Welfare through Voluntary Efforts," *Annals of the American Academy of Political and Social Science* 105 (January 1923): 77; Perkins quoted in Robert Asher, "The Limits of Big Business Paternalism: Relief for Injured Workers in the Years before Workmen's Compensation," in *Dying for Work: Workers' Safety and Health in Twentieth-Century America*, ed. David Rosner and Gerald Markowitz (Bloomington: Indiana University Press, 1989), pp. 28–29.

advocate of a lot of foolish, misapplied, maudlin sympathy that has paraded under the name of 'welfare work,' " he wrote in 1913.[29]

Viewed within a landscape of burgeoning state activity, however, the politics of welfare capitalists appear considerably less benign. Indeed, the benevolence that welfare employers championed often placed them, at least insofar as legislated labor reform was concerned, in the same voluntarist political camp as the NAM. Promoting welfare work's benefits to workers and the wider public, welfare capitalists not only endorsed employers' virtues and initiative; by championing the alternative, they disputed the need for public provisions.

For precisely this reason, proponents of legislated social welfare came to view welfare capitalists as political foes. At a national conference on social insurance, T. J. Duffy, a member of the Ohio Industrial Commission, warned of the "representations of those who, for selfish reasons, set up the scarecrow of [government] paternalism. . . . in order to prevent men from . . . considering the real merits of State insurance." Even some NAM leaders learned to appreciate the political support welfare capitalists gave them. Recognizing that welfare work, for all its "maudlin sympathy," strengthened the association's support of voluntarism, the NAM's president, George Pope, praised in 1916 the timely arrival of "a new era in American industry" characterized by "a keener sense of social responsibility among the great body of manufacturers than ever before . . . a new era in American industry." Responding to comparisons between European progress and American backwardness, Pope denounced those who would "Germanize, Gallicize, or Anglicize our industries or institutions," warning of the injurious effects public programs would have on individual initiative. "When misfortune, accident, sickness, and old age lessen the power of the individual to provide for himself or for those dependent upon him," he urged, "then let us help him to help himself." Welfare capitalists could not have agreed more. Like Pope, they saw in the political drama unfolding before them a contest between state and voluntary social provision, only one of which could prevail.[30]

Compared to the panoply of proposed plans of the Progressive era, the paths not taken, the reform voluntarism of welfare capitalism was remarkably conservative and politically restrained. Understandably,

29. *Survey*, August 16, 1913, p. 623; Post quoted in Henderson, *Citizens in Industry*, p. 21.

30. T. J. Duffy and Col. George Pope quoted in U.S. Bureau of Labor Statistics, *Proceedings on the Conference on Social Insurance*, Bulletin 212 (1917), pp. 145, 850–54.

many contemporaries had a difficult time seeing it that way. Although welfare capitalists supported the NAM's political voluntarism, their conspicuous investment in worker pensions, cafeterias, roof gardens, and safety devices visibly refuted the NAM's harsher antilabor views. In this difference lay the seeds of welfare work's success. Welfare work's political appeal derived from the fact that its push for workplace reform made its sponsors appear remarkably progressive. Protecting in the long run a private ordering of industrial affairs, welfare work owed its popularity to its marketability in an age of reform: a response to the labor problem more palatable than the one evinced by Henry Frick and his colleagues.

Welfare Work and the Politics of Language

No less a personage than John Commons first introduced and defined the term "welfare work." In a July 1903 article in *Review of Reviews*, Commons praised programs for employees at the International Harvester Company in Chicago as an example of the growth of "welfare work," a term he defined as "all of those services which an employer may render to his work people over and above the payment of wages."[31]

Common's explanation at once suggests the appearance of the term and its unfamiliarity. By 1903 the word "welfare," understood to mean well-being, prosperity, and good health, was centuries old; its use dated to the early fourteenth century. By the 1890s the word "welfare" was also being related specifically to laborers' well-being in the context of describing efforts to promote the "welfare of workers." The phrase, however, was but one of many labels inspired by contemporary interest in industrial reforms. What in the 1900s and 1910s would be classified unhesitatingly as welfare work was, in the 1890s, called interchangeably "industrial betterment," "social uplift," or "uplift work."[32]

31. John R. Commons, " 'Welfare Work' in a Great Industrial Plant," *Review of Reviews* 28 (July 1903): 79. On Commons's ideas on labor reform, see Wunderlin, *Visions of a New Industrial Order*, and Ronald W. Schatz, "From Commons to Dunlop: Rethinking the Field and Theory of Industrial Relations," in Lichtenstein and Harris, *Industrial Democracy in America*.

32. *Oxford Encyclopedia of the English Language*, p. 108; Helen Grant Cushing and Adah V. Morris, *Nineteenth-Century Readers' Guide to Periodical Literature, 1890–1899*, vol. 2 (New York: H. W. Wilson, 1944), p. 1435; Leo S. Rowe, "Conference of the Central Bureau for the Promotion of the Welfare of the Laboring Classes," *Annals of the American Academy of Political and Social Science* 3 (July 1892): 73–81; A. I. Finley, "Shop Improvement and Its

The term "welfare work" became a permanent fixture in industrial discourse only after the founding of the National Civic Federation's Welfare Department in January 1904. The department, a business organization whose executives included H. H. Vreeland of the New York City Railroad Company, Cyrus McCormick of International Harvester, and John Patterson of National Cash Register, sought to ease industrial tensions through voluntarily provided labor reforms. Believing that the department's name would be important to its success or failure, members debated at the outset which label would best capture the spirit and goals of their work. Discussions of language were politically encumbered. Members voiced concern that the terms "betterment" and "social uplift" would offend American workers' autonomy and "fighting spirit." These terms, they argued, mirrored the pejorative language of charity and philanthropical work. Applied to the workplace, they suggested that workers' character flaws, rather than their conditions of employment, were to be the primary objects of reform. Hoping to avoid these connotations, the department decided on the term "welfare work" instead. Its suggestion of prosperity and well-being seemed more in keeping with what they viewed as the distinctive "independent spirit" of the American working class, a spirit department members were eager to preserve.[33]

Thus, almost at its inception, the term "welfare work" encapsulated a distinctive vision of politics, reform, and welfare. As Linda Gordon has argued, the meaning of welfare has changed radically over the last century, evolving from a "vision of the good life" to "grudging aid to the poor." Welfare capitalists clung to the former definition. They viewed the word "welfare" positively, chiefly because they understood it to be a phenomenon of the private sector. This identification, alien to Americans today, made sense in the Progressive era, decades before the term "welfare state," linking welfare specifically to government provisions, began to be used. Indeed, welfare capitalists spent considerable time distinguishing private sector provisions, which they called welfare,

Critics," *Social Service* 4 (September 1901): 79.

The *Readers' Guide to Periodical Literature* shows a separate heading for "welfare work in industry" as early as the 1890–99 volume. But because the volume was published after the years it indexes, it reflects the projection of a later generation's linguistic taxonomy onto the past and not contemporaries' understanding.

33. National Civic Federation, *Proceedings of the Eleventh Annual Meeting of the National Civic Federation* (New York, 1911), pp. 314–15; U.S. Senate, Commission on Industrial Relations, *Final Report and Testimony of the U.S. Commission on Industrial Relations*, 64th Cong., 1st sess. (Washington, D.C.: Government Printing Office, 1916), 3:2219; Green, *National Civic Federation and the American Labor Movement*, pp. 269–70.

from government entitlements. Foreshadowing the equation of public assistance with individuals' personal failings, an equation that figures prominently in attacks on public assistance programs today, they assailed state reforms as "free" government handouts to the needy and dependent. Welfare work, in contrast, promised contractual embellishments to hardworking, deserving wage earners—workers who neither needed nor, according to employers, wanted state support. Promoting an employer variant of the American Federation of Labor's voluntarism, welfare capitalists insisted that self-respecting workers would not willingly prostrate themselves to the state to secure concessions they could otherwise "earn." Praising workers' fierce independence and private initiative as the backbone of political virtue, proponents of welfare work invoked a Sombartian view of labor conversatism that conveniently buttressed their own critique of welfare statism. Europe might have embraced the state model, but the United States never would, the argument ran, because American workers opposed it. As one industrialist explained, glaring disparities between the European and the American welfare systems could be explained only by "the difference of mental attitude between the European laborer and the American. The American does not like to have things done for him. . . . The continental worker does not have this feeling."[34]

Attributing the absence of a public welfare safety net to workers' rather than employers' preferences enabled welfare capitalists to present their antilabor legislation crusade in a pro-labor light. The Social Insurance Department of the National Civic Federation (NCF), for instance, opposed universal sickness insurance partly because of the "vehement opposition on the part of the working people to compulsory health insurance." The department decided to "defer" to workers' opinions because insurance "through legislative enactment . . . would destroy the initiative of the industrial worker necessary to our development as a nation." Emphasizing workers' ideological distinctiveness, welfare capitalists made labor exceptionalism as they defined it a justification for state exceptionalism.[35]

---

34. Linda Gordon, *Pitied but Not Entitled: Single Mothers and the History of Welfare, 1890–1935* (New York: Free Press, 1994), p. 1; U.S. House of Representatives, *Report of the Industrial Commission*, 14:ci. On the voluntarism of the American Federation of Labor, see Christopher Tomlins, *The State and the Unions: Labor Relations, Law, and the Organized Labor Movement in America, 1880–1960* (New York: Cambridge University Press, 1985); and Forbath, *Law and the Shaping of the American Labor Movement*.

35. "If Not Compulsory Insurance—What?" *National Civic Federation Review* 4 (June 5, 1919): 1.

Praise for the virtues of labor voluntarism surfaced frequently in discussions of welfare work. In an interview published on the front page of the *New York Times* on November 17, 1912, Gertrude Beeks, secretary of the Welfare Department, emphasized the incongruity between welfare capitalism and government provision. Beeks was no stranger to the philosophy and practice of welfare capitalism. Widely regarded as the movement's leader, Beeks, more than anyone else, directed its course. After serving from 1894 to 1901 as assistant secretary of the Chicago-based Civic Federation (predecessor to the NCF), Beeks gained hands-on experience in the movement as a welfare worker at the McCormick Works, soon to become International Harvester. She remained with the company until 1903 and then joined the NCF. Owing chiefly to her tenacity, the Welfare Department was founded soon thereafter. As department secretary, Beeks became, in the words of one journalist, "nominally secretary and actually the very pulse" of the department. Beek's experience and expertise made her uniquely qualified to comment on the complexion of welfare work. Her *Times* interview, accordingly, provides a revealing glimpse of the political dynamic undergirding the movement as a whole.[36]

Elucidating the political origins of welfare work, Beeks described it as a logical response by employers to government regulation, a mechanism for curtailing demand for public provisions. The rise of welfare work, she explained, "was an economic move, for it anticipate[d] legislation forcing some provision for the sick, maimed, or worn out, but loyal industrial employee." The special appeal of welfare work, she continued, was that it was preferable to legislative reform. First was the financial consideration. Echoing the AFL's critique of minimum wage legislation, Beeks argued that legally mandated improvements would establish the ceiling, not the floor, for workplace reform. By curbing employers' initiative, compulsory meliorations would impede future im-

36. Beeks's tasks as department secretary were wide-ranging: she investigated factories, department stores, and shops to study working conditions and the successes and failures of welfare work; she published dozens of articles and pamphlets; she gave guest lectures to women's clubs, employer associations, and labor organizations (the Stationary Firemen's Union even made her an honorary member); and in 1913, a year after the *Times* interview, she taught the first systematic course on welfare work in the history of higher education at the New York University School of Commerce. As a consultant, she was paid $100 a day (an astronomical sum for 1912, especially given her sex), plus expenses to advise employers on how to establish welfare work. See Sarah Comstock, "A Woman of Achievement: Miss Gertrude Beeks," *World's Work* 26 (August 1913): 444–48; Commons, " 'Welfare Work' in a Great Industrial Plant"; "The Social Agent," *Rochester Union Advertiser*, September 27, 1902; *Chicago Evening Post*, September 24, 1902; Green, *National Civic Federation and the American Labor Movement*, p. 276.

provements. In addition, with legislation forcing business's hand, industrial harmony born of workers' appreciation of employers' generosity would be absent; employees would be less likely to respect the indifference of legal compliance, she argued, than they would the thoughtfulness behind unprompted magnanimity. "It is infinitely better," she contended, "that [workplace provisions] should be worked out by voluntary action, rather than under the compulsory influence of law, for such determinations on the part of employers tend greatly to promote [a] peaceful relationship between employer and employed." Moreover, Beeks continued, the private sector could afford to be more generous than the public. Lauding the financial benefits of private accident compensation, Beeks insisted that "no government compensation in the world is half so generous as that which has been worked out . . . by these enlightened employers. . . . No law exists providing such a generous compensation."[37]

But a still more vital consideration for Beeks was the toll government handouts would exact on workers' morale. Here, Beeks distilled the essence of the welfare work movement's critique of government "charity." Private sector reforms would spare workers the feelings of ineptitude and the stigma of disgrace spawned by dependency on the state. Promoting a set of values grounded in the political virtue of economic independence, Beeks warned that unearned welfare, by eroding individual initiative and the penchant for self-help, would destroy workers' self-respect. Thus for Beeks, welfare work entailed more than calming the waters of industrial conflict. Its triumph was tantamount to safeguarding American political virtue, which she claimed was imperiled by the advance of government provisions. As Beeks explained, welfare work

> is a fine thing . . . for it removes from the State and municipal governments an important part of the vast burden of charitable expenditures which lies so heavily upon them and so humiliates those who are dependent on it, thus relieving the . . . public from taxation and the unfortunate recipients from a humiliation even harder to be borne. That last point is, above all, worthy of strong emphasis. Plans like this one make for self-respecting citizenship among the workers and for happiness among the families of those who may be ill, injured, or aged.[38]

37. Marshall, "Welfare Work May Conquer Great Labor Problems," p. 1.
38. Beeks admitted that yet another point in favor of welfare work was that the state and the taxpaying public would benefit financially by being freed from the burden of

The self-respecting citizenship to which Beeks referred, moreover, could be obtained by both male and female workers. Welfare capitalists accepted popularly prescribed gender roles in which manliness was staked to achievement within the marketplace, femininity to homemaking and economic dependence. But they insisted that irrespective of sex, workers' welfare and political citizenship would best be supported by private rather than government provisions. To make their case, welfare capitalists delineated a hierarchy of welfare provision in which the site and source of provisions were crucial. As they explained with reference to male workers, insofar as government provision transformed self-reliant citizens into state dependents, it was intrinsically emasculating. Devaluing the "rugged independence" that supposedly made America special, government provision weakened male character and sapped the country's political strength. In contrast, welfare work, adulating voluntarism and self-help, validated manhood by supplying the material tools for independence—pensions, stockholding plans, private property—which employees "earned" through hard work and loyalty. Within this paradigm, public and private provisions became emblematic of the distinctive social conditions of recipients. Needy wage earners received government charity; deserving wage earners earned nonmonetary merit pay.[39]

Welfare capitalists' arguments for the preferability of private provisions for women were more complex but equally revealing of the desire of employers to preserve private sector control over labor matters. Welfare capitalists agreed that women's political citizenship necessitated their performance of sex-specific roles. If "being a man" meant economic independence, "being a woman" meant accepting domestic duties bounded by homemaking and motherhood. They disagreed, however, about who was best able to promote responsible female citizenship.

Anathema to male political virtue, state guardianship was deemed by many Progressive reformers to be the best conservator of female wage earners' maternal calling. Many reformers agreed with the American Federation of Labor's proclamation that the working woman "is, as a possible mother, to be protected by the State. She is, when a helpless

paying for public provisions. See Marshall, "Welfare Work May Conquer Great Labor Problems," p. 1.

39. An excellent analysis of the gendering of political and economic citizenship is Gwendolyn Mink, "The Lady and the Tramp: Gender, Race, and the Origins of the American Welfare State," in *Women, the State, and Welfare*, ed. Linda Gordon (Madison: University of Wisconsin Press, 1990), pp. 92–122.

mother, to be nurtured with her children by the State. She is, in many respects as a citizen, to share in a changed environment, brought about by justice in the State."[40]

Accepting an ideology of gender difference inherent in such statements, welfare capitalists nevertheless hailed private workplace reforms as a better protector of femininity than state provisions. Promising a radical overhaul of the conditions of work through an infusion of private capital, employers vowed to transform the factory into a training camp for superior maternal citizenship. While protective legislation advocates aimed to ease the burden of wage labor, welfare capitalists promised enriched womanhood as a *condition* of wage labor. Welfare firms sponsored hygiene, cooking, and sewing classes on company time. According to Beeks, programs for women, "endeavoring to fit [them] to be good wives and mothers," benefited everyone: the employer, the public, and, most important, women workers themselves. "Many an ex-working girl has gone back to her old employer," Beeks boasted, "to thank him for having made her a good wife." Thus, without disputing the charge that women possessed a maternal destiny more important than wage work, welfare capitalists recast wage work as a stepping-stone to a higher state of femininity.

Unifying Beeks's discussions of labor voluntarism, citizenship, masculinity, and femininity was an impassioned defense of the virtues of private sector reform. From the beginning, welfare work was more than a descriptive term. It was also a political ideology. Promoting voluntary reform as the best response to the labor question, welfare work challenged the need for government provisions. At precisely the point when comprehensive legislative protections for workers became a political possibility, welfare capitalists demonstrated their willingness to reform the workplace to the point necessary to retain the privileges of power.

The Organizational Framework of Welfare Work

The coining of the term "welfare work" and the ensuing definitional discussions were important steps in the consolidation of the welfare work movement, attempts to hammer out a consistent, unifying ideology. Equally important to the rise of welfare work were the numerous agencies that reported on, coordinated, and encouraged the expansion of private sector reforms.

40. Editorial in *American Federationist*, August 1910.

Industrial betterment schemes first captured national attention in the 1890s. Journals such as *Harper's Weekly, Forum,* and *Review of Reviews* featured descriptions of individual employers' experiments to solve the labor problem through workplace amelioration; contemporaneously, more specialized business periodicals such as *Engineering Magazine* began documenting its value to management. The journalistic interest in workplace betterment intensified after 1900, along with both the expansion of private reforms and the growing recognition of welfare work as an independent activity. Between 1900 and 1910 approximately 160 articles on welfare work, most of them laudatory, appeared in mainstream journals. By 1905, at least four books trumpeting welfare work's merits were in circulation. By 1920, the publication of two others had rounded out the list.[41]

These general works were supplemented by a spate of government and private surveys. State labor bureaus led the way, publishing independent investigations of employers' activities. As early as 1887, the Pennsylvania Bureau of Industrial Statistics issued a special bulletin titled "Alleviation of Distress among Workingmen" as part of its *Fifteenth Annual Report*; between 1903 and 1906 New York, New Jersey, and Rhode Island followed suit. The Federal Bureau of Labor Statistics issued three bulletins on welfare work between 1900 and 1919. The first, Victor Olmstead's *Betterment of Industrial Conditions*, released in 1900, surveyed welfare activities at a dozen firms. Elizabeth Lewis Otey's 1913 *Employers' Welfare Work* supplied information on fifty establishments. The last, Alice Whitney's *Welfare Work for Employees in Industrial Establishments in the United States*, was the most ambitious. Begun in 1916 and issued in 1919, it assessed welfare policies in 431 establishments. In addition to the three major bulletins, the Bureau of Labor Statistics' *Monthly Review* published dozens of summaries of individual reforms that often

41. For a representative but incomplete survey of nineteenth-century periodical literature, see *Nineteenth-Century Readers' Guide to Periodical Literature, 1890–1899*, p. 1435. For articles published between 1900 and 1921, see vols. 1–5 of the *Readers' Guide to Periodical Literature* (Minneapolis: H. W. Wilson, 1905–22). Contemporary monographs include Nicholas Paine Gilman, *Profit Sharing between Employer and Employee: A Study in the Evolution of the Wage System* (Boston: Houghton Mifflin, 1889), idem., *A Dividend to Labor: A Study of Employers' Welfare Institutions* (Boston: Houghton Mifflin, 1899); William Howe Tolman, *Social Engineering: A Record of Things Done by American Industrialists Employing Upwards of One and One-Half Million of People* (New York: McGraw, 1909); Budgett Meakin, *Model Factories and Villages: Ideal Conditions of Labour and Housing* (Philadelphia: George W. Jacobs, 1905); Edwin L. Shuey, *Factory People and Their Employers: How Their Relations Are Made Pleasant and Profitable* (New York: Lentilhon, 1900); Henderson, *Citizens in Industry*; Daniel Bloomfield, *Labor Maintenance: A Practical Handbook of Employees' Service Work* (New York: Ronald Press, 1920).

provided evidence for the more comprehensive reports. Two employers' organizations, the Boston and Cleveland Chambers of Commerce, making none of the claims of objectivity of government agencies, issued independent reports praising employers' magnanimity.[42]

Meanwhile, two national organizations, the American Institute of Social Service and the Welfare Department of the National Civic Federation (NCF), were aggressively promoting welfare work. The institute was founded in 1898 by Protestant minister Josiah Strong, but it was William Tolman, the institute's executive director and director of industrial betterment, who launched the organization's zealous crusade for welfare work. Under Tolman's tutelage, the institute highlighted welfare "success stories" in its monthly magazine, *Social Service*. It also distributed a weekly circular dispensing advice for commercial clients on topics ranging from the use of mottoes on factory walls to the operation of employee suggestion systems.[43]

The NCF's Welfare Department was larger and better financed and ultimately more important to the advance of welfare work. The National Civic Federation was founded in 1900 by the Chicago journalist and former schoolteacher Ralph Easley to explore political, economic, and social issues of national significance. Throughout the Progressive era the NCF was, in the words of one historian, "the leading organization of politically conscious corporate leaders." Although some of the NCF's first standing committees (including committees on foreign relations, taxation, and military affairs) reflected the organization's initially diverse interests, the NCF quickly became identified by the public as an organization devoted exclusively to industrial relations.[44]

42. See Pennsylvania, Department of Internal Affairs, Bureau of Industrial Statistics, "Alleviation of Distress among Workingmen," *Fifteenth Annual Report*, 1887, in *Annual Report of the Secretary of Internal Affairs*, vol. 15, pt. 3 (Harrisburg, 1888); New York Department of Labor, *Third Annual Report of the Commissioner of Labor* (Albany, 1903), pt. 4: "Employers' Welfare Institutions," by George A. Stevens and Leonard W. Hatch, in New York, *Assembly Documents, 1904*, vol. 22, no. 61 (Albany, 1904); "Welfare Work in Rhode Island," in Rhode Island, Commissioner of Industrial Statistics, *Nineteenth Annual Report* (Providence, 1906), and "Industrial Betterment Institutions in New Jersey Manufacturing Establishments," in New Jersey, Bureau of Statistics of Labor and Industries, *Twenty-seventh Annual Report* (Trenton, 1904). The Bureau of Labor Statistics issued three bulletins on welfare work between 1900 and 1919: *The Betterment of Industrial Conditions*, Bulletin 31 (1900); *Employers' Welfare Work*; and *Welfare Work for Employees in Industrial Establishments in the United States*, Bulletin 250 (1919).

43. Letters of May 31, June 6, and October 24, 1906, American Institute of Social Service Weekly Commercial Letter Service, Cyrus H. McCormick Jr. Papers, Box 41, State Historical Society of Wisconsin, Madison (hereafter SHSW).

44. James Weinstein, *The Corporate Ideal in the Liberal State, 1900–1918* (Boston: Beacon 1968), p. xv.

One reason for this narrowing identification was Easley's member-ship recruitment strategy. Easley wanted the federation's appeal to tran-scend party and class cleavages. To this end he named Samuel Gompers NCF vice president, a position Gompers held until his death in 1924. Easley also established an NCF Executive Committee equally represen-tative of labor, capital, and an undefined "public." Although big busi-ness interests, ably represented by Andrew Carnegie and George W. Perkins, university administrators, and politicians, furnished the finan-cial backbone of the NCF, at least one-third of the Executive Commit-tee was drawn from organized labor.[45]

The NCF's association with labor issues became even more pro-nounced when the federation established its Welfare Department in January 1904. Viewing the implementation of welfare programs as em-ployer-driven, the Welfare Department limited its membership to em-ployers—those who were "taking the lead in welfare work in industries and those who [have] not yet begun it." The department declared its purpose to be the following:

1) To educate the public as to the real meaning and value of welfare work, which is understood to be any effort on the part of the employer, working with the employees, to better the conditions of the latter.

2) To interest employers not engaged in welfare work by emphasizing their moral obligation to give consideration to the general welfare of their employees.

3) To maintain a central bureau, for the exchange of experiences by employers actually engaged in welfare work, a special feature being the report of failures and their causes; and for the collection of data, reading matter, and illustrations for the benefit of all inquiring em-ployers.[46]

The department also announced that it would promote reforms in five key areas: sanitation (emergency hospitals, locker rooms, ventilation), recreation (concerts, gymnasiums, vacations), education (classes and li-braries), provident funds (pensions, insurance), and employee housing.

The Welfare Department quickly became one of the most active within the federation. Membership statistics reflect its growth. At its

45. Ibid., pp. 8–9.
46. National Civic Federation, *Conference on Welfare Work* (New York: Andrew H. Kellogg, 1904), p. xxv.

founding in 1904 the Welfare Department had 125 members; by 1911 its membership exceeded 500. Among them were some of the most prominent welfare firms of the day, including H. J. Heinz, the United Shoe Machinery Company, the National Biscuit Company, and Macy's.[47]

The Welfare Department gave the welfare movement momentum and unity. As H. H. Vreeland, first chairman of the Welfare Department put it, before the department's founding, the employer viewed "welfare work [as] an individual effort on his part in his particular locality . . . he was rather like the mole groping in a dark passage." After the department's establishment, this situation changed. As Bruno Ramirez has argued, the department supplied "a framework through which employers could compare their experiences, analyze common problems, and improve their programs." Linking together welfare capitalists from across the country, the Welfare Department cleared a path for collaboration and furnished a collective identity that transcended individual efforts.[48]

The Welfare Department functioned as the movement's clearinghouse, issuing reports and compiling statistics. It published a quarterly journal, the *Review*, as well as several pamphlets and numerous articles on welfare work. It sponsored a permanent public exhibit in New York City. Its secretary, Gertrude Beeks, corresponded frequently with companies to keep the department's files up to date and spoke frequently to employer associations. For a fee, department officials visited work sites to offer suggestions on establishing or improving welfare programs. In 1904 and 1911, the department hosted national welfare work conferences, bringing together dozens of welfare workers and employ-

47. Gertrude Beeks, *Welfare Work: An Address before the National Association of Wool Manufacturers* (New York, 1906), pp. 4–5, SHSW; Gertrude Beeks to Samuel Gompers, July 25, 1911, American Federation of Labor Papers, President's Office General Correspondence, Box 14, Folder 6; SHSW; Green, *National Civic Federation and the American Labor Movement*, pp. 268–70; membership list from Gertrude Beeks to S. M. Darling, November 16, 1904, Cyrus H. McCormick Jr. Papers, Box 39, SHSW.

48. Bruno Ramirez, *When Workers Fight: The Politics of Industrial Relations in the Progressive Era, 1898–1916* (Westport, Conn.: Greenwood Press, 1978), p. 149; National Civic Federation, *Conference on Welfare Work*, p. 1. The organizational framework within which welfare work flourished redirected previously uncoordinated instances of employer paternalism along a focused path. As one company welfare worker explained in 1910, the tendency of employers to care for workers "has existed in some form or another ever since the first employer was willing to do a little more for his employees than he had to under wage and other contract stipulations." The welfare work movement, however, arose only after this willingness had "crystallized into a well-planned and supervised work."

ers from across the country. When it was unable to join employers together under the same roof, it propagated its message on speaking tours.

The NCF's activities directly engaged the debate over private versus public provisions. In print and in person, NCF officials proffered welfare work as the enlightened alternative to reform through legislative enactment. The conspicuousness of the Welfare Department's political conservatism was reflected in the Department of Labor's 1913 description of it as "educational, conservative and nonaggressive"—an organization that "does not believe in resorting to legal enactment to assist in securing the conditions desired."[49]

Historians disagree over the NCF's role in campaigns for legislated reforms. James Weinstein, for instance, has argued that NCF support of workers' compensation laws was indicative of the organization's willingness to back social reform legislation to fend off political threats from the left. But the workers' compensation case can be interpreted in a different way—as an example of the NCF's opposition to government interference in capital-labor relations. By 1910, when the NCF began its active lobbying for compensation reform, widespread political support had made the enactment of some form of accident legislation practically inevitable. By intervening, the NCF won public approval while securing for itself a role in shaping the outcome of legislative negotiations. Model compensation legislation drafted in 1910 by P. Tecumseh Sherman, a conservative lawyer who chaired the NCF's legal committee, affirmed the federation's view that less government intervention was best. Sherman's proposal was sent to governors and legislators in all states that had established compensation committees. Informed by his rejection of the German model as both constitutionally untenable and unlikely to meet with labor's approval, it was, by his own admission, a "halfway measure," "the most conservative and least expensive scheme." It did not propose universal, compulsory, or state-financed coverage, and it was dismissed by many critics, including the Socialist Morris Hillquit, who correctly identified the NCF's ostensible support for compensation legislation as a shrewd attempt to prevent passage of "legislation which will sweep away all the defenses of the employer."[50]

49. U.S. Bureau of Labor Statistics, *Employers' Welfare Work*, p. 6.
50. Sherman and Hillquit quoted in Weinstein, *Corporate Ideal in the Liberal State*, pp. 45, 51–55; Robert Asher, "Business and Workers' Welfare in Massachusetts, 1880–1911," *Business History Review* 43 (1969): 452–75; idem, "Radicalism and Reform: State Insurance of Workmen's Compensation in Minnesota, 1910–1933," *Labor History* 14 (1973): 19–41;

The shortcomings of the numerous workers' compensation statutes adopted during this time—twenty-one states passed compensation or accident insurance laws between 1911 and 1913—enabled welfare capitalists to continue to milk their reputations as benefactors while proving, through the voluntary adoption of more generous accident insurance schemes, the pointlessness of further legislation. As a representative of the B. F. Goodrich Company explained in 1916 to John B. Andrews, secretary of the AALL, the fact that his company was "already paying vastly more for [worker] benefits" than the AALL's suggested state schemes undercut the need for legislated protections. In addition, the passage of compensation laws gave the NCF and welfare capitalists acceptable grounds upon which to urge reformers advocating legislated health insurance, pensions, or other provisions to discontinue their campaign. Savvily labeling workers' compensation laws as a "great but uncertain experiment" in social legislation whose long-term impact was unknown, the NCF made its lukewarm support of workers' compensation laws the basis for a full-fledged assault, couched in the vocabulary of prudence and caution, on other social insurance measures. As Gertrude Beeks warned at a national conference on social insurance in 1916, "It seems rather unfortunate to advocate a system experimentally. . . . Why in the world do we want to jump over the fence and bring into this country something the result of which we can not possibly estimate at the present time?"[51]

Even before it had entered the workers' compensation campaign, the NCF had revealed its voluntarist colors. The organization's early rejection of compulsory arbitration in favor of independent negotiation illustrated its commitment to achieving industrial harmony through self-regulation. The NCF Committee on Arbitration and Conciliation endorsed trade agreements precisely because they offered an alternative to compulsory third-party arbitration. On the controversial issue of child labor, the NCF again toed the voluntarist line. Easley himself deprecated the public outcry as an insult to "many fair-minded and humane employers" and urged critics to observe the "great progress [that] has been made" in the past fifteen years before resorting to legislative action to protect child welfare. And after the workers' compensation battle ended, the NCF continued its voluntarist crusade. In

idem, "Origins of Workmen's Compensation in Minnesota," *Minnesota History* 44 (1974): 142–53.

51. U.S. Bureau of Labor Statistics, *Proceedings of the Conference on Social Insurance*, pp. 345–47, 533, 541.

1913–14, with financial support from Andrew Carnegie and W. K. Vanderbilt, it conducted a "Survey of Social, Civic, and Industrial Progress," designed to neutralize pro-legislation sentiments strengthened by the findings of the 1912–15 Commission on Industrial Relations (CIR). At exactly the same time that the CIR's public hearings were revealing the full extent of industrial squalor, the NCF survey emphasized the positive and the improved; as the title of the survey stated, the study's focus was industrial *progress*. The NCF also lobbied against compulsory health insurance; Beeks commented at a gathering in 1916 to debate its merits that "health is the most important thing to our Nation, except individual initiative." These examples suggest that if we are to generalize at all from the NCF's compensation campaign, we must see it as a reflection more of the organization's long-standing antistatist politics than of support for legislated welfare protections.[52]

To be sure, not every employer influenced by the NCF's relentless promotional work had to accept its political message in its entirety. But many did. Although welfare capitalists often let the NCF fight legislative battles—and take the political heat—on their behalf, they sometimes aired their antistatist politics as individuals. Testifying before the Commission on Industrial Relations, John G. Shedd, longtime president of welfare firm Marshall Field and Company, was asked to comment on the desirability of compulsory protections for labor. After asserting that existing protections had "pretty well safeguarded industrial conditions," he questioned the need for protective laws. "You can not," he insisted, "legislate to stifle unrest any more than you can legislate people into a happy frame of mind. To my mind, the greatest happiness and satisfaction comes from a full day's work well done and fully recompensed." Disputing the "assumption" that industrial conditions were bad enough to warrant reform, he reminded the commission that "this country is today the best country in the world for the man who has to make his living." Percy Straus, manager of Macy's department store and another welfare work leader, likewise admitted that he thought social insurance "can be overdone." George W. Perkins, director at the United States Steel Company and International Harvester, both well-known welfare firms, characterized government intervention as the source of, rather than the cure for, existing labor tensions. "For

---

52. Wunderlin, *Visions of a New Industrial Order*, pp. 53, 128; Tishler, *Self-Reliance and Social Security*, pp. 136–38; Easley quoted in Weinstein, *Corporate Ideal in the Liberal State*, p. 28; Beeks quoted in U.S. Bureau of Labor Statistics, *Proceedings of the Conference on Social Insurance*, p. 532.

every ounce of trouble brought about in industry through the selfish-
ness and cupidity of business men," he told the commission, "a pound
of trouble has been brought about through half-baked laws and mut-
tonhead legislation on the part of our legislators. Our legislators have
not even possessed hindsight, and they have been veritable babes in
foresight."[53]

The 1916 Conference on Social Insurance, a national meeting of
employers, legislators, insurance magnates, social workers, and officials
of charity and health organizations, convened to discuss workers' compensation, health insurance, old-age insurance, maternity benefits,
mothers' pensions, and unemployment insurance, afforded another opportunity for welfare capitalists to verbalize their antistatist views. During a discussion of proposed sickness insurance legislation, R. B.
Stearns, vice-president of the Milwaukee Electric Railway & Light Company, claimed that he did "not believe this country is ready for legislation of this kind." Existing voluntary schemes, he suggested, were
adequately attending to the health needs of workers. "Up-to-date employers," he told the conference, already "employ the same principles
of health insurance through the various forms of welfare work, relief
systems, cooperative activities, and preventive measures" proposed by
model legislation. Magnus Alexander of the General Electric Company
likewise based his arguments against state provisions on the preferability of private sector reforms. Discussing a proposed noncontributory
old-age pension system, he depicted voluntarism as the best protector
of self-sufficiency. "The progress in social betterment in this country,"
he asserted, "has been brought about in large part by individual initiative, independence, and self-reliance. . . . This process will continue unless the forces that have brought it about are undermined by unwise
social legislation." Praising voluntary schemes and employers who installed them, he warned that if state intervention were to supersede
the prevailing voluntarist policy, Americans would be forced to bear
both the "stigma of pauperism and the loss of citizenship rights." Like
Gertrude Beeks, Alexander depicted welfare work as the guardian of
American political virtue, a way to improve the workplace without "sacrificing" self-sufficiency and individualism in the process.[54]

The parallels between employers' testimonials and the NCF's agenda,

53. Testimony of John G. Shedd, Percy Straus, and George W. Perkins in U.S. Senate,
Commission on Industrial Relations, *Final Report and Testimony*, 4:3372, 3:2383, 8:7600.
54. U.S. Bureau of Labor Statistics, *Proceedings of the Conference on Social Insurance*,
pp. 634, 770–71.

the organization's prodigious growth and its popularity among welfare employers, and especially the extent to which its energies animated the movement as a whole suggest the degree to which the spread of welfare work occurred within the NCF's political borders. Moreover, because political and more narrowly circumscribed labor management goals were not mutually exclusive, employers could support the political agenda of welfare capitalism without sacrificing their commitment to factory efficiency. Indeed, it was precisely welfare work's versatility, a system of labor control that was also an antistatist scheme, that cemented its popularity among a growing segment of employers in the Progressive age. Expecting welfare programs to improve labor output, reduce turnover, and embellish recruitment and retention incentives, welfare employers lost nothing in hoping that its efficacy would also be measured by the preservation of employers' prerogatives.

The Demography of Welfare Work

More than a name and organizational campaign, welfare work was also a practice that affected at least 1,500 firms by 1914. But which employers? And why some but not others? Comparing causality in welfare and nonwelfare firms is problematic. Only a minority of employers in the Progressive era established welfare work. The historical record privileges their stories. In an era when political leaders and social reformers sought to ease industrial tensions, welfare employers were encouraged to recount their experiences for the public record. Moreover, employers in the Progressive era were a fragmented class. They operated within the structural boundaries of capitalism, but their actions were mediated by differences in location, firm size, the composition of the labor force, market orientation, and employers' individual convictions. Each company functioned within its own economic and political constellation, the precise configuration of these relationships peculiarly its own.[55]

And yet the striking structural similarities among welfare firms suggest that certain companies were better positioned than others to invest in welfare programs. Although an analysis of the common features of welfare companies cannot generate a composite of the prototypical welfare firm, it *can* suggest the problems and experiences shared by many welfare employers.[56]

55. Robert H. Wiebe, "Business Unity and the Progressive Movement, 1901–1914," *Mississippi Valley Historical Review* 4 (March 1958): 664–85.
56. Wiebe, *Businessmen and Reform.*

Two national surveys completed in 1913 furnish important data on welfare work companies. The first, the Bureau of Labor Statistics' bulletin *Employers' Welfare Work*, surveyed welfare activity at fifty firms. The second, sponsored by the Boston Chamber of Commerce, includes private correspondence between members of the chamber's Industrial Relations Sub-Committee on Welfare Work and sixty-eight companies. Although there is some overlap, the surveys provide information on one hundred welfare firms. Together they reveal both the structural similarities among welfare firms and the economic and political imperatives that unified welfare work as a movement.[57]

Size. Most welfare firms were large corporations that concentrated a large number of employees in a single location. Although welfare work did not follow automatically on the heels of corporate bigness, the majority of welfare firms employed more than 1,000 workers. Given patterns of employee concentration at the turn of the century, a dis-

---

57. Firms surveyed for the Bureau of Labor Statistics Bulletin were American Woolen; Atchison, Topeka & Santa Fe Railroad; Bloomingdale's; Browne & Sharpe; Chicago Telephone; Cleveland Hardware; Cleveland Twist Drill; Commonwealth Edison; Curtis Publishing; Edison Electric; Filene's; Forbes Lithograph; General Electric; Gimbel Bros.; Gorham Manufacturing; Greenhut Siegel; H. Black & Co.; H. J. Heinz; Hotel Astor; Huyler's; Interborough Transit; International Harvester; Joseph & Feiss; Lowe Bros.; Lowney Chocolate; Macy's; Marshall Field; Metropolitan Life; National Biscuit Co.; National Cash Register; New England Telephone; New York Evening Post; New York Telephone; Niagara Falls Power; Pocasset Worsted; Sears, Roebuck; Sherwin-Williams; Shredded Wheat; Solvay Process; Talbot Mills; Thomas G. Plant; Thomas Manufacturing; Union Pacific Railroad; and United Shoe Machinery. See U.S. Bureau of Labor Statistics, *Employers' Welfare Work*.

The Boston Chamber of Commerce investigation surveyed the following firms: A. E. Little & Co.; Acme White Lead & Color Works; Alaska Refrigerator; American Can; American Soda Fountain; Baldwin Locomotive Works; Barcalo Manufacturing; Boston Woven Hose & Rubber; Bourne Mills; Brighton Mills; Browne & Sharpe Manufacturing; C. Howard Hunt Pen; Cadillac Cabinet; Celluloid Company; Dennison Manufacturing; Eastman Bros. & Bancroft; Eastman Kodak; Edison Electric Illuminating Co. of Boston; Elgin National Watch Co.; Fitchburg & Leominster St. Railroad; Forbes Lithograph Manufacturing Company; General Electric; German-American Button Co.; Grand Rapids Refrigerator Co.; H. J. Heinz; Hershey's; Huyler's; International Harvester; Keystone Leather Co.; L. Adler Bros. & Co.; Ludlow Manufacturing Associates; Marshall Field; Michigan Stove Co.; N. O. Nelson Manufacturing Co.; National Blank Book Co.; New England Telephone & Telegraph; Norton Co.; Page Belting; Parke, Davis & Co.; Plymouth Cordage; Pocasset Worsted; R. Wallace & Sons Manufacturing Co.; Regal Shoe; Remington Typewriter; Royal Worcester Corset; Rumford Chemical Works; S. D. Warren & Co.; Sears, Roebuck; Solvay Process; Syracuse Chilled Plow; Talbot Mills; Taylor Instrument; Trenton Potteries; Union Switch & Signal Co.; U.S. Steel; Vermont Marble Co.; W. L. Douglas Shoe Co.; Wagner Electric Manufacturing Co.; Walker & Pratt; Walter Baker & Co.; Waltham Watch Co.; Wanamaker's; Wells Bros. Co.; Westinghouse Air Brake Co.; Westinghouse Electric & Manufacturing Co.; Westinghouse Lamp Co.; Willet, Sears & Co.; and Yale & Towne Manufacturing Co. See Boston Chamber of Commerce Collection, Case 48, Folder 332–19, Baker Library Archives of the Harvard Graduate School of Business.

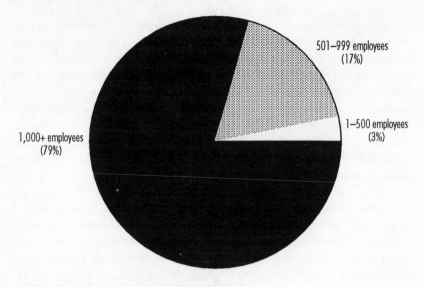

Average number of employees in welfare firms surveyed: 7,597
Average number of employees in U.S. industrial establishments: 26

Figure 1. Size of labor force in welfare firms, 1913

Sources: U.S. Bureau of Labor Statistics, *Employers' Welfare Work*, Bulletin 123 (1913); Boston Chamber of Commerce Papers, Case 48, Folder 332–19, Baker Library Archives of the Harvard Graduate School of Business; U.S. Bureau of the Census, *The Integration of Industrial Operations* (Washington, D.C.: Government Printing Office, 1924), pt. 2.

proportionate number of large companies were welfare firms. In 1913, when firms with over 1,000 employees accounted for about 0.2 percent of American businesses, they represented fully 81 percent of welfare firms surveyed. While the average number of employees in an industrial establishment in 1913 was 2.6, the average number of employees in surveyed companies exceeded 7,000 (Figure 1).[58]

There are several explanations for the correlation between the size

58. U.S. Bureau of the Census, *The Integration of Industrial Operation* (Washington, D.C.: Government Printing Office, 1924), pp. 40, 76; Glenn Porter, *The Rise of Big Business, 1860-1910* (Arlington Heights, Ill: Harlan Davidson, 1973), pp. 10–11; Sanford Jacoby, *Employing Bureaucracy: Managers, Unions, and the Transformation of Work in American Industry, 1900-1945* (New York: Columbia University Press, 1985), p. 3; and Walter Licht, "Studying Work: Personnel Policies in Philadelphia Firms, 1850–1950," in *Masters to Managers: Historical and Comparative Perspectives on American Employers*, ed. Stanford M. Jacoby (New York: Columbia University Press, 1991), pp. 43–74. By 1900 at least 75 plants in the Northeast and Midwest employed 2,000 or more employees. Portending further employee concentration, these firms were still the exception to the rule.

of the labor force and the presence of welfare work. First, large firms were more visible and thus more likely to be subjected to public scrutiny and government inquiry. As one contemporary observed, "The larger the corporation is the more . . . it is in the limelight, and consequently it is better business for them to treat their labor well than [it is in] a smaller concern." Relatedly, big businesses were often headed by moguls such as John Patterson and Edward Filene, who functioned as celebrities in their respective communities. The public monitoring of these larger-than-life magnates predisposed them to support policies that protected their reputations.[59]

Second, the cost structure of big business favored year-round production; when large pools of capital were invested in fixed costs, it was expensive to weather bad business cycles. Given high constant costs, a permanent labor force was more than an elusive ideal—it was a precondition for production. Efficacious strategies to reduce labor turnover were invaluable.

Third, large firms were best equipped with the financial resources to administer plant-wide labor policies. Sustained corporate growth in the Progressive era endowed big business with the profits necessary to develop comprehensive welfare programs. In addition to having more money than other firms to allocate to welfare expenditures, big businesses were also best situated to offer a broader selection of welfare provisions. Welfare work operated on an economy of scale; its per capita cost decreased as the size of the labor force grew. The construction of a company cafeteria, for instance, required an initial outlay prohibitive to the small firm. And once constructed, the cafeteria's daily operation demanded constant operating costs beyond the financial reach of many firms. In general, the size of a firm had a bearing on the benefits it could offer. Not surprisingly, quasi-pecuniary benefits such as profit sharing and pensions were among the first employee benefits offered in the United States. Their administration, relegated chiefly to the realm of paperwork, required few costs above the sum to be "shared" with employees. As a result, they could be introduced in small and large firms alike. Only large firms had the capital to build more physically substantive benefits such as clubhouses, tennis courts, and hospitals at a low per capita cost. As one contemporary said, "Large establishments with abundant capital and more than the usual margin of profits . . . can do many things not possible for small factories." When the Bureau of Labor Statistics noted with approval the growth

59. U.S. Senate, Commission on Industrial Relations, *Final Report and Testimony*, 8:7459.

in the construction of company restaurants, auditoriums, and gymnasiums in its 1913 survey of welfare work, it was observing the expansion of benevolence as a big business phenomenon.[60]

Fourth, employers and industrial reformers often viewed labor problems as a symptom of corporate estrangement. Under antebellum proprietary capitalism, workers in shops and small factories were employed by a person who both owned and managed production. The diverse tasks required of the owner-entrepreneur frequently gave him a degree, albeit limited, of personal contact with employees. When such contact was regular and the labor force was small, as a shoe company executive pointed out, "cases of sickness, accident and death were sure to come to his attention," allowing him "every opportunity to be personally helpful to those in his employ."[61]

The growth of big business caused the demise of routine personal contact. The postbellum incorporation wave depended on the issue of public stock to finance industrial expansion. Diversified ownership enabled a single individual to own more than one company and thousands of individuals to own a single company; consequently, ownership in the corporate community became "scattered over the globe." The uncoupling of ownership and management physically separated those who controlled firms on paper from those who ran them daily and limited possibilities for routine contact between employer and worker. It used to be the case that "master and man lived and worked together," William Tolman wrote in 1909. But "the day has passed when the employer is able to individualize those who work for him; not knowing them by name or even by sight, the personal touch, the point of contact has been lost."[62]

60. Shuey, *Factory People and Their Employers*, p. 26. The earliest profit-sharing plan in the United States was established by the Bay State Shoe & Leather Co. in 1867. The plan gave workers 25 percent of the company's net profits. It lasted six years and was terminated when workers struck for higher wages. Other early plans were established at the A. S. Cameron Co. of Jersey City (1869), Brewster Co. of New York (1870), Peace Dale Manufacturing Co. of Peace Dale, R.I. (1878), Rand McNally & Co. (1879), N. O. Nelson Manufacturing Co. (1886), and Procter & Gamble Co. (1887). The first pension fund was established by the American Express Company in 1875. See "Profit Sharing in the United States," *Monthly Review of the Bureau of Labor Statistics* 2 (January–June 1916): 46–47; "Industrial Pensions," *Monthly Review of the Bureau of Labor Statistics* 3 (July–December 1916): 131.

61. United Shoe Machinery Co. to Yale University, August 1916, Mudd Library, Yale University. For a good overview of labor control as it functioned in the nineteenth-century firm, see David Edwards, *Contested Terrain: The Transformation of the Workplace in the Twentieth Century* (New York: Basic Books, 1979).

62. Tolman, *Social Engineering*, p. 48.

Industrial analysts attributed much of the era's labor troubles to corporate bigness. Changes in the size of industrial establishments, they argued, had reduced workers' loyalty, encouraged inferior work habits, hampered productivity, and increased the appeal of collective organization as a vehicle for venting frustration. "The greatest single contributing factor . . . in the development of the present [labor] situation," Dudley Kennedy wrote in *Industrial Management*, "has been the . . . remarkable growth of manufacturing units . . . and the increase in the number of non-resident owners." An editorial in a Chicago newspaper, the *Inter-Ocean*, concurred. "Undoubtedly many of the strained labor situations in this country," it opined, "result from lack of personal contact between employer and employee."[63]

Welfare work promised to renew the personalism of small firms within the colossal aggregations of Progressive America. Its establishment symbolized ongoing accord between employer and employee in a workplace whose expanse precluded the regular contact necessary for its spontaneous development. Its philosophy of congeniality, propagated in company newspapers, speeches, posters, and songs, suggested mutuality and even familial love. The logic of welfare capitalism dictated that increasing distance between owner and worker could be relieved partially by weekend picnics in which both parties intermingled freely; the iron role of the foreman would be tempered by the creation of representative councils to which workers were encouraged to submit ideas for improving productivity. By providing social and recreational opportunities for company affiliates and their families, welfare programs united on a personal level employees otherwise segregated by wage, authority, and rank. Perceived as a counterpoise to the alienation of size, welfare programs were begun most frequently in large establishments.

Worker control. Companies and industries in which workers exercised some control over production were in the forefront of the welfare movement. Employees whose knowledge and skill were indispensable to management were singled out as especially worthy of the incentives and attention welfare programs extended. Consequently, turn-of-the-century industries in which production processes were markedly resis-

63. Dudley R. Kennedy, "Employment Management and Industrial Relations," *Industrial Management* 58 (November 1919): 353–54; editorial, "The 'Social Engineer' and Strikes," reprinted in *Social Service* 4 (October 1901): 105; Letters of May 31 and June 6, 1906, American Institute of Social Service Weekly Commercial Letter Service, Cyrus H. McCormick Jr. Papers, Box 41, SHSW.

tant to specialization and mechanization proved fertile territory for welfare work; welfare programs were concentrated in railroad companies and in steel, machine-shop, electrical, and printing establishments but were less pronounced in textile manufacture. Skilled workers also represented the most unionized portion of the American working class, which enhanced the likelihood that they would be targeted as welfare clients: even an employer who accepted unions in principle could not help but hope that good working conditions would reduce the prospect of a costly strike. Under the roof of a single company, skilled employees could have access to welfare programs denied to unskilled co-workers.

Businessmen in nonfactory settings experienced a different form of worker control. Employees who had daily contact with customers in department stores, hotels, telephone exchanges, and transportation facilities influenced the company's profitability through their disposition and demeanor. In these industries, the right attitude on the part of employees could make the difference between a satisfied and an unsatisfied customer. When profitability was tied to employee performance, employers had an added incentive to ensure that their workers were content and loyal. As Boston Edison's president, Charles Edgar, reminded his employees, "Every day you meet . . . customers or possible customers. As they find you, smiling or grim, so they will judge us as a body. To them you are the company—good or bad."[64]

In designating certain workers more desirable and hence more deserving of benefits than others, welfare work upheld the gendered, racist stereotypes of employer ideology at the turn of the century. In food companies that sold goods to a mass market, for instance, employers championed the superiority of their products by emphasizing the "pleasing" attributes of the workers who made them. In advertising literature, Heinz ketchup was touted not as the product of labor performed in dingy factories replete with illiterate, swarthy foreigners—the likes of whom filled the pages of Upton Sinclair's bestseller *The Jungle*—but as the glorious outcome when native-born, refined, and educated young women exercised their culinary prowess in pure, pristine surroundings. To recruit and retain workers who might aspire to this ideal and to persuade consumers that their products were of high quality, enterprises such as Heinz, Hershey's, Shredded Wheat, and Na-

---

64. David B. Sicilia, "Selling Power: Marketing Leadership at Boston Edison, 1886–1926," paper presented to the Organization of American Historians and the National Council on Public History, New York, April 12, 1986, in author's possession.

tional Biscuit made the practice and publicity of welfare work company policy.

Firms such as Heinz and Hershey's shared with Boston Edison and Macy's a comparable relationship between company and consumer. Each of these firms sold products directly to end users. At Boston Edison and Macy's, the success of welfare work might boost customer satisfaction. At Heinz and Hershey's welfare work was publicized as the purchaser's assurance of superior goods. In each of these firms employers viewed workers' behavior as a determinant of consumer satisfaction and hence indispensable to company profits. Welfare work was a means by which firms minimized the likelihood that employees would jeopardize these profits. Not surprisingly, industries in which good customer relations were essential to profits were leading exemplars of welfare work (Figure 2).

Labor markets. Labor supply was also related to worker control. In cities with a high concentration of companies, greater employment prospects gave workers a degree of mobility and leverage. Skilled employees or those with desired attributes could express their dissatisfaction by quitting their jobs without suffering the penalty of permanent unemployment. This condition marked an important distinction between small-town benevolence, which characterized much of postbellum southern industry, and the bureaucratic benefits incarnated in the welfare programs of northern big business. In company towns, employees had less leverage. Their dependence on employers gave companies more freedom to control workers' lives. So-called benefits often assumed a coercive nature. Employee participation in programs was usually mandatory; deductions were automatically taken from wages to pay for programs. In contrast, the laws of supply and demand put companies in urban, industrial centers at a comparable disadvantage in relation to labor markets. These firms had to compete for labor. Welfare work thus assumed strategic importance as employers tried to outdo each other in the provision of benefits in their efforts to recruit and retain employees.[65]

65. On southern welfare work, see Douglas Flamming, *Creating the Modern South: Mill-hands and Managers in Dalton, Georgia, 1884–1984* (Chapel Hill: University of North Carolina Press, 1992); Allen Tullos, *Habits of Industry: White Culture and the Transformation of the Carolina Piedmont* (Chapel Hill: University of North Carolina Press, 1989); Jacquelyn Dowd Hall et al., *Like a Family: The Making of a Southern Cotton Mill World* (Chapel Hill: University of North Carolina Press, 1987); Melton Alonza McLaurin, *Paternalism and Pro-*

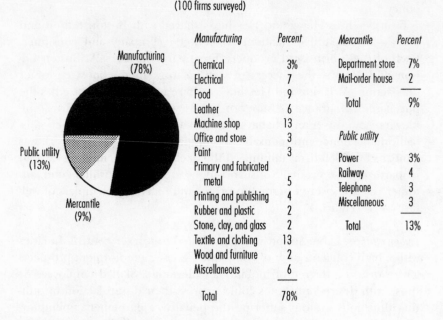

(100 firms surveyed)

Manufacturing	Percent
Chemical	3%
Electrical	7
Food	9
Leather	6
Machine shop	13
Office and store	3
Paint	3
Primary and fabricated metal	5
Printing and publishing	4
Rubber and plastic	2
Stone, clay, and glass	2
Textile and clothing	13
Wood and furniture	2
Miscellaneous	6
Total	78%

Mercantile	Percent
Department store	7%
Mail-order house	2
Total	9%

Public utility	
Power	3%
Railway	4
Telephone	3
Miscellaneous	3
Total	13%

Figure 2. Industrial classification of welfare firms, 1913

Sources: U.S. Bureau of Labor Statistics, *Employers' Welfare Work,* Bulletin 123 (1913); Boston Chamber of Commerce Papers, Case 48, Folder 332–19, Baker Library Archives of the Harvard Graduate School of Business.

In addition, the leverage enjoyed by firms that could use welfare programs to secure a satisfactory labor force altered the competitive environment in which individual firms vied for profits. Because only a small number of firms were able to institute recruitment-worthy benefits, welfare work supplied big business with a mechanism for controlling the market by driving out competitors unable to afford comparable measures.[66]

---

test: *Southern Cotton Mill Workers and Organized Labor, 1875–1905* (Westport, Conn.: Greenwood Press, 1971); and David L. Carlton, *Mill and Town in South Carolina, 1880–1920* (Baton Rouge: Louisiana State University Press, 1982). See also H. F. J. Porter, "Industrial Betterment," *Cassier's Magazine* 38 (August 1910): 311.

66. For a discussion of how welfare work programs often pitted manufacturers against each other, see Wiebe, *Businessmen and Reform,* pp. 166–67.

Table 4. Number and percent of welfare firms located in cities, by number of city residents, wage earners, and industrial firms, 1910

City residents		Wage earners[a]		Industrial firms	
Number	Percent	Number	Percent	Number	Percent
10,000+	94%	10,000+	95%	100+	98%
50,000+	85	50,000+	73	500+	89
100,000+	81	100,000+	51	1,000+	80

[a]Employed wage earners registered by census enumerators. The actual available labor supply was probably higher.

Sources: U.S. Bureau of Labor Statistics, *Employers' Welfare Work*, Bulletin 123 (Washington, D.C.: Government Printing Office, 1913); U.S. Department of Commerce, Bureau of the Census, *Thirteenth Census of the United States*, vols. 2, 3, 9 (Washington, D.C.: Government Printing Office, 1913).

Of the welfare firms identified by the Bureau of Labor Statistics in 1913, 94 percent operated in cities with over 10,000 residents, and over three-quarters (81 percent) operated in cities with over 100,000 residents (Table 4). These figures are probably low, for they reflect census data collected in 1910. The typical labor market in which most welfare firms surveyed by the bureau were immersed was decidedly different from that of the southern company town in which a single employer could dictate the terms and prospects of employment.

Legislative activity. The regional character of labor legislation also accounted for the relative scarcity of welfare work in the South. Progressivism did not elude the South, but it yielded fewer legislated protections for workers than in the North. The South's less developed industrial infrastructure, the comparative absence of organized labor activity, and the New South creed, tying business growth to southern progress, thwarted the advance of southern labor laws. By 1900 regulations on accident prevention, factory inspection, and women's working hours were the norm in the North but still the exception in the South.

The South's weaker regulatory environment helps explain the comparative absence of welfare capitalism in the region. As an effort to inhibit labor legislation, welfare capitalism had its strongest appeal in northern (including midwestern) states, where efforts to pass statutory labor reforms seemed most likely to, or had already managed to, succeed.[67]

67. Nelson, *Managers and Workers*, chap. 7; Brandeis, "Labor Legislation."

Business cycles. National and regional economic trends affected local labor markets and the development of welfare programs. Employers adjusted production quotas as the economy expanded and contracted. When production demands exceeded the supply of labor, the likelihood of welfare work increased, as did the number of workers targeted for welfare programs. World War I marked the peak of welfare activity as manufacturers, suffering from a curtailed supply of labor resulting from wartime conscription and the cessation of European immigration, tried to create a stable labor force to meet unprecedented production demands. The conjuncture of labor shortages and increased demand prompted the expansion of welfare work in factories across the country. By the end of the war, the number of departments organized to administer welfare benefits had roughly doubled.

The exigencies of war also forced employers to modify their standards and extend business benevolence to workers previously outside the reach of the welfare umbrella. In areas with a high foreign-born population, employers organized welfare programs for immigrant men and women. When production returned to prewar levels in 1919 and companies reemployed returning workers, immigrants were once again marginalized beyond welfare work's grasp. Indeed, the combination of a labor surplus and normalized production prompted many businesses in postwar America to dismantle welfare programs altogether.[68]

Concentration of women wage earners. Employers of women were most likely to develop welfare programs. Of 431 welfare firms surveyed by the Bureau of Labor Statistics for a 1919 bulletin, 37 percent came from industries employing a predominantly female labor force. In welfare firms where women represented only a minority of workers, employers extended them a disproportionately high number of welfare benefits. At National Cash Register, for instance, over half of the welfare programs were established for women employees even though women made up only 20 percent of the labor force.[69]

The employment of female wage earners presented employers with a

68. Robert F. Lovett, "Present Tendencies in Personnel Practice," *Industrial Management* 65 (June 1923): 327; Henry Eilbirt, "The Development of Personnel Management in the United States," *Business History Review* 33 (Autumn 1959): 350–52; Norman J. Wood, "Industrial Relations Policies of American Management, 1900–1933," *Business History Review* 34 (Winter 1960): 408–9.

69. Minutes of the Fifth Meeting of the Conference on Welfare Work at Chicago Commons, Lecture by Mr. Thomas of the National Cash Register Company, May 1, 1906, Cyrus H. McCormick Jr. Papers, Box 40, SHSW.

unique set of problems for which welfare work frequently became the chosen solution. Women workers had the highest turnover rate of any class of employees. Their growing number in the country's wage labor force—from 1.9 to 7.3 million between 1880 and 1920—prompted middle-class reformers to argue that industrial capitalism was desecrating workers' femininity and placing the moral status of future generations in peril. The advance of protective labor legislation embodied reformers' critique. Countering these problems were the economic incentives employers had for employing women: their wages were lower; they were less likely and able to unionize; they were considered more suitable for certain occupations, such as department store and telephone switchboard work, than men. By creating welfare work programs tailored to women's "special needs"—cooking and sewing classes, workshops on personal grooming and infant care, extra rest periods—companies tried to retain women wage earners while reassuring critics lobbying for more legislation that instead of stripping a woman of her femininity, the factory setting reinforced it. As with other forms of welfare work, women's welfare work was initiated to contend with both external political pressures and internal factory demands.

The Profitability of Paternalism

Employers adopted welfare work because they believed that for a variety of reasons, sympathy within the workplace paid. Certainly a few employers boasted that welfare work was nothing more than an act of kindness. When asked if welfare work profited his company, for instance, Henry Heinz responded that he had "never given that side of the matter any thought. We are fully repaid when we see our employees enjoying themselves. . . . You know, this makes a little Heaven here below, and that is something worth having." The treasurer of the Ludlow Manufacturing Company ascribed the origins of welfare work at his firm to a similarly lofty ideal. "We became interested in welfare work some twenty years ago," he told a conference of welfare workers in 1904. "The expectation of profiting . . . was never in our minds [then], and is not today. We have the feeling that animates you all . . . that 'As we are passing through this world just once, and shall never pass this way again, we should like to do what good we can as we pass along.' "[70]

70. Henry Heinz quoted in Shuey, *Factory People and Their Employers*, p. 201; testimony of Charles W. Hubbard in National Civic Federation, *Conference on Welfare Work*, p. 61.

While we cannot overlook the genuine goodwill that motivated some employers to establish welfare programs, we can also not ignore the benefits they received from doing so and the inherent limitations of private sector philanthropy. Significantly, most employers did not dissimulate their intentions under a cloak of morality. They admitted publicly and privately that altruism within the workplace was a profit-making venture. As Macy's manager, Percy Straus, explained to the 1912–15 Industrial Commission, welfare work was "good business and nothing else." Others concurred. Welfare work was "not merely philanthropy . . . [but] a paying investment."[71]

Indeed, one of the most resonant metaphors emerging from employers' justifications of welfare expenditures likened the caring for employees to wise husbandry: the nurtured employee, like the pampered animal, was a product of his "owner's" business acumen, not sentimental softening. As one manufacturer put it, "When I keep a horse and I find him a clean stable and good food I am not doing anything philanthropic for my horse. I am doing [this] for my own interest. If I hire a man and I improve machinery so that he can turn out more and better work I am not doing anything philanthropic. I am just improving the tools." In characteristically crass fashion, National Cash Register's John Patterson also likened welfare work to animal husbandry. As employers, he explained, "We buy physical and mental labor. If it pays to take care of a good animal that only returns physical work, how much more important is it for the employer to take care of the employee returning both physical and mental labor?" The condiment king Henry Heinz sank the metaphor to new depths when he reneged on his own "Heaven here below" explanation. He told *Social Service* that welfare programs at the Pittsburgh plant arose out of the recognition "that the perfecting of labor is as essential to the advancement of our business as the perfecting of fruits and vegetables. . . . Our most liberal expenditures in advancing the comfort and happiness of our working people have been abundantly justified from the most narrow and selfish standpoint of actual improvement of product and business income."[72]

71. U.S. Senate, Commission on Industrial Relations, *Final Report and Testimony*, 3:2377; O. M. Becker, "The Square Deal in Works Management," *Engineering Magazine* 30 (January 1906): 553.

72. Graham Taylor, "The Policy of Being Human in Business," *Chicago Daily News*, June 16, 1906, in Cyrus H. McCormick Jr. Papers, Box 40, SHSW; Patterson quoted in William H. Tolman, *Industrial Betterment* (New York: Social Service Press, 1900), p. 81; W. Bayard

Employers' perception of welfare work as a profitable undertaking helps resolve the paradox of capitalist paternalism, specifically the question: How can industrial capitalism and paternalism coexist? Are not the goals of an employer who seeks to advance workers' welfare, thereby implicitly acknowledging their humanity, fundamentally at odds with those of an employer who views wage earners chiefly as commodities whose value lies in the degree to which their labor can be successfully extracted? Is not paternalism, premised on compassion, antithetical to capitalism, defined by its "central tendency toward depersonalization"[73]

The weakness of the dichotomous paradigm lies in its projection of a perfect capitalist order in which paternalism and capitalism would indeed be diametrically opposed, a mythical market with an unlimited supply of labor, devoid of restraints curtailing employers' freedom, free of external pressures affecting capital's fate. In such a market employers would have an unfettered reign to treat labor as a commodity to be consumed and discarded at will. Capital would have all the leverage, labor none. There would be no room, and certainly no need, for gratuitous affection.

But such a perfect market has probably never existed, and it certainly did not exist in the United States at the turn of the century. Employers in Progressive America were confronted with unprecedented labor agitation, unionization, high turnover, labor shortages, public animosity, and the possibility of a burgeoning welfare state vitiating, if not eliminating, business prerogatives. Under these conditions, being sympathetic to workers was a way to reinforce, not contradict, the capitalist ethos. Welfare work promised the recruitment and retention of a labor force who would return the investment through more and better work. Beyond factory walls, the presence of welfare programs assured employers a better public image, according them a means to enhance their leverage, political and economic, in a larger industrial arena. In both instances benevolence promised desired dividends, while profitability itself subsumed multiple ambitions.

Cutting, "Madison Square Garden Meeting, March 26," *Social Service* 3 (April 1901): 100; Henry Heinz to William H. Tolman, March 18, 1901, *Social Service* 3 (April 1901): 104.

73. See Eugene D. Genovese, *Roll, Jordan, Roll: The World the Slaves Made* (New York: Pantheon, 1974), pp. 661–65; Steven Peter Vallas, "Paternalism and Modern Industry: Factory Regimes at Ford and Bell," paper presented at the annual meeting of the American Sociological Association, Cincinnati, August 1991.

2 /

Welfare Work and
Industrial Efficiency

In 1892 John Patterson, president and founder of the National Cash
Register Company (NCR), made an alarming discovery. An order of
cash registers valued at $50,000 had been returned from England, in-
operable because of defective workmanship. The Dayton company had
been struggling to stay solvent since Patterson founded it in 1884. The
cost of replacing the faulty registers now threatened to push the company to the brink of bankruptcy. A year later, employees dealt the company another blow. Within a twelve-month period, they set the factory
on fire three times. Patterson blamed the defective registers, too, on
employee sabotage, a painful indication of workers' dissatisfaction with
life and labor at NCR. The company might weather such manifestations
of its workers' unhappiness this time but not again. The firm's only
chance for survival lay in a rapid solution to its labor troubles. Patterson
decided that "more interest would have to be taken in our employees
to make them better workers." His financial fate depended on it.[1]

In the ensuing decade the National Cash Register Company became

1. National Cash Register Company (NCR), untitled pamphlet on welfare work (Dayton, ca. 1910), pp. 2, 3; Paul Monroe, "Possibilities of the Present Industrial System,"
American Journal of Sociology 3 (May 1898): 22. Though never proven, arson was assumed
to be the work of "disaffected employees."

the nation's leading exemplar of welfare work. By 1904 the firm's 3,800 workers could take advantage of numerous benefits: a library with 900 books and subscriptions to monthly and weekly journals; a clubhouse for entertainment, lectures, and meetings; calisthenic "recesses" during work hours; a kindergarten for employees' children; a men's and women's dining room serving low-cost lunches during the day and dinners to overtime workers at night; art, dance, English, history, and needlework classes; Sunday outings; and scenic gardens and recreational parks designed by none other than Frederick Law Olmsted for the employees' use.[2]

Patterson's hypochondria extended to an obsessive interest in protecting his employees' health. A committed food faddist, Patterson once fasted for thirty-six days to demonstrate mastery of mind over body. At company gatherings he liked to plant an employee in the audience to ask a prearranged question, "What keeps you so healthy and youthful, Mr. Patterson?" to enable Patterson to launch into a diatribe on unhealthful eating. The company magazine printed Patterson-inspired health and exercise tips such as "too much sleep softens and enfeebles" and recommended vigorous walks for "nervousness, lassitude, [and] headaches." The company maintained drinking water at uniform temperature to prevent stomach disorders, provided massage vibrators at the employee gym, gave illustrated lectures on digestion and venereal disease, sterilized equipment oil, and installed ventilation appliances to modulate hourly the atmosphere of factory rooms. Employees could take twenty-minute weekly baths on company time. In 1912 William Tolman called NCR the "safest, healthiest, most unique and efficient factory in the United States."[3]

Patterson was the first to admit that his welfare measures were not inspired by unbridled altruism. Welfare work paid by increasing profits. The company offered welfare programs because "comfort, health and relaxation bring greater efficiency." The welfare division calculated that the 3 percent of its annual payroll spent on employee programs— about $45,000 a year—yielded "between five and ten percent profit in actual dollars and cents." To underscore this point and to assuage

2. NCR, *A Trip through the NCR Factory* (Dayton, 1904), pp. 26–35. The best analysis of welfare work at NCR is Judith Sealander, *Grand Plans: Business Progressivism and Social Change in Ohio's Miami Valley, 1890–1929* (Lexington: University Press of Kentucky, 1988).

3. Stanley C. Allyn, *My Half Century with NCR* (New York: McGraw-Hill, 1967), p. 22; *NCR*, December 1903, p. 714; William H. Tolman, "How a Manufacturing Concern Promotes Industrial Hygiene," paper presented to the International Congress of Hygiene and Demography, Washington, D.C., 1912; NCR, *Trip through the NCR Factory*, p. 18.

workers' suspicions that welfare connoted charity, Patterson hung posters throughout the factory stating simply, "IT PAYS."[4]

Scores of company pamphlets narrated the NCR factory fairy tale. Most began with a brief history of the company—its founder, product, and plan—followed by a bleak portrayal of factory life at NCR before the dawning of Pattersonian enlightenment. One photograph of unshaven and haggard-looking workmen offered the caption: "The Company did little for the welfare of its employees." Another of a somber-looking woman conveyed an equally pessimistic message: "Cold lunches did not produce good work."[5]

But the regenerative powers of welfare work had transformed employees. Because of welfare programs, NCR had "a better class of workmen; better skill; more contentment." Better still, the "new" happy, healthy workers had increased profits. To its delight, the company had discovered that "it pays for employers to enlist the sympathy of their employees by looking after their physical and mental comfort." Rather than trying to destroy the factory, "employees are proud of their connection with the Company." Improvements in light and air had been repaid by "a higher standard of health [and] hence . . . fewer accidents and less time lost from sickness." Pure drinking water had produced workers whose "wage-earning capacity [is] unimpaired by sickness." Ventilation and "pure air" had increased overall efficiency: "What would barrels of metal dust have meant," one publication queried, "had they gone into the lungs of the workers?" Freeing employees from fear for their personal safety, the pamphlet continued, "increases output. It is not only right and just that we safeguard our workers, but it pays." Pleasant surroundings had created an environment conducive to "the economical production of good work." Recreation, games, and department competitions had served to "arouse the enthusiasm of the employees and to cultivate an *esprit de corps* which increases the efficiency of the entire Company."[6]

4. Report of Gertrude Beeks, 1901, Nettie Fowler McCormick Papers, Box 27, State Historical Society of Wisconsin, Madison (hereafter SHSW); Patterson quoted in Edwin L. Shuey, *Factory People and Their Employers: How Their Relations Are Made Pleasant and Profitable* (New York: Lentilhon, 1900), pp. 199, 210; minutes of the fifth meeting of the Conference on Welfare Work at Chicago Commons, Lecture by Mr. Thomas of the National Cash Register Company, May 1, 1906, Cyrus H. McCormick Jr. Papers, Box 40, SHSW; NCR, *A New Era of Factory Life* (Dayton, 1900), p. 3.

5. NCR, untitled pamphlet on welfare work, pp. 2, 3.

6. NCR, *Trip through the NCR Factory*, p. 36; NCR, untitled pamphlet on welfare work, pp. 13, 15, 16; NCR, *Welfare Work* (Dayton, 1900), pp. 12, 16; Tolman, "How a Manufacturing Concern Promotes Industrial Hygiene," p. 15.

The expanse and range of its welfare programs made NCR unique among welfare firms. John Patterson shared with hundreds of other employers, however, a desire to boost factory efficiency by improving the physical and psychological well-being of employees. Not every employer who adopted welfare work encountered the dramatic gestures of worker resistance that Patterson did. But most conceded that employee dissatisfaction—whether manifested in burned buildings, high turnover, absenteeism, strikes, or careless work—undermined productivity. Like Patterson, they pinned their hopes for higher efficiency and profits on welfare work.

For Patterson and his colleagues, improving labor productivity within the spatial boundaries of the factory was a goal that complemented welfare work's larger political objectives. At NCR the evolution of company welfare programs merged pragmatic and political concerns. To be sure, the establishment of NCR's welfare programs preceded the politicization of welfare work in the Progressive era. Programs for workers were established in the 1890s to defuse workers' discontent. Over time, however, the purpose of NCR's welfare work broadened. After a strike in 1901 shut down the factory for two months—forever dispelling Patterson's notion that welfare work was a magical solvent for labor dissatisfaction—Patterson reorganized but continued to support welfarism, announcing that the company would "do more welfare work. I am more than ever convinced that it pays." The dividends Patterson solicited were soon forthcoming. Accolades spotlighting Dayton's model factory catapulted Patterson and his products to international fame. Partly because it was able to capitalize on this publicity, NCR acquired monopoly control over the cash register market—about 95 percent of domestic sales by 1913. Indeed, the company's hold over the national market became so complete that in 1913 the federal government successfully prosecuted Patterson and twenty-six NCR officers under the Sherman Antitrust Act. A wave of support, strengthened by Patterson's stature as a do-good businessman, shielded him and his men from jail. In 1916 the federal government dropped criminal charges against the company. The firm's monopoly and its faith in welfare work were confirmed. The ease with which Patterson channeled workplace reforms into effective product and company advertising highlights how factory productivity and public support could be mutually reinforcing.[7]

The NCR example is instructive. Welfare work in the Progressive pe-

7. See Sealander, *Grand Plans*, pp. 30, 33–35.

riod enabled employers to sell the virtues of a private system of employee welfare even as they strove to improve labor productivity. At a time when political woes and efficiency worries commanded employers' attention, welfare work promised to remedy both.

Welfare Work, Labor Productivity, and the Progressive Impulse

The multiple applications of welfare work reveal employers' awareness that companies operated in a society in which the boundaries between the public and the private, the economic and the sociopolitical, frequently overlapped. On the factory, office, and store floor, employers' recognition of the fluidity between the world of work and the world beyond inspired the drive for labor efficiency.

Welfare capitalists accepted at the outset that the quality of employee output directly reflected the value of the emotional, physical, educational, and spiritual "input" workers received from their surroundings—surroundings that often lay beyond the geographic boundaries of the workplace. Their sensitivity to the power of the environment to sculpt personal behavior and character philosophically linked employers to Progressive sociologists, social settlement workers, factory inspectors, temperance crusaders, and public hygiene reformers. Each group championed environmental modification as the basis for reform; each rejected the concept of a social laissez-faire order in which the environment, constructed by immutable forces of nature, loomed as the constant around which individuals must either adjust or be crushed. Without repudiating its influence over individuals, reformers insisted that the environment itself was malleable. Claiming social science as their ally, reformers offered a vision of an improved environment in which societal ills were "objectively" cataloged and corrected. Rather than being products of fixed forces, social and economic surroundings were viewed as alterable variables that could be manipulated through social engineering to uplift humankind.

Welfare work participated in and promoted the era's environmentalist fervor. "Give a person good surroundings," John Patterson promised fellow employers, "and you will receive good work in return." Employers deemed workers' emotional and physical well-being not only crucial to factory efficiency but factors that, under company direction, could be manipulated to suit employers' needs.[8]

8. Patterson quoted in William Ruehrwein, *A Wonderful Factory System* (1895; Dayton: National Cash Register Co., 1897), p. 7.

For most wage earners work meant long hours of hard labor performed under one roof. By the early 1900s the nineteenth-century campaign for shorter hours had resulted in the ten-hour day for most
northern workers in manufacturing, mercantile, and mining establishments. This victory notwithstanding, most workers still had to labor fifty-
eight to sixty hours a week. Because most wage work was performed in
a central location, the work site was the most logical place to effect
environmental reform. Because its organization and appearance lay entirely within the employer's control, moreover, it was also the most
convenient starting point. Emphasizing the integral links between material culture and worker culture, welfare work endeavored to improve
the aesthetics of factory conditions. Physical beautification—roof gardens, elegant dining rooms, employee libraries lined with mahogany
bookcases—invited workers' emotional, spiritual, and intellectual
transcendence on company grounds and on company terms without
challenging the structural hierarchy that kept workers subordinate. Less
ethereal improvements such as ventilation, regulated drinking water,
and electric lighting harnessed modern technologies to protect workers' longevity by making the experience of wage work physically tolerable.[9]

Collapsing the boundaries of home, leisure, and work, welfare work
attempted to modify not only employees' work space but the totality of
their environment. Acknowledging that what workers did after hours
affected their work performance, welfare employers cast their reform
net wide. As one industrial consultant put it, when "what the employees
do in their time affects what they do in the employer's time, then it
may be to his interest to make it his business to look into such matters."
For welfare work to be effective, "the whole life of the man and the
whole life of society must be considered." Welfare work sought to regulate and control workers' use of personal time, often making receipt
of benefits contingent on round-the-clock "good" behavior verified
with home inspections. The B. F. Goodrich Company, for instance, denied compensation for disabilities resulting from "the use of alcohol,
stimulants or narcotics; immoral practices and venereal diseases; [and]
accident or injury received in a saloon or disreputable resort."[10]

Welfare work also entered the realm of workers' leisure, an issue that

9. U.S. Bureau of Labor Statistics, *The Betterment of Industrial Conditions*, Bulletin 31
(1900) p. 1153; Charles Henderson, *Citizens in Industry* (New York: D. Appleton, 1915),
p. 210.

10. H. F. J. Porter, "The Higher Law in the Industrial World," *Engineering Magazine* 29
(August 1905); Committee on Industrial Welfare, *Industrial Profit Sharing and Welfare Work*
(Cleveland: Cleveland Chamber of Commerce, 1916), p. 61.

Educational uplift at work. (*Cassier's Magazine*, September 1905.)

engendered considerable concern and lively debate among reformers at the turn of the century. Hoping to offset the purportedly injurious effect of the burgeoning commercial leisure market on labor efficiency, welfare firms organized wholesome alternatives to wrest control of leisure from workers. While employees yearned to have "eight hours for what we will," welfare employers sought to abolish the disjunction of labor and leisure by placing both under company control.[11]

Underwriting these disparate machinations was a trenchant belief that welfare programs, whatever their shape, would generate higher output. Welfare work would reform workers' mental, emotional, and

11. For a discussion of contested visions of working-class culture, see John Kasson, *Amusing the Million: Coney Island at the Turn of the Century* (New York: Hill & Wang, 1978); Lewis A. Erenberg, *Steppin' Out: New York Nightlife and the Transformation of American Culture, 1890–1930* (Westport, Conn.: Greenwood Press 1981); Roy Rosenzweig, *Eight Hours for What We Will: Work and Leisure in an Industrial City, 1870–1920* (New York: Cambridge University Press, 1983); Francis G. Couvares, *The Remaking of Pittsburgh: Class and Culture in an Industrial City, 1877–1919* (Albany: SUNY Press, 1984); Kathy Peiss, *Cheap Amusements: Working Women and Leisure in Turn-of-the-Century New York* (Philadelphia: Temple University Press, 1986); Elliot Gorn, *The Manly Art: Bare-Knuckle Prize Fighting in America* (Ithaca: Cornell University Press, 1986); and Michael Denning, *Mechanic Accents: Dime Novels and Working-Class Culture in America* (London: Verso, 1987).

physical faculties; in exchange, workers would reward employers' efforts with more and better work. Plant-wide efficiency—as measured by more output, reduced absenteeism and turnover, the recruitment and retention of high-quality laborers, and fewer strikes—would prevail. The only medium not exchanged in the equation was power. Employers expected welfare work to make employees better workers, not employers in their own right.

Welfare work's call to productivity fit snugly within the framework of yet another Progressive impulse: efficiency. As Samuel Haber, Robert Wiebe, and Sharon Hartman Strom have shown, the language of efficiency was not exclusive to the world of industry; it was, in many regards, the dominant watchword of Progressive reform. As principle, efficiency connoted effectiveness, discipline, and coordinated improvement. As practice, it justified the leadership of middle-class men and women in reform movements to redress overcrowding, inadequate urban amenities (sanitation, housing, schooling, and transportation), and political corruption. Invoking their expertise as professionals, engineers, economists, sociologists, physicians, and social workers made reform and the rationalization of society along scientific lines virtually synonymous. The promise of a redesigned environment purged of its most corrupt, cumbersome, and outdated features made the ideology of efficiency nothing short of visionary in reformers' eyes.[12]

Contributing to the popularization of the gospel of efficiency was growing interest in the multiple uses of scientific management. First advanced as a cogent program by Frederick Winslow Taylor in the 1890s, scientific management—not called as such until 1910—promoted the standardization of work and management as a partial solution to labor troubles. Taylor's ideal factory attained optimal productivity by eliminating functions, jobs, purchases, and procedures revealed to be gratuitous through "scientific" investigation. Knowledge acquired from careful observation of existing workplace routines supplied managers with the factual foundation for the reorganization of the workplace. Time and motion studies, incentive wages, systematic accounting and purchasing, and formalized foremanship were key features of Taylor's program, each designed to eliminate wasted time, energy, and material.[13]

12. On the popularization of efficiency, see Samuel Haber, *Efficiency and Uplift: Scientific Management in the Progressive Era, 1890–1920* (Chicago: University of Chicago Press, 1964); Robert H. Wiebe, *The Search for Order, 1877–1920* (New York: Hill & Wang, 1967); Sharon Hartman Strom, *Beyond the Typewriter: Gender, Class, and the Origins of Modern American Office Work, 1900–1930* (Urbana: University of Illinois Press, 1992); and Raymond E. Callahan, *Education and the Cult of Efficiency* (Chicago: University of Chicago Press, 1962).

13. On scientific management, see Frederick Winslow Taylor, *The Principles of Scientific*

Although Taylor and his program had won respect within the engineering academy by the early 1900s, it took the highly publicized Eastern Rates case of 1910 to earn scientific management a widespread following. The Interstate Commerce Commission (ICC) hearings pitted eastern railroads against the Progressive reformer Louis D. Brandeis, who represented a group of trade associations opposed to the railroads' proposed rate increase. Brandeis won, but the means by which he did so ultimately had a greater impact on the currents of Progressive reform than the decision itself. The testimony of the efficiency experts Henry L. Gantt, Frank B. Gilbreth, Harrington Emerson, and others enabled Brandeis to suggest, in lieu of proposed rate increases, the application of "scientific management"—a term agreed upon by the witnesses in advance "as the most suitable designation for the new philosophy of management they were to expound and defend at the forthcoming hearings"—as a cure for the railroads' woes. Brandeis argued that scientific management would enable railroads simultaneously to boost profits, lower costs, and even increase wages. Thus, in one fell swoop, Brandeis's appeal made scientific management appear to be the ally of consumers, workers, shippers, and reformers nationwide. The hearings, followed in the spring of 1911 by the serialized publication of Taylor's *Principles of Scientific Management* in the Progressive *American Magazine*, underscored the many potential uses of scientific management for a society in disarray. As the *American Magazine*'s editor, Ray Stannard Baker, remarked in his introduction to Taylor's essays, it was "to the fine scientific habit of mind . . . that the country must look to for its salvation." By the end of 1911 the ICC hearings and Taylor's widely read essays had encouraged many Americans to brand Taylor a Progressive hero, elevate the status of engineer to that of social reformer, and see in scientific management a method for achieving far-reaching social, political, and economic reform.[14]

Management (1911; New York: Norton, 1967); Callahan, *Education and the Cult of Efficiency;* Haber, *Efficiency and Uplift;* Daniel Nelson, *Frederick W. Taylor and the Rise of Scientific Management* (Madison: University of Wisconsin Press, 1980); Samuel Jacoby, *Employing Bureaucracy: Managers, Unions, and the Transformation of Work in American Industry, 1900–1945* (New York: Columbia University Press, 1985); and Strom, *Beyond the Typewriter.*

14. For a discussion of the Eastern Rates case, see Callahan, *Education and the Cult of Efficiency*, pp. 19–20; Thomas McGraw, *Prophets of Regulation* (Cambridge: Harvard University Press, 1984), pp. 91–94; Nelson, *Frederick W. Taylor and the Rise of Scientific Management*, pp. 174–76 (Baker quoted on p. 176); Strom, *Beyond the Typewriter*, pp. 33–34; and Steven Usselman, "The Untimely Enshrinement of Engineering: Railroads and Their Regulators in Progressive Era America," paper presented at the Atlanta Roundtable in the Comparative History of Labor, Industrialization, and Technology, May 12, 1996, in author's possession.

Reifying efficiency, welfare work was a strategy that converged rather than conflicted with scientific management. The underlying compatibility of the two management strategies was rarely acknowledged by Taylor, however. Indeed, one of the curious dualities of Taylor's personality was his commitment to reform on the one hand, and, as one of his biographers has put it, a tendency toward "indifferent, often ruthless . . . relations with workers" on the other. Taylor was particularly concerned with the problem of workers' soldiering: their "innate" desire to "work as slowly as they dare while they at the same time try to make those over them believe that they are working fast." To undercut workers' control over the knowledge of production, which gave them considerable say in determining how long it should take to complete a task, Taylor urged managers to "assume . . . the burden of gathering together all of the traditional knowledge which in the past has been possessed by the workmen and then of classifying, tabulating, and reducing this knowledge to rules, laws, and formulae." With ownership of the knowledge of production thus having been transferred, as David Montgomery has aptly described, from the "workman's brain" to the "manager's cap," managers would be in a position to direct the timing, organization, and performance of work.[15]

As a means to gain workers' compliance, Taylor steadfastly championed individual financial incentives—"generous piece-work prices or a premium or bonus of some kind for good and rapid work"—as the best inducement of labor efficiency. Money alone would spur the intrinsically lazy employee to do better work. Taylor argued that welfare programs were of distinctly secondary importance to remuneration and dismissed welfare work as frivolous, even counterproductive. Many of his disciples agreed. One cautioned that what the workman wants from the boss is "a chance to earn all the money possible." So long as the workman feels he is not "getting enough money, he would be just about as grateful to the boss for interest displayed in the safety and healthy of his body . . . as a starving man would be to you for handing him a bunch of violets." Other proponents of scientific management worried that welfare benefits would indulge workers, reducing their incentive to supply the employer with maximum effort. Taylor himself warned that "too great liberty results in a large number of people going

---

15. Nelson, *Frederick W. Taylor and the Rise of Scientific Management*, p. x; Taylor, *Principles of Scientific Management*, p. 36. David Montgomery explores the deskilling dimensions of scientific management in *Workers' Control in America: Studies in the History of Work, Technology, and Labor Struggles* (New York: Cambridge University Press, 1979), pp. 9–27. Also see Hugh G. J. Aitken, *Taylorism at Watertown Arsenal: Scientific Management in Action, 1908–1915* (Cambridge: Harvard University Press, 1960).

wrong who would be right if they had been forced into good habits."
Hard work and just compensation alone would promote desirable habits and support the industrial work ethic.[16]

Taylor's disdain for paternalistic schemes bespoke the existence of a
larger ideological conflict in which alternative conceptions of employees' psychological motivations sometimes put welfare workers and line
managers at odds within the managerial realm. Foremen, production
managers, and plant superintendents frequently shared what Sanford
Jacoby has termed a "manufacturing orientation": they were concerned with the quick and cheap manufacture of products. To many
of these people, the industrial worker was a necessary but often
uncooperative partner in this endeavor, too "lazy, grasping, and un-
trustworthy" for managers' liking. Only strict discipline or Taylorist
incentives, many managers argued, could curb these tendencies and
induce high output. On the other side of the spectrum were welfare
workers who insisted that attention paid to the human element of industry would boost efficiency and enhance productivity. The clash between the two perspectives frequently made welfare work a source of
managerial conflict on the factory floor.[17]

Significantly, however, neither Taylor's nor line managers' wariness
of welfare practices prevented employers from adopting both scientific
management and welfare work in the Progressive era. Many industrialists—including those at the Joseph Bancroft and Sons Company, Scovill, Plymouth Cordage Company, Curtis Publishing, Heinz, Santa Fe
Railroad, Remington Typewriter, Forbes Lithograph, and General Electric—promoted both systems of management simultaneously. This
coexistence was not inherently conflictual, Taylor's comments notwithstanding. Rather, it reflected employers' willingness to experiment with
overlapping approaches for achieving greater productivity. To many
employers, the complementarity of scientific management and welfare
work lay in both strategies' enshrinement of efficiency, evidenced in
each movement's quest for order, higher output, and greater profits.
Sharing the same objective, the two strategies simply had different start-

16. Taylor, *Principles of Scientific Management*, p. 34; Frederick Winslow Taylor, "Shop
Management," *Transactions of the American Society of Mechanical Engineers* 24 (1903): 1454;
Haber, *Efficiency and Uplift*, pp. 20–21; Frank Barkley Copley, *Frederick W. Taylor, Revolu-
tionist* (Norwood, Mass., 1916), p. 5; Jacoby, *Employing Bureaucracy*, pp. 6–7.

17. Daniel Nelson and Stuart Campbell explore the oppositional character of welfare
work and scientific management in "Taylorism versus Welfare Work in American Industry: H. L. Gantt and the Bancrofts," *Business History Review* 46 (1972): 1–16. Also see
Jacoby, *Employing Bureaucracy*, pp. 6–7, 39–64.

ing points. Welfare work sought to control and mold the personal attributes workers brought to their labors; scientific management tried to direct the application of those attributes. In addressing the totality of workers' lives—their mental, physical, and emotional faculties, overlapping and interwoven—the deployment of both management strategies gave employers added power to regulate *all* variables potentially affecting workplace efficiency.[18]

The frequent blending of the two management styles can also be explained by the limited impact Taylor, the best known but certainly not the only proponent of scientific management in the Progressive era, had on the practical installation of scientific management procedures. Many scientific management consultants disagreed with critical aspects of Taylor's approach. Their implementation of scientific management was guided as much by independent judgment and experience as by Taylor's few articles of instruction. After Taylor died in 1915, the pace of modification quickened, and many disciples found in Taylor's published works support for programs—including welfare work—he had never endorsed. The dilution of Taylor's principles was compounded by the reality that, from the very beginning, few firms felt compelled or able to retool every aspect of production, accounting, and distribution along strictly Taylorist lines. Most favored a pick-and-choose approach, selecting individual features of scientific management that seemed to offer the best, most cost-efficient solution to immediate problems.[19]

The introduction of scientific management in the Progressive era was never as complete as Taylor would have liked. Its uneven and partial installation, the independent-mindedness of those doing the installing, and Taylor's death soon after the popularization of the idea made scientific management a strategy whose porous boundaries enabled it to be joined easily to other labor management techniques. Welfare work, having already appropriated the language of efficiency to assert its cred-

18. This complementarity is explored well by Steven W. Usselman in "Scientific Management without Taylor: Management Innovations at Bancroft," in *Working Papers from the Regional Economic History Research Center: Essays in Textile History*, ed. Glenn Porter and William H. Mulligan Jr. (Greenville, Del.: Eleutherian Mills–Hagley Foundation, 1981), pp. 47–77, and by Strom in *Beyond the Typewriter*, pp. 120–29.

19. See Daniel Nelson, *Managers and Workers: Origins of the New Factory System in the United States, 1800–1920* (Madison: University of Wisconsin Press, 1975), chap. 4; Harry Braverman, *Labor and Monopoly Capital: The Degradation of Work in the Nineteenth Century* (New York: Monthly Review Press, 1975); Nelson, *Frederick W. Taylor and the Rise of Scientific Management*; Strom, *Beyond the Typewriter*, pp. 125–29.

ibility, was easily incorporated into employers' multifaceted attempts to boost workplace productivity.

Making Workers Efficient

Because industrial efficiency was a broad mandate subsuming related but distinct objectives—from the recruitment of workers to their health—welfare work targeted different areas of concern. Several, however, stood out.

Companies experiencing frequent labor shortages and high turnover frequently turned to welfare work. In contrast to the mid-1890s, the Progressive era was a time of sustained economic growth. Relative prosperity bestowed a modicum of leverage to wage earners, especially native-born and skilled workers deemed indispensable for certain lines of work. Although the structure of local labor markets varied by region, labor market instability, characterized more by employers' difficulties securing the right kind of labor than by their ability to acquire labor at all, was chronic in the Progressive era. Especially in industrial urban centers, employees dissatisfied at one firm frequently found employment at another. Fluctuating labor markets made the provision of incentives to recruit and retain workers an enticing option, at times even an economic necessity. "There is nothing so expensive," complained Plymouth Cordage Company welfare worker W. E. C. Nazro, "as a heavy overturn of labor. . . . It is proverbial that 'the hireling careth not.' " Employers reasoned that given a choice, workers would sell their labor power to the company offering the greatest employment rewards. Herbert Vreeland, chairman of the NCF Welfare Department, believed that, other things being equal, employees "will seek work where the conditions are best."[20]

When employers relied on benefits to attract and keep workers, they consciously disregarded a more obvious lure: higher wages. It would have been significantly easier for employers just to increase wages. Such a move would have required little advance planning and minimal ad-

20. W. E. C. Nazro, "History of Welfare Work at the Plymouth Cordage Company," in *Plymouth Cordage Company: One Hundred Years of Service* (Cambridge, Mass., 1924), p. 61; New Jersey Department of Labor, Bureau of Statistics, *Industrial Betterment Work in New Jersey* (Trenton: MacCrellish & Quigley, 1904), p. 107; Herbert H. Vreeland, *Welfare Work*, address delivered before the New England Cotton Manufacturers' Association at Atlantic City, September 20, 1905 (New York: Welfare Department of the National Civic Federation, 1905), p. 24, SHSW.

ministration, and workers would have acquired the freedom and financial means to tend to their own welfare. Indeed, many scientific management advocates professed grave reservations that nonpecuniary benefits such as gun clubs or cooking classes could influence employees' attitudes. As one manufacturer stated, "I decry this idea of feeding oranges to men when they prefer to have the money for the oranges, apples, bananas or whatever is wanted." That many employers, notwithstanding these concerns, favored benefits over higher wages hints at their expectation of welfare work's promised pay-offs.[21]

To the charge that welfare work deflated wages, welfare employers countered—often falsely—that they offered the same, if not better, financial remuneration than their competitors. Welfare work was simply a "bonus." They also insisted that the per capita rewards of welfare work greatly outweighed their per capita cost—that the 2 cents per employee required to build company baths would not, distributed as wages, enable employees to install bathtubs in their own homes. According to a Plymouth Cordage Company official, a "distribution of funds expended for welfare work . . . by the Plymouth Cordage works during the past year would amount to $9.30 per employee per year, or 17.9 cents per employee per week, an amount so small, that it is quite certain that if expended individually it could not result in anything like the pleasure or benefit per individual [now provided]."[22]

A less frequently professed but equally important reason why employers favored welfare work over higher wages was their determination to control workers' actions, to define their welfare on *company* terms. Employers had little faith in workers' ability to "do the right thing" as far as business interests were concerned. Had they believed that workers would spend extra money on baths, they might have been less reluctant to support wage increases. But they suspected that wage raises would be used in brothels and dance halls, activities bound to exact a toll on the next day's work performance. Welfare programs, in contrast, funded such benefits as nutritious meals and supervised recreation that buttressed the company's vision of the ideal employee as healthy and

21. W. D. Forbes of W. D. Forbes Company quoted in William Tolman, *Social Engineering: A Record of Things Done by American Industrialists Employing Upwards of One and One-Half Million of People* (New York: McGraw, 1909), p. 360. On the social meanings embedded in the construction of the wage, see Alice Kessler-Harris, *A Woman's Wage: Historical Meanings and Social Consequences* (Lexington: University Press of Kentucky, 1990).

22. H. K. Hathaway, report of May 31, 1913, Plymouth Cordage Company Papers, File I, Drawer I, Folder G, Baker Library Archives of the Harvard Graduate School of Business (hereafter BL).

industrious. The public dimension of welfare work also played a for-
mative role in employers' decisions to offer welfare programs instead
of higher wages. Welfare work was bound to win the approval of men
and women who criticized work conditions, boosting a company's reputation in a way higher wages alone could not.

Prized for its purported ability to recruit workers, welfare work was also
lauded for its capacity to improve the health of those already in the company's employ. The rising stature of the medical profession in the wake
of the American Medical Association's reorganization in 1901 and published findings on communicable illnesses highlighted the importance
of occupational health to workplace efficiency. As one reformer proclaimed, health maintenance was nothing more than "an economic
method for lessening . . . human waste." The American Association for
Labor Legislation estimated in 1910 that the annual "social and economic cost of sickness" in industry exceeded $7.7 million. Although
welfare capitalists dismissed the AALL's call for government-provided
health care, they nevertheless agreed that health economics was important. As one cautioned, "The worker's health must be attended to, or
dollars slip into the 'loss' column." Attention to the physical condition
of workers reduced absenteeism and made working hours more pro-
ductive. "To those who do not see the connection between the question
of health and the matter of conducting a paying business," a writer for
the *American Journal of Sociology* put it crassly, "we would say that a healthy
operative turns out more work than a dyspeptic."[23]

Justified by economic reasoning, health provisions became one of
the most popular forms of welfare work in the Progressive period. The
Bureau of Labor Statistics found that of 431 welfare establishments
surveyed in 1916–17, 265 had hospital or emergency rooms, 110 had
first-aid equipment, 64 provided tuberculosis therapy, 106 offered daily
rest periods, and 193 permitted sick leave with pay. Other cost-saving

23. Testimony of Dr. Winthrop Talbot, director of the Health and Economics Department of the National Electric Company, in *Proceedings of the National Civic Federation Conference on Welfare Work* (New York, 1911), p. 320, SHSW; Mary Barnett Gilson, "Recreation
of the Working Force," *Industrial Management* 54 (October 1917): 55; American Association for Labor Legislation, *Memorial on Occupational Diseases* (New York: American Association for Labor Legislation, 1910); C. W. Price, Orval Simpson, Dale Wolf, Charles
Woodward, F. J. Moss, and W. R. Basset, *Working Conditions, Wages and Profits* (Chicago:
A. W. Shaw, 1920), p. 1; "Cost of Industrial Health Supervision," *Industrial Management*
55 (January 1918): 48; Paul Monroe, "Possibilities of the Present Industrial System,"
American Journal of Sociology 3 (May 1898); H. F. J. Porter, "The Higher Law in the Industrial World," *Engineering Magazine* 29 (August 1905); Otto P. Geier, "Health of the Working Force," *Industrial Management* 54 (October 1917): 15.

reforms were also instituted. Seats in factories enabled workers "to maintain strength and health." Footstools prevented backaches and "other ailments." Elevators also paid dividends because employers found that those "who laboriously climb the stairs to the upper floors of the factory are not in as good condition for work as when a way is found to conserve the energy by the use of elevators." Drinking fountains were also an investment in industrial efficiency. "The use of common drinking-cups carries the risk of infection," whereas the fountain, in "permit[ting] the water to bubble into the mouth of the operative . . . reduces the danger of contracting tuberculosis." Baths and showers enabled the worker to go home from a day's work "a cleaner and more self-respecting man" while warding off "muscular rheumatism . . . thus prevent[ing] absence and broken time in the factory." Individual lockers "prevent the accumulation of vermin." Factory rest rooms gave relief to "temporarily incapacitated" workers who would otherwise "deprive the employer of . . . output if obliged to go home." Adequate ventilation was also desirable. In a well-ventilated building "the brain is more active, attention is more alert. . . . and where combustible dust and shavings are cleaned up, the insurance rate is lower enough to pay [for] the cost of tidiness." In one factory, overall productivity increased after galvanized iron pipes were installed to circulate fresh air. "Previously, in very hot weather, the men were frequently overcome, and sometimes it was necessary to shut down the entire mill." Since the ventilation system's installation, however, "not a single hour's time has been lost because of the excessive heat." In another firm, calisthenics purportedly left employees imbued with "cheerfulness and alacrity; buoyancy of spirits and happiness of mind prevail where formerly languor and despondency ruled, and much more and better work is accomplished than before."[24]

The provision of hot, nutritious meals was another popular welfare measure. It responded to both the virtual absence of public eating facilities for wage-earning women in the early 1900s and the prominence

24. Gertrude Beeks, *Welfare Work: An Address before the National Association of Wool Manufacturers* (New York, 1906), p. 16, SHSW; National Civic Federation, *Conference on Welfare Work* (New York: Andrew H. Kellogg, 1904), p. 132. Union Switch & Signal Co. to Boston Chamber of Commerce, April 16, 1913, Boston Chamber of Commerce Collection, Case 48, Folder 332–19, BL; U.S. Bureau of Labor Statistics, *Betterment of Industrial Conditions*, p. 1133; Ernest G. W. Souster, *The Design of Factory and Industrial Buildings* (London: Scott, Greenwood & Son, 1919), pp. 30, 35; Henderson, *Citizens in Industry*, p. 99; Gertrude Beeks, "Practical Welfare Work: What Leading Manufacturers and Other Employers Are Doing to Improve the Working Conditions of the Wage Earner," *American Industries* 5 (June 15, 1907): 3.

Women workers at NCR exercise their way to better health and productivity. (*Cassier's Magazine*, September 1905.)

of the working-class saloon as an eating site for men. By controlling workers' food source, employers hoped to provide healthy meals and keep workers out of socially undesirable settings. Fears of moral and bacterial contagion emanating from working-class eateries colored the cautionings of one company official, who warned against letting "employees carry their baskets to some dark dismal corner to eat their lunch. . . . You take good care of your livestock, you buy good coal for your boilers," he continued, enlisting the higher causes of accounting and efficiency to legitimate the provision of health food, "why not provide good fuel to your employees?" The Metropolitan Life Insurance Company worried that employees with limited earnings would skip lunches altogether. Hence it was merely good policy for the company to provide workers with "nourishing [noon] meals." On any given day, Metropolitan Life employees could avail themselves of free lunches, including "soup, a choice of meat or fish, vegetables, and milk, tea or coffee." A sample meal in 1914 offered the company's 16,000 workers vegetable soup, cold corned beef and smoked beef tongue, lettuce salad, strawberry ice cream or cornstarch pudding, bread and butter, and a choice of beverages. Vegetarians were offered additional selections of rice and milk. At a cost of 21 cents per worker each day, meals were considered a valuable investment "to insure efficiency." Between 1911 and 1914 Metropolitan Life spent over $1 million to realize this goal.[25]

Employers hoped that healthy food served during the day would inspire workers to adopt new nutritional standards at home at night. Many companies dispensed handy take-home nutritional advice. At NCR, "Health in the Factory" became a regular employee newsletter feature in which NCR nutritionists and nurses gave guidelines for healthful eating. "Overeating is the fruitful source of most of our headaches," one nurse claimed. To avoid headaches, another suggested, "All flesh foods should be given up. The drinking of tea and coffee should be discontinued, spices and condiments should be banished from the table. . . . Ordinary toast is indigestible." The article went on to recommend that all foods be "reduced to a liquid state before. . . . [being] swallowed" and even included a rhyme to encourage workers to commit this thought to memory:

> So if you want to live long,
>   Living always well and strong,
> Don't take too big a bite—
>   Only just a little mite—
> And chew, chew, chew,
>   As one ought to chew,
> Then slowly feed the living mill;
>   But let it grind as fast as 'twill,
> And do not swallow in such haste;
>   Take plenty of time the food to taste,
> And chew, chew, chew,
>   For that's the thing to do.[26]

25. Statement of John Patterson, quoted in notes taken from "Conferences on Welfare Work at Chicago Commons under the Auspices of Professor Graham Taylor," May 1, 1906, Cyrus H. McCormick Jr. Papers, Box 40, SHSW; Thomas Neal, "Rounding Out a Business," *Social Service* 5 (February 1902): 52; Frances Gwen Ford, "Hot Luncheons for Employees," *Social Service* 9 (January 1904): 76; "Working Conditions in New York Stores," *National Civic Federation Review* 4 (July 15, 1913): 6; Metropolitan Life Insurance Company, *Welfare Work for Employees* (New York, 1915), pp. 12–13; idem, "The Welfare Work Conducted by the Metropolitan Life Insurance Company for the Benefit of Its Employees" (1912), pp. 9–12; idem, *How to Be Happy and Well* (New York, ca. 1920), p. 8.

26. *NCR*, May 1904, pp. 10–19, 25. In some firms, "nutrition" became a relative concept. The welfare worker at one major railway line tried to reduce alcohol consumption by selling employees chocolate, believing that "if a man would eat enough candy to supply heat and force he would not yearn for fire-water." Late twentieth-century nutritionists

Factory beautification was deemed as vital to employee performance as proper nutrition was to good health. Indeed, a picturesque and comfortable work setting was considered indispensable for promoting employees' vigor. While adequate ventilation protected workers' lungs, flowers in the factory appealed to their spiritual aestheticism. Although the efficacy of protected lungs might be easier to measure than that of workers' emotional equilibrium, the upkeep of both was regarded as equally important to plant productivity.

Technological innovations spurred the development of architectural reforms. Welfare firms were not only the country's largest industrial establishments, they were also typically among its newest. The date of the construction or expansion of many factories, including those of the Westinghouse Electric and Manufacturing Company (1895), National Cash Register (1896), and the United Shoe Machinery Company (1904), enabled builders to incorporate contemporary technologies that improved cleanliness, ventilation, and light. Electrification in the 1890s, for instance, greatly enhanced factory illumination. Reinforced concrete, first used systematically in factory construction in the 1900s, had several advantages. It was less flammable and easier to clean than other building materials. In addition, its strength could support more and larger windows. When in 1904 the United Shoe Machinery Company became the first major factory to be built with reinforced concrete, it was the windows covering almost all of the buildings' wall space, more than any other feature, that impressed observers.[27]

But technological breakthroughs were not the only reason for the considerable enthusiasm greeting architectural reforms. Contemporaries' conviction that environment influenced character imbued factory improvements with a special aesthetic. In reformers' eyes, industrial architecture was not only an inert cluster of structures and space but an active agent of personal reform. The excitement surrounding workplace beautification reflected the degree to which architecture and design were viewed as blueprints for society as a whole, projecting an image of a chaotic, urban, and industrial world redeemed by manicured gardens and factory windows overlooking pristine greenery. The political limitations of the "aesthetic approach to industrial reform" were obvious. As Eileen Boris has noted, factory face-lifts may have cre-

---

might scoff at this advice, but their Progressive era counterparts viewed chocolate as a health food. See Henderson, *Citizens in Industry*, p. 81.

27. Nelson, *Managers and Workers*, pp. 15, 16, 23.

ated ideal work spaces, but they also "left the larger political economy intact."[28]

As one would expect, employers' discussions of beautification reiterated the efficiency mantra. "The beautifying of your plant and grounds," one employer assured colleagues, "is expensive at the start, but like all good things, economical in the end." Another manufacturer, touring a firm surrounded by "well-trimmed lawns, flower gardens, shrubbery and shade trees [with] ivy-covered buildings," found that the company's reforms had not been in vain. "Working in surroundings such as these," the visitor noted, "the employee feels the dignity of his job. He finds in his surroundings an inspiration to cleanliness—which makes for better work. This builds up his self-esteem and is bound to be reflected in his earning capacity." In 1903 *Home and Flowers* surveyed five hundred businessmen across the country to determine if there was "any financial value in attractive surroundings to a business plant." Employers responded resoundingly in the affirmative; 95 percent declared that "the product of a factory or business concern is much more valuable when the factory or office is clean, attractive and beautiful, and when the employees can come into daily contact with orderly surroundings and see floral beauties on the grounds."[29]

The employer about to embark on factory beautification encountered a plethora of advice. Progressive era business and architecture journals were replete with practical tips and philosophical ruminations about refurbishing the industrial landscape. The purpose of landscape improvement, one consultant wrote, "is not to secure pretty spots, but [to create] an attractive general landscape composition in which the relation of trees, vines, shrubs and flowers to the great masses of buildings are considered and provided for on a just scale and in such a manner as to interfere in no respect with practical requirements." Achieving visual balance was key. The landscape should include "an attractive composition of foliage . . . to relieve the harshness and bareness of blank walls, severe architectural lines and crude temporary

28. Eileen Boris, *Art and Labor: Ruskin, Morris, and the Craftsman Ideal in America* (Philadelphia: Temple University Press, 1986), p. 155. For an interesting discussion of the social meanings of corporate architectural innovation, see Angel Kwolek-Folland, *Engendering Business: Men and Women in the Corporate Office, 1870–1930* (Baltimore: Johns Hopkins University Press, 1994), chap. 4.

29. *Home and Flowers* survey discussed in "What Manufacturers Say about Improved Factory Surroundings," *Social Service* 7 (May 1903): 108–10; Thomas Neal, "Rounding Out a Business," *Social Service* 5 (February 1902): 52.

Factory beautification at NCR. (*Cassier's Magazine*, September 1905.)

structures.'' Tips on plant selection abounded. ''Where the spaces are narrow, where vehicles must pass near at hand . . . high, narrow foliage can be established by the use of such trees as the Lombardy poplar,'' one landscaper recommended. Wisteria ''thrived'' on brick surfaces, while against windowless blank walls ''broad masses of foliage can be secured by the use of such rapid-growing trees as poplars, willows, sycamores and ailanthus.'' Another landscape architect suggested ivy to soften buildings' harsh silhouettes. ''Whenever atmospheric conditions permit,'' he explained in *Factory*, ''ivys [*sic*] will make attractive the

ugliest wall surface. Those varieties known as the Boston ivy and En-
gleman's ivy are hardy and will grow under very adverse conditions."
If ivies failed to capture a manufacturer's fancy, flowers were the recommended alternative. "Geraniums and periwinkles," he continued,
"will grow under the most discouraging conditions and the exterior of
a factory with so simple an addition as window boxes containing these
plants can be made very attractive."[30]

Improving factory surroundings was a package deal: what existed outside the factory was as important as what lay within. A beautiful factory
exterior needed to be matched by an orderly but pleasing interior. As
one welfare advocate warned, "It is no good making the factory cheerful and bright if lavatories and W. C.'s [water closets] are dull, dirty
and sloppy."[31]

Like the refashioning of factory landscapes, internal improvements
reflected employers' willingness to experiment with new inducements
to boost labor productivity. The installation of windows, for instance,
increased output rates because "light and sunshine add greatly to the
cheer, and consequently, to the health of workers." In addition, accidents were less frequent "in well-lighted [rather] than in gloomy buildings." "Abundant" lighting was also credited with reducing waste
because materials were not "lost, mislaid, and wasted so much as in
dimly-lit buildings." Gertrude Beeks praised ventilation systems as a
cost-efficient means for promoting efficiency. "In one notable case,"
she explained, "the cost of installation was six thousand dollars, but
the reduction ... of absences because of illness was so great that the
employer was compensated for the outlay. . . . Previously the employees
were likely to become stupid [in] the latter part of the afternoon, [but]
the new system maintained alertness during the entire day."[32]

The quest for factory efficiency continued through other programs.
Benefits such as vacations, pensions, profit sharing, and stockholding
ensured the stability of the labor force because they were given only to
long-term employees. The length of employment necessary to qualify
for such benefits varied by firm, but all placed a premium on loyalty
to the company. To be eligible for vacations, for instance, employees
were usually expected to remain employed for at least a year. In the

30. Warren H. Manning, "The Landscape Improvement of Factory Grounds," *Social
Service* 7 (March 1903): 61–65; Jens Jensen, "Making Factory Buildings Attractive," *Factory*
4 (June 1910): 311–13, 337–38.
31. Souster, *Design of Factory and Industrial Buildings*, p. 41.
32. Ibid., pp. 30, 35; Henderson, *Citizens in Industry*, p. 99; Beeks, "Practical Welfare
Work," p. 3.

case of pension, profit-sharing, and stockholding schemes, the longer an employee worked, the greater the remuneration. In each instance, benefits gave employees added incentive to perform years of labor free of incidents or disruptions that might call their loyalty into question.

More than other programs, profit-sharing and stockholding plans attempted to attenuate class tensions by emphasizing the mutual objectives of capital and labor, conferring on workers a vested interest in the firm's productivity. Higher company profits translated into higher dividends for workers; the more a worker gave to the company as an individual, the more he or she got back. Employers conceded that the general appeal of profit sharing and stockholding lay in the possibility of the "development of a larger spirit of harmony and cooperation . . . resulting, incidentally, in greater efficiency and larger gains."[33]

Profit sharing and stockholding also encouraged employees to shed the "penalizing" attributes of working-class character and internalize "sound" capitalist values. Consider the miraculous transformation of "Henry B." and "Thomas M." at Procter and Gamble. Henry arrived at the company a "more than incipient drunkard." Then he learned about the company's stockholding plan. Henry suddenly became a changed man: "He could talk of nothing else." Succumbing to enthusiasm, he became a stockholder. "With the very first payment came a sense of security from financial worries—those things that drive many a poor workman to drink—and a real reason for saving kept Henry away from old haunts." Discovering capitalism saved Henry's soul: "Now he needs no drink cure—he has a substantial bank account."[34]

Thomas M. was apparently just as "fortunate." After an accident in the machine room cut off his arm, he refused the company's offer of a sizable pension, for "a mere gift would have robbed the man and his family of that self-respect which is compatible only with independence." Instead, Thomas became a profit sharer, saved money each month, "and now this one-armed laborer is the owner of $12,000 worth of 7 per cent stock." "No 'Help me, I'm a cripple' sign for Thomas M.," Procter and Gamble happily reported, "and his little family go[es] forth . . . [to] add to the real improvement of the world."[35]

33. Solvay Process Co. to Boston Chamber of Commerce, November 21, 1916, and Eastman Kodak Co. to Boston Chamber of Commerce, April 22, 1913, Boston Chamber of Commerce Collection (hereafter BCCC), Case 48, Folder 332–19, BL; U.S. Bureau of Labor Statistics, *Profit Sharing in the United States*, Bulletin 208 (1916), p. 5.

34. Janet Ruth Rankin, "Profit Sharing for Savings," *World's Work* 28 (July 1914): 319.

35. Ibid.

Employers also lauded property ownership for its ostensibly character-changing properties. Like profit sharing and stockholding, the possession of real property was expected to reorient workers' values, transforming the deracinated proletarian into a property-loving capitalist. One industrial expert observed that "men are more likely to be sober, steady, industrious and faithful if they own visible property." A committee created to study the benefits of constructing worker housing at the Plymouth Cordage Company determined that employees' homes would provide an ideal solution to "restlessness in the air." "One of the things which has so appealed ever since people lived in caves has been the desire on the part of every normal man and woman for something which they could call a home," the committee reported. "History shows us no race of people who have owned land . . . who became revolutionists."[36]

In addition to promoting docility among workers, the provision of employee housing promised a lower turnover rate. Notwithstanding its ubiquity as a symbol of middle-class success, home ownership was a minority experience at the turn of the century. In 1890 only 48 percent of American families owned homes. Tying ownership to employment, companies offered the status that came with ownership in exchange for company loyalty. Welfare firms providing homes to own typically financed employees' mortgages. Workers made an initial down payment, usually 10 percent of the house's selling price. They paid the balance, including interest, in monthly installments over a period of ten to fifteen years. Companies with home-owning plans such as U.S. Steel and Goodyear formed subsidiary realty companies to handle all financing, ostensibly curbing charges of paternalism by keeping housing transactions on a strictly "business basis." In buying from their employer, workers usually got below-market rates; employers, for their part, accrued profits from interest and the satisfaction of knowing that an outstanding mortgage would keep workers geographically in town and economically and politically in tow. Indeed, some employers calculated that employee housing reduced labor turnover so significantly that they could afford to a sell a house to an employee below cost in an amount equal to the per capita cost of labor turnover.[37]

36. C. W. Post, "A Step Forward," *Square Deal* 4 (April 1909): 6; Henderson, *Citizens in Industry*, p. 169; Report of the Industrial Homes and Gardens Committee, ca. 1917, Plymouth Cordage Company Papers, File I, Drawer I, Folder B, BL.

37. Gwendolyn Wright, *Moralism and the Model Home: Domestic Architecture and Cultural Conflict in Chicago, 1873–1913* (Chicago: University of Chicago Press, 1980), p. 83; Leifur

Employers tried to change not only the availability of housing but also the home's internal environment. Regardless of where workers lived or who owned their dwellings, welfare firms typically endeavored to extend their regulatory reach over employees' private time. The prevailing reform discourse associated working-class conditions with a litany of evils. Workers' homes were routinely described in turn-of-the-century texts as dark, dirty, and diseased—veritable breeding grounds for moral and physical decay. Such images supplied potent ammunition for reformers eager to abolish homework in order to "rescue" consumer goods from the contagion of home manufacture. Welfare capitalists, in contrast, sought not to separate home and work but rather to reform the former to boost the efficiency of the latter. Overcrowding, filth, noise, and licentious behavior at home, they maintained, adversely affected the labor force's efficiency. As an article in *Industrial Management* put it,

> It is not to be wondered at that a man who has slept for six or seven hours in a room with ten others, only turning out of bed in the morning in time for a night-shift man to take his place between the same sheets, does not go to his work fresh, happy and cheerful. And after working hours he has no place to go except the saloon, and nothing to do but drink. It is not likely that his health will be so good or his efficiency so great as that of the man who sleeps in healthy surroundings and has a comfortable home.[38]

Paralleling their efforts to reshape the workplace, employers tried to make the employee home a nursery for moral purity. As Gwendolyn Wright has argued, faith in the interconnectedness of domestic space and personal character undergirded many Progressive reforms and gave rise to an architectural school devoted to advancing middle-class morality through the design of model homes. Welfare employers similarly supported the goal of improved behavior through the reorganization of domestic space, justifying inspections of workers' dwellings under the auspices of moral reform. The ideal home, they contended,

Magnusson, "Methods of Sale of Company Houses," *Monthly Labor Review* 8 (April 1919): 1178; Louis A. Boettiger, *Employee Welfare Work: A Critical and Historical Study* (New York: Ronald Press, 1923), pp. 202–4.

38. Leslie H. Allen, "The Problem of Industrial Housing," *Industrial Management* 54 (December 1917): 397.

would recast wage earners into a middle-class mold of temperate efficiency.[39]

The best example of home reform was the Ford Motor Company's famous five-dollar day. Henry Ford introduced the five-dollar day in 1914 to combat an almost 400 percent turnover rate that followed the 1913 introduction of the moving assembly line at his Highland Park plant. The wage was twice the going rate in the Detroit area, and workers clamored around Ford's doors to get it. In practice, however, the five-dollar day was not a flat wage increase but a profit-sharing payment that workers earned only if they complied with rules of conduct at work and at home. Employees eager to collect their promised wage had first to meet the approval of company investigators charged with interviewing family members and scrutinizing home conditions. Poor sanitation, overcrowding, and improper behavior were grounds for disqualification. To be approved as profit sharers, employees had to "live in clean, well conducted homes." "The company is anxious," stated one pamphlet, "to have its employees live . . . under conditions that make for cleanliness, good manhood, and good citizenship." Married men were instructed to rent housing that would protect the morals of the entire family—to provide home "conditions that will tend to clean helpful ideas, rather than those likely to be formed in the streets and alleys of the city." What Ford defined as disorderly conduct in the home included drinking, smoking, "domestic troubles," and living with a woman to whom one was not married. In the first two years of the program, fully 28 percent of employees were disqualified.[40]

Ford defended his intrusive policy as "good business." Home cleanliness, he contended, curbed absenteeism; purity of the soul inculcated efficient work habits. "Some persons may argue that we have no right to inquire how a man lives at home so long as he does his work at the factory," Ford testified before the U.S. Commission on Industrial Relations, but "our experience leads us to conclude that [this] interest taken in employees . . . is most desirable from every standpoint, not only that of the employee and his family, but that of the business itself." To the charge that home visits were coercive, he responded that "no coercion is laid upon any employee, but if he is not living a sober life,

39. Wright, *Moralism and the Modern Home.*
40. Stephen Meyer III, *The Five Dollar Day: Labor Management and Social Control in the Ford Motor Company, 1908–1921* (Albany: SUNY Press, 1981), pp. 149–62; Stuart D. Brandes, *American Welfare Capitalism, 1880–1940* (Chicago: University of Chicago Press, 1976), p. 89.

or is neglecting his duties as a father or husband . . . he can not be an associate in our business."[41]

Though it was one of the most egregious invasions of workers' privacy, the Ford case was not unique. In companies across the country, welfare workers and social secretaries were instructed to win workers' trust so as to gain admission to their homes. Isabelle Nye, social secretary at the Siegel-Cooper department store in New York, noted that company policy required that newly hired workers visit her office so that she could "find about their home conditions, how they are surrounded." After the initial interview, Nye reported, "I visit their homes very frequently . . . and get into their home lives." The team of welfare workers and visiting nurses at International Harvester regularly investigated workers' homes to inspect hygienic conditions; visits often devolved into impassioned disputes about sleeping conditions, air circulation, and cleanliness, disputes that reflected contested definitions as to what constituted good hygiene.[42]

Hoping that a stable family life would encourage industrial discipline, employers integrated the entire family into welfare activities. Winning the confidence of employees' wives was deemed vital; according to one welfare worker, "It is through the women [that] we . . . reach the home." Firms established welfare programs for workers' wives to prod them into crafting a home environment conducive to desired male behavior. At the Joseph Bancroft and Sons Company, cooking classes for employees' wives were initiated because "Mr. Bancroft has a theory that if women knew how to cook well and provide good, wholesome meals to their husbands, it would solve the drink problem." Herbert Vreeland, chair of the NCF Welfare Department, encouraged companies to take an active role in cultivating women's prowess at housekeeping. Paying tribute to the regenerative attributes of hygienic surroundings, he promised that "the disappearance of slovenliness from the household will make the fireside an attractive and winning competitor to the saloon when the day's work is over."[43]

41. Testimony of Henry Ford, in U.S. Senate, Commission on Industrial Relations, *Final Report and Testimony of the U.S. Commission on Industrial Relations*, 64th Cong., 1st sess. (Washington, D.C.: Government Printing Office, 1916), 26:7627.

42. Testimony of Isabelle Nye, in National Civic Federation, *Conference on Welfare Work*, pp. 109–13; testimony of Mary Goss, in *Proceedings of the Eleventh Annual Meeting of the National Civic Federation*, pp. 338–42; Barcalo Manufacturing Co. to Boston Chamber of Commerce, May 1, 1913, BCCC, Case 48, Folder 332–19, BL.

43. Testimony of Elizabeth C. Wheeler of the Shepard Co. of Providence, R.I., in National Civic Federation, *Conference on Welfare Work*, p. 113; lecture by Elizabeth Briscoe at

Employees' children were often covered by welfare programs, too. Child-oriented programs were intended not only to evoke parental appreciation but also to mold children into disciplined prospective workers. At the Kaynee Company of Cleveland, a well-equipped outdoor playground gave neighborhood children the opportunity to "stretch their little limbs and develop their little muscles without fear of street traffic." A philanthropic measure? "Not at all!" the company insisted. "All that Kaynee does is done in the cause of better business. Children who are brought up in the open grow into better men and women, and the better men and women are, the healthier they are— [and] the better employees they will make." Another employer concurred. Constructing swings for employees' children was economically astute. "The children in these families are coming into your shop in a very few years; how much better for you that their bodies have been somewhat strengthened by exercise and their minds disciplined by regulated play."[44]

"Regulated play" was deemed critical for adult employees too. Reduced hours of work at the turn of the century had amplified the centrality of leisure to workers' lives. An increase in workers' real wages— from 1901 to 1907 wages for unskilled workers rose approximately 12 percent and for skilled and unionized workers about 17 percent— equipped wage earners with the financial means to participate in the expanding world of commercial entertainment. Dance halls, amusement parks, movie theaters, and saloons promised release from the drudgery of work and the implied tedium of nights at home in the exciting world of commodified leisure.

Employers believed that left to their own devices, workers in turn-of-the-century America would succumb to the perilous thrills of cheap amusements. According to one contemporary, in the absence of proper guidance the temptation would be irresistible: "Multitudes are exposed to all the vicissitudes and temptations of city life, without mentors, and with their earnings free from control." Leisure activities dissipated employees' moral fabric, drained their pocketbooks, and depleted their spiritual and physical reserves. From the perspective of employers, commercial amusements eroded the industrial ethic by promoting absen-

---

New York University, April 21, 1913, Box 84, National Civic Federation Papers, New York Public Library; Herbert H. Vreeland, *Welfare Work*, address to New England Cotton Manufacturers' Association at Atlantic City, September 20, 1905 (New York: NCR Welfare Department, 1905), p. 9.

44. A. Booster, *The Song of the Kaynee Blouse* (Cleveland: Kaynee Co., 1917), p. 26; William Tolman, "The Social Secretary," *Social Service* 2 (November 1900): 12.

teeism, drunkenness, and illness. Drunk, financially strapped, or fatigued from indulgence, the "merry" worker was a sorry substitute for the robust, efficient human machine employers desired.[45]

Here, too, welfare work became the championed solution. In welfare capitalists' eyes, the leisure crisis could be remedied by company amusements. Instead of directing money reserved for welfare expenditures into higher wages—giving workers the choice of how their leisure would be purchased—welfare employers determined that they alone knew what was in workers' best interests. Events such as company dances, theatricals, picnics, and clubhouses gave employers opportunities to become key actors in all spheres of a worker's life, and hence to increase employees' dependence on and loyalty to the company. Harking back to a time when masters and apprentices mixed leisure and labor in a single domain, employers invoked the language of corporate domesticity to coat their actions with a familial gloss. But more than nostalgia for an industrial era that they themselves had not experienced prodded employers to establish leisure activities. Such events, given free to workers, countered common amusements, from dance halls to taverns, with a menu of ritualized leisure choices intended to reinforce the industrial ethic by "rescuing" workers from the perils of unpredictable street culture. As the Brooklyn Rapid Transit Company put it simply, "billiards are better than saloons." The Curtis Publishing Company found that its smoking rooms "justify their expense many times over by keeping the men in the building during noon hour and keeping them away from the corner poolroom."[46]

Company sports ostensibly supplied comparable benefits. Of the 431 establishments surveyed by the Bureau of Labor Statistics in 1916–17, more than half (219) had facilities for outdoor recreation. "Wholesome recreation develops both the health and the spirit of a body of workers," one female welfare worker advised. When conducted in "proper surroundings," it provided "a safety valve worthy of attention." Of course, as the welfare worker suggested, the proper environment was crucial; unrestrained athleticism was tantamount to chaos. "I know of no quicker nor more effective way to disorganize a factory," one employer warned, "than to do as did Frankenstein, build up a body

45. Henderson, *Citizens in Industry*, p. 187; Tolman, *Social Engineering*, p. 50.

46. C. B. Lord, "Athletics for the Working Force," *Industrial Management* 54 (October 1917): 44–45; "The Brooklyn Rapid Transit Company," *Social Service* 13 (November–December 1906): 14; Vreeland, *Welfare Work*, p. 15; Robert C. Clothier, "The Employment Work of the Curtis Publishing Company," *Annals of the American Academy of Political and Social Science* 65 (May 1916): 105.

that you cannot afterward control.'' The benefits of *supervised* recreation, however, were purportedly infinite. Employers reasoned that skills and habits learned on the playing field would enhance work performance. The physically fit employee would be alert and energetic. "Coordination of mind and hand . . . are very necessary qualities even in repetitive work," one welfare worker rationalized. Enthusiasm on the baseball field would not end when the game did. Instead, it would be channeled into work, giving gratuitous zeal a "legitimate" outlet. Sports instilled a fierce competitive drive, a desirable trait because "an unambitious worker is a drag, sometimes even a menace to an organization." Athletics were also praised for their ability to quench the restless spirit; one physician went so far as to call sports "superlative weapons in fighting radicalism." Instead of going on strike, employees could relieve their aggressions in a boxing ring.[47]

Team sports such as baseball, basketball, and soccer, common at large welfare firms such as International Harvester, Sears, Roebuck, and NCR, fostered interdependence and mutual responsibility, ideal attitudes for work and play alike. Indeed, sports metaphors such as "teamwork" and "group togetherness" provided managers with a language for articulating a vision of workplace relations they hoped workers would come to accept. Group activities also promoted deference, "a sense of fairness in accepting the 'umpire's' decision." In addition, team sports tried to mitigate the oppositional culture nurtured by working-class amusements. At the beginning of the twentieth century, sports still boasted particular class signatures. Although the middle class had found in boxing, traditionally a working-class pursuit, an athletic answer to cultural concerns about their own effeminacy and self-indulgence, other sports such as riding, hunting, and yachting remained unapologetically middle class. Welfare programs offered workers hybridized forms of leisure that blurred class distinctions: rifle clubs *and* open-air baseball; horseback riding *and* boxing; yachting *and* billiards. On company terrain, athletics ceased to be a marker of class difference as

47. Mary Barnett Gilson, "Recreation of the Working Force," *Industrial Management* 54 (October 1917): 52; Lord, "Athletics for the Working Force"; "Outdoor Sports Remedy for Unrest," *Industrial Management* 49 (January 1920): 9. For an interesting analysis of masculinity and the popularity of sports at the turn of the century, see John Higham, "The Reorientation of American Culture in the 1890s," in *The Origins of Modern Consciousness*, ed. John Weiss (Detroit: Wayne State University Press, 1965), pp. 25–48. On interpretations of workplace leisure, see Gareth Stedman Jones, "Class Expressions versus Social Control? A Critique of Recent Trends in the Social History of 'Leisure,' " *History Workshop* 4 (Autumn 1977): 162–70; Steven Gelbert, "Working at Playing: The Culture of the Workplace and the Rise of Baseball," *Journal of Social History* 6 (June 1983): 3–22.

More than just an invitation to play, a company sports program had many meanings. (*Industrial Management* 54 [October 1917].)

employers consciously destabilized boundaries separating working-class and middle-class cultures.[48]

In addition, by encouraging interdepartment rivalries, team sports made competition among workers, rather than against employers, their basis. By creating artificial divisions within the workforce itself, divisions that surfaced when "machine room A" picked up bat and ball to defeat "machine room B" on the baseball field, athletic leagues attenuated class-based tensions. Nor did one have to be an athlete to reap the thrills of the game; spectators could share "through sympathy the excitement of participation." Because each team comprised workers of mixed rank, organized sports created an arena for articulating the company's commitment to democracy; increased hierarchy on the shop floor was offset by the fluidity of equal opportunity sports. As one welfare worker boasted, "Sports bring out foremen and porters, office workers and machinery operatives alike. They are not confined to any class or stratum of society." The Goodyear Tire and Rubber Company underscored this sentiment in a discussion of its annual athletics day. "This is a real Labor Day bringing men and management together in

48. Gilson, "Recreation of the Working Force," p. 55. On boxing, masculinity, and the working class, see Gorn, *Manly Art.*

close contact," it boasted. "They are all hard workers. Is it not better than a street parade, [which] encourage[s] class distinctions?"[49]

From ventilation systems to playgrounds, welfare measures strove to make employees more efficient. In 1906 industrial expert O. M. Becker aptly characterized the economics of the welfare work movement, reporting in *Engineering Magazine*:

> The thoughtful employer is finding that it is not merely philanthropy to do what he can to make his employees cheerful, happy and content; but that it is a paying investment, yielding tangible returns as well as intangible. . . . They appear in a more happy and contented corps of workers, and in a consequently cheapened production by reason of the better quality and increased quantity of the output; in an absence of strikes and labor disturbances; in greater interest in the business; in increased personal loyalty; and in a dozen other ways, all tending to greater economy of operation in the establishment. The testimony on this point is indisputable, and amounts to this: However much it means in the sum total of civilization to have a community of cheerful, intelligent, and virtuous operatives, it means a great deal more to the employer himself in the way of economic output and increased profits. That is to say, *it does pay*.[50]

Employers agreed. Claiming that work relations and productivity had improved dramatically, most pronounced welfare work a success. The catalog of welfare work success stories was long. The Ford Motor Company credited a steady reduction in labor turnover between 1913 and 1914 to the introduction of its five-dollar day. The Metropolitan Life Insurance Company boasted that welfare work had yielded a better "grade of employees" and reduced labor turnover by 50 percent. After three years of welfare work, the Sherwin-Williams Paint Company announced that "we [used to have] a standing advertisement for help wanted in every paper in the country, and then could not get enough. Today there are upwards of 100 applications on our list." A Philadelphia manufacturer likewise claimed that welfarism had "changed the financial status of the company within six months from a loss of $2100 per month to a small profit." Other employers cited similar results. In

49. Gilson, "Recreation of the Working Force," p. 55. Goodyear Tire & Rubber Co., *The Work of the Labor Division* (Akron, 1920), p. 40.

50. O. M. Becker, "The Square Deal in Works Management," *Engineering Magazine* 30 (January 1906): 554.

1917 the Department of Labor found that employers reporting favorable outcomes from welfare work outnumbered those who did not by 5 to 1.[51]

That welfare employers so frequently boasted of the profitability of private sector benevolence should not surprise us. It was vital to employers' larger defense of the private ordering of industrial relations to show that it was natural for industrial capitalism, even in its most profit-oriented incarnation, to take heed of workers' welfare. Implicitly refuting charges that welfare work was a temporary fad concocted only to satisfy reformers' pleas for change, employers justified their benevolence on the mantle of Progressive efficiency, demanding that contemporaries view welfare work—as employers themselves claimed to do— as a logical and permanent stage in the evolution and rationalization of corporate capitalism. As O. M. Becker put it, the proven profitability of welfare work meant that the time had come "where a business, in order to be continuously successful, will necessarily become . . . moralized, whether the owner wishes it or not." Welfare capitalists advertised this message whenever they could.[52]

51. Boettiger, *Employee Welfare Work*, pp. 146–48; Brandes, *American Welfare Capitalism*, p. 135; William H. Tolman, *Industrial Betterment* (New York: Social Service Press, 1900), p. 81; Metropolitan Life Insurance Co., *The Welfare Work of the Metropolitan Life Insurance Company for Its Employees: Reports for 1918* (New York, 1918), p. 14; Becker, "Square Deal in Works Management," p. 553; American Institute of Social Service Weekly Commercial Letter Service, letter of September 26, 1906, "Business Value of Industrial Betterment," Cyrus H. McCormick Jr. Papers, Box 41, SHSW; U.S. Bureau of Labor Statistics, *Welfare Work for Employees in Industrial Establishments in the United States*, Bulletin 250 (1919), p. 119.
52. Becker, "Square Deal in Works Management," p. 554.

3 /

The "Human Face" of American Capitalism

In 1916 exhibits sponsored by the Detroit Chamber of Commerce and the Welfare Department of the National Civic Federation conveyed the "good news" about welfare work to the public. Each exhibit was open to visitors year-round; both featured an array of "models, photographs, illuminated stereopticon views, moving pictures, literature and other data" depicting the merits of capitalist beneficence. By the fall, under the directorship of such luminaries as William Howard Taft, Jane Addams, Nicholas Murray Butler, and Charles W. Eliot, planning began for a third exhibition, the Traveling Exhibit of Welfare Work in American Industry. As its title implied, the most distinguishable characteristic of the new exposition would be its mobility. Now the gospel of welfare work could be propagated across the country.[1]

By early 1917 the Traveling Exhibit of Welfare Work was finalizing plans to display its wares in more than twenty American cities. The

1. G. B. St. John to Boston Chamber of Commerce, October 31, 1916, and A. A. Ainsworth to Howard Coonley, January 3, 1917, Boston Chamber of Commerce Collection (hereafter BCCC), Case 48, Folder 332–19, Baker Library Archives of the Harvard Graduate School of Business (hereafter BL); "Welfare Work for New York City Employees," *National Civic Federation Review* 4 (May 1914): 22; Manufacturers' Association of the City of Bridgeport, *Report on Welfare Work in Bridgeport and Elsewhere* (Bridgeport: Brewer-Colgan, 1918), p. 11.

traveling show consisted of company-sponsored presentations display-
ing "what American manufacturers are doing in . . . bettering the conditions of their employees." Its organizers offered the exhibit to any
city whose Chamber of Commerce met two conditions: a minimum ten-
day sponsorship and full cooperation with the exhibit's publicity
agents.[2]

Although the exhibition was free to the public, participating companies paid dearly for the privilege of renting space at it. A 10-by-33-
foot unit cost $500, a 10-by-40 foot unit $600. This rate applied only
to a single show: if a company wanted to be represented at twenty cities,
rental space alone would cost a minimum of $10,000. In addition, par-
ticipating firms were required to pay the cost of setting up their section
of the exhibit, a cost the directors estimated would range from $1,500
to $5,000. Despite the substantial expense, forty-four companies, in-
cluding Prudential Life Insurance, General Electric, H. J. Heinz, National Cash Register, and the Goodyear Tire and Rubber Company had
signed on by the spring of 1917 to publicize their welfare programs to
the public.[3]

The organization of the Traveling Exhibit of Welfare Work and the
support it quickly received illuminate the centrality of publicity to
American welfare work. The Janus face of welfare capitalism encouraged employers to advertise their altruism even as they justified welfare
programs to shareholders for its lucrative returns. Emphasizing the
compassionate, even "indulgent" character of their labor policy, welfare capitalists courted employee respect and public support at a time
when shooting workers was frighteningly commonplace; advertising the
cleanliness of factory environs, they allayed consumer doubts in an era
when the horrors and extent of product adulteration evoked national
concern and political scrutiny. In its calculation of the gains to be accrued through advertising labor reform, the marketing of benevolence
represented both a critical component of welfare capitalist ideology
and an important, albeit often overlooked, dimension of turn-of-the-
century corporate public relations.[4]

2. St. John to Boston Chamber of Commerce, October 31, 1916, and Ainsworth to
Coonley, January 3, 1917, BCCC, Case 48, Folder 332–19, BL.

3. St. John to Boston Chamber of Commerce, October 31, 1916, and Ainsworth to
Coonley, January 3, 1917.

4. On labor and corporate public relations in the Progressive era, see Richard S.
Tedlow, *Keeping the Corporate Image: Public Relations and Business, 1900–1950* (Greenwich,
Conn.: JAI Press, 1979); David E. Nye, *Image Worlds: Corporate Identities at General Electric,
1890–1930* (Cambridge: MIT Press, 1985); and Angel Kwolek-Folland, *Engendering*

Employers used many mediums to praise private provisions and those who bestowed them. Welfare work was promoted in articles, pamphlets, and photographs submitted to business organizations, educators, labor organizations, industrial critics, politicians, social science journals, and employees themselves. Some establishments went a step further, hosting factory tours so that the world could witness firsthand the fruits of welfare capitalism.

Companies' visual and verbal chronicling of "happy workers" mirrored another Progressive development in which the dissemination of written and visual documentation became an important aspect of political lobbying. Invoking a spirit of documentary realism, professional reform groups assembled ostensibly objective evidence to advance their cause. Organizations such as the National Child Labor Committee, the American Association for Labor Legislation, and the National Consumers' League used photographic exhibits, picture postcards, slide lectures, and investigative journalism to communicate the gravity of industrial carnage and to marshal support for government regulation of the workplace.[5]

Welfare firms' idyllic depictions of labor conditions were never intended to be an unmediated representation of social reality; they were meant to counter criticisms of "predatory" capitalism. Journals condemning the plights of wage slavery were answered by company pamphlets lionizing gains employees enjoyed from private provisions. For every photograph critical of the treatment of industrial wage earners, companies such as National Cash Register and Heinz submitted portraits of a strikingly different scene: nurtured factory laborers happily at play on company grounds. Welfare work publicity did not contradict outright the veracity of reformers' claims. But by presenting a remarkably different view of working conditions, they refuted the normality of labor exploitation and vitiated the urgency of reformer's legislative program.

Welfare work advertising targeted three distinct communities: employees, reformers of industry, and consumers. Company employees were the first targeted audience for welfare work publicity. Employers acknowledged that worker contentment, loyalty, and productivity were not automatic by-products of welfare capitalism; before employees

Business: Men and Women in the Corporate Office, 1870–1930 (Baltimore: Johns Hopkins University Press, 1994).

5. Maren Stange, *Symbols of Ideal Life: Social Documentary Photography in America, 1890–1950* (New York: Cambridge University Press, 1989).

could be transformed by capitalist beneficence, they had to be apprised of the magnitude of welfare activity. Company-controlled employee newspapers communicated this information, announcing programs and encouraging participation. In addition, employee magazines tried to fortify workers' appreciation of welfare programs and their attachment to their employer by routinely reminding them that welfare schemes "worked"—that because of their employer's generosity, they, as workers, were happier and better off.

If workers were the internal target of company publicity, those outside the firm's employ constituted an equally important audience. Acute industrial strife and the attendant threat of government regulation had compounded the importance of public opinion to business. By advertising their benevolence in a public arena, welfare firms endeavored to revamp their image and rally support for their broader political mandate. Pictorial and printed "evidence" of contented and healthy wage earners buttressed employers' claims that even without government initiative forcing their hand, business could play a salutary role in workers' lives. Welfare work publicity thus decried the need for widening government involvement in industrial relations at a time when private efforts—as a spate of company propaganda attested—had already "accomplished" so much.

Publicity had an added appeal for companies selling products directly to end users. These welfare firms identified a third audience for welfare work publicity: the consumer. Immersed in a culture and economy increasingly geared toward mass consumption, employers made welfare work a key component of product marketing. Companies manufacturing packaged food, household appliances, and ready-made clothing acknowledged the existence of the educated, discriminating consumer who took into account the conditions under which products were assembled before making a purchase. Foregrounding the conditions of the workplace and the treatment of wage earners as crucial determinants of product quality, advertising cast welfare work as the savvy shopper's ally. In addition, by forging a link between labor provisions and consumer satisfaction, employers ensured that welfare capitalism was viewed as a management policy whose immediate beneficiaries extended beyond the workplace.

Publicity and Employees

To secure and maintain employee participation, welfare work required a regular and reliable medium for publicizing industrial betterment programs to workers. The favored method of communication was the employee magazine, also called the internal house organ. These magazines, published regularly, usually monthly, provided an ideal forum for publicizing company-sponsored employee activities.[6]

Welfare firms were among the first business to establish employee magazines in the United States. National Cash Register published the first plant-wide employee newsletter in the United States, *Factory News*. The twelve-page bulletin began circulation in 1890, around the time that the company's president, John Patterson, established welfare work. Following a similar trajectory, the H. J. Heinz Company introduced *Pickles* to employees in the late 1890s after Heinz adopted factory-wide welfare provisions. In other firms employee magazines also followed closely on the heels of welfare work. The popularity of employee magazines roughly paralleled that of the welfare movement itself, reaching an apex during World War I, a period marked by unprecedented demands for capital-labor cooperation. By the end of the war, approximately three hundred employee magazines were being published in companies across the country.[7]

The employee magazine itself functioned as a form of welfare work, attempting to restore closer communication between the two parties by conveying written and visual messages from management to employees. At the Goodyear Tire & Rubber Company, management viewed the *Wingfoot Clan* as an "indispensable means of communication between Goodyear and her host of 'Goodyearites.' . . . [The paper has tried] to promote good feeling and to cultivate the *esprit de corps* of the plant." Magazines published messages, poems, and essays lauding the merits of company camaraderie and industrial partnership. Stressing the personal interconnectedness of workers of different ranks, employee magazines asserted a familial basis for corporate relations. Stories about the private lives of department supervisors, often accompanied by photos, humanized corporate management. That such anecdotes often appeared alongside stories on workers' activities placed both groups on a rhetorically equal footing. Baseball team scores, news of the sick, technical reports, and fiction that filled the pages of the employee magazine proclaimed—and, in so doing, tried to inculcate—the existence of a

6. See Samuel M. Jones, *Letters of Love and Labor* (Toledo: Franklin Printing & Engraving, 1900). In his first letter, dated May 5, 1900, Jones explained that "I want to write as friend to friend; I want to have with you simple heart to heart talks, as brother to brother; and I want to do it in order that our lives may be made more perfect, more complete, because I am true to the best impulses of my soul."

7. National Industrial Conference Board, *Employee Magazines in the United States* (New York, 1925), pp. 1–3.

company culture forged by common interests, values, and goals, a culture whose mutuality was more important than employment hierarchies. Nor, importantly, was this culture confined to wage earners. Magazines and newsletters distributed in firms with predominantly male employees often featured homemaking sections—"tested recipes" submitted by employees' wives, gardening tips, sewing hints, children's essay contests, want ad columns—to ensure that the company's presence would be all-encompassing, extended to spouses and into the home. Articles such as "Makin' 'Em Read the Plant Paper" in *Industrial Management* offered strategies for publishing an employee magazine that would be "actually howled for by the employees" and "taken home to their families where their appearance [would be] hailed with joyous shouts." Although the expectation that a factory newspaper could single-handedly evoke such enthusiasm was clearly rendered tongue-in-cheek, the mushrooming of advice literature on employee magazines published in business periodicals indicates the value employers assigned to them.[8]

Employee magazines also conveyed substantive news about welfare work, thereby performing several tasks. First, they brought welfare work to employees' attention, cataloging services and events. The frequency of these announcements, moreover, served as habitual reminders of the depth and breadth of employers' magnanimity. In addition, welfare work notices were couched in a celebratory language intended to eradicate employees' indifference and inspire participation. Indeed, if announcements were to be accepted verbatim, company events portended unsurpassed merriment and never-ending thrills.

Employee magazines reported the outcome of welfare functions in an equally zealous light. Just as each upcoming event was advertised as guaranteed fun, so, too, was every past event "remembered" as an unequivocal success. Descriptions of past company activities encouraged selective memory—even if workers had not enjoyed themselves at an annual picnic or a company baseball game, they were still informed by management's revisionist account that they had. The *Scovill Bulletin*, for instance, the employee magazine of the Scovill brass factory in Waterbury, Connecticut, enthusiastically recounted an apparently infinite number of enjoyed welfare functions. The first Scovill Girls' Club's

8. Goodyear Tire & Rubber Co., *The Work of the Labor Division* (Akron, 1920), p. 28; National Cash Register, *NCR*, May 1904; Frank H. Williams, "Makin' 'Em Read the Plant Paper," *Industrial Management* 60 (July 1920): 70. The importance of corporate domesticity to labor relations is explored well by Kwolek-Folland in chap. 5 of *Engendering Business*.

dance had been "a social . . . success." At the Foremen's Ladies Night, dancing to a ten-piece orchestra, "the older girls, as well as the younger, [had] enjoyed themselves frolicking in square sets." The Soldiers' Benefit Ball and Entertainment of 1917 had been an "artistic success beyond all anticipation." Each Scovill foremen's outing always seemed to be "the best the Club has had." No matter which bulletin one read, a similar theme prevailed: because of their employer's generosity, Scovill employees were perpetually amused.[9]

To supplement written descriptions of workers' merriment, employee magazines published photographs. Paradoxically, these photographs rarely showed workers doing what they were paid to do: work. Instead, they depicted employees at play—at a picnic, bowling on the company team, attending a dance. By focusing on leisure instead of labor as a desirable mode of worker expression, employee magazines extended company approval to what the technological innovations implemented by many welfare capitalists had already begun: the gradual eclipse of workers' control fostered by the reorganization of the workplace along scientifically, often technologically, rationalized lines. The altered relationship between factory hands and their products in specialized, automated industries required companies to locate new arenas for employees to express themselves as well as new techniques for combating their alienation. To employers, company-sponsored leisure offered an ideal substitute for workshop independence.

Employee magazines proved ideal for giving this supplantation tangible form. In an age when the costs of machinery were outpacing those of labor, when leisure entrepreneurs were vying for working-class patronage of amusements whose character challenged a work ethic rooted in discipline, self-control, and sobriety, company photographs encouraged employees to shift their locus of self-worth from the increasingly monotonous rhythms of labor to the unpredictable, "exciting" world of company-controlled leisure. At the same time, photographs of workers at play urged employees to acquire leisure thrills within a corporate setting. By 1914 most group photographs of sporting workers showed them in team uniforms, visually underscoring corporate bonds by making individual identity secondary to group affiliation.[10]

Pictures taken for the Westinghouse Electric Corporation's employee

9. *Scovill Bulletin*, August 1915, December 1916 November 1917, May 1919, Scovill Manufacturing Co. Papers II (hereafter SMCP), Case 33, BL.
10. Nye, *Image Worlds*, pp. 83–85; Kwolek-Folland, *Engendering Business*, pp. 152–53.

Charles Yessel, photographer for the Westinghouse Electric Company, captures welfare work in action for the employee magazine, *Machine News*. This baseball game was played at the South Philadelphia plant's employee picnic on September 13, 1919. (Courtesy of the Hagley Museum and Library, Wilmington, Delaware.)

magazine provide a revealing glimpse of pictorial publicity at work. The South Philadelphia plant, constructed in 1917 by the Pittsburgh-based corporation, manufactured power-generating systems. The factory complex, reflecting the parent corporation's commitment to welfare work, included cafeterias, health and recreation facilities, and other employee-support operations. In January 1918 the company began publication of a monthly employee magazine, *Westinghouse Machine News*. The magazine's editors relied on the expertise of company photographer Charles Yessel, transferred from Pittsburgh headquarters, to supply them with visual endorsements of the desirability and efficacy of welfare programs. Yessel's glass-plate negatives developed for *Machine News* illuminate how company photographs operated as a visual shorthand, encoding and endorsing carefully contrived, politically encumbered messages. In almost every picture Yessel projected the marvels of welfare work. One picture showed employees playing baseball, a nearby crowd of co-workers eagerly awaiting the outcome. Another captured the excitement of a push ball game; yet another revealed employees'

The Westinghouse All Stars at the company picnic, September 13, 1919. (Courtesy of the Hagley Museum and Library, Wilmington, Delaware.)

children immersed in the fun of a pie-eating contest at a Westinghouse picnic. Notwithstanding the absence of a single descriptive caption, these photographs bespoke the tremendous pleasure employees and their families could find in the world of company recreation. *Machine News* also contained visual testimonials of other forms of company benevolence. A picture of the machine shop dispensary disclosed that workers' wounds were professionally treated; another displayed the company cafeteria, ready to serve. The clarity and authority of the pictures, presented as an undistorted mirror of the realities of workers' experience, seemed to offer incontrovertible evidence of the veracity of employers' claim that welfare work and employee satisfaction went hand in hand."[11]

11. Photographs from the Westinghouse Collection are in acc. 69.170 in the Hagley Pictorial Archives, Hagley Museum and Library, Wilmington, Del. (hereafter HML). Information on the role of Charles Yessel at the Westinghouse Corporation's South Phila-

Pushball game, Westinghouse picnic, September 13, 1919. (Courtesy of the Hagley Museum and Library, Wilmington, Delaware.)

Company photographs, in which employers used visual images to interpret employees' experiences for them, were supplemented by written narratives published in employee magazines. Here, workers were advised that welfare work had yielded its intended effects—that welfare work, in short, "worked." Employers chose their words carefully when touting the benefits of welfare capitalism to employees; they cited employee contentment and industrial partnership rather than higher output or lower turnover as the intended and achieved results of workplace benevolence. The apparent benignity of such terms reassured workers that in instituting welfare programs, employers did not harbor a secret antilabor agenda. Indeed, in proclaiming industrial harmony as the most important accomplishment of welfare work, employee magazines tried to discredit the notion that class conflict was an inevitable or permanent characteristic of capitalist organization. The establishment

delphia Works is from folder "Yessel-Narrative," Hagley Pictorial Archives, HML. These materials include two untitled manuscripts, a chronology of the Westinghouse Company, and a paper headed "Printing Charles Yessel's Glass Plate Negatives." My thanks to Jon Williams for drawing my attention to this material.

Button-sewing contest, Westinghouse picnic, September 13, 1919. (Courtesy of the Hagley Museum and Library, Wilmington, Delaware.)

of welfare programs simply reflected employers' goodwill; workers' appreciation, in turn, illustrated the intrinsic mutuality of capital and labor. Citing high worker turnout at a factory minstrel show and dance, the *Scovill Bulletin* proclaimed that the event's "success in every respect . . . indicates . . . just what a great, big family the Scovill Company family really is." By offering habitual proclamations of welfare work's ability to generate industrial peace and by insisting that such a spirit of togetherness was the natural and desirable state of industrial relations, employee magazines attempted to transform employers' wishes into concrete realities.[12]

Workers unconvinced by employers' testimonials were encouraged to accept those of other workers. Employee magazines frequently featured endorsements of welfare work by employees themselves. The National Cash Register magazine, *Woman's Welfare*, first published in 1903 solely to promote women's welfarism, published letters from female employees expressing their appreciation of NCR largesse. A woman known only through her initials, "T. L.," wrote that "during the month

12. *Scovill Bulletin*, December 1916, SMCP, Case 33, BL.

The pie-eating contest made the Westinghouse picnic a family affair. (Courtesy of the Hagley Museum and Library, Wilmington, Delaware.)

of December sixty-five baths were taken in one of our women's departments. This means a great expense to the Company, but I am sure we all appreciate this privilege." Another female worker, "J. M.," noted that "one may come to this institution a pessimist, but the consideration of its officers for the welfare of its employees soon eradicates such opinions and in their place spring thankfulness and a desire to return this kindness with conscientious labor." For convincing workers of the value of welfare work, the enthusiasm of the company convert undoubtedly proved more effective than the predictable rhetoric of management.[13]

The flip side to such company-generated encomia was the chastisement employee magazines extended to those who did not attend welfare activities. The scolding was gentle, even playful: to have admitted that such a group constituted more than a minority of laborers would have undermined the company's claim to factory-wide support. Still, management subtly endeavored to make nonparticipants feel excluded—presumably sensitive ostracizing would bring "outsiders" back

13. National Cash Register, *Woman's Welfare* 2 (March 1904): 11, 14.

into the fold. In this spirit, the *Scovill Bulletin* advised employees that "if there were any employees of this Company who, through force of circumstances or a cruel fate, failed to see the Scovill Minstrels at Buckingham Hall, they must have been a sad, sorry lot."[14]

The celebration of welfare work in employee magazines was, above all, company propaganda. The editor of the employee magazine was the employer's most powerful in-house publicity agent. As one *Industrial Management* article reported, "The employees' magazine reaches all the workers, every month or oftener. The 'advertiser' has all kinds of space in which to work toward his object." The "advertiser," of course, was the employer, his "object" to create a labor force whose acceptance of company welfare work would yield efficient, hardworking, loyal, and "uplifted" employees. To realize these goals, employee magazines advertised the desirability and achievements of welfare work. Their publication carried the expectation that after another repetition, the company's message would become accepted wisdom.[15]

Courting the Public

In his masterful critique of Gilded Age captains of industry, historian Matthew Josephson took particular offense at the private dealings of nineteenth-century financiers. The pages of Josephson's *Robber Barons* are replete with stories of businessmen's clandestine gatherings, held secretly not only to forge plans for perpetuating their wealth but also to conceal their avaricious strategies from the public. By Josephson's account, Commodore Cornelius Vanderbilt "carried all his bookkeeping accounts in his own head and trusted no one with them." "Brooding" John D. Rockefeller "was given to secrecy" and had an "instinct for conspiracy." Pierpont Morgan operated under a "silent, phlegmatic exterior," while "tight-lipped" Jay Gould "kept his mouth shut and his money hidden."[16]

Notwithstanding his acrimony, Josephson highlighted the intense privacy that characterized American business culture for most of the nineteenth century. Businessmen before and of the robber baron gen-

14. *Scovill Bulletin*, February 1917, SMCP, Case 33, BL.
15. John T. Bartlett, "The Dramatic Gesture and the Photo: Two Ways to Personalize Management," *Industrial Management* 62 (November 1921): 274.
16. Matthew Josephson, *The Robber Barons: The Great American Capitalists, 1861–1901* (1934; New York: Harcourt Brace Jovanovich, 1962), pp. 14, 15, 48, 60, 63, 112, 114, 129.

eration defended the prerogatives of a Smithian model of classical liberalism: they performed in a market economy as autonomous, self-serving individuals whose actions should be left unchecked by interfering parties, including a potentially hostile public. As Richard Tedlow has argued, the reigning nineteenth-century management philosophy held that "the primary fiduciary responsibility of the business executive [was] to his firm's stockholders rather than to some undefinable public." What transpired behind company doors was supposed to remain private knowledge.[17]

The traditional disjuncture between private and public in the business realm was challenged at the beginning of the twentieth century. Companies vulnerable to outside scrutiny began to recast their relationship to the public, hiring professional public relations and advertising firms to mold their image for consumers, organized labor, journalists, and politicians. The growing tendency, especially among journalists, to talk about a singular "American public" as a united force whose opinion constituted the final arbiter of American values, amplified pressure on businessmen. Progressive thinkers such as Walter Lippmann and Louis Brandeis expressed faith in the power of public discussion to create enlightened citizenship and a concomitant political consciousness necessary for social reorganization. According to Brandeis, public awareness spawned by scientifically assembled facts would operate as nothing less than a "continuous remedial measure" against economic corruption. While this definition of a united public clearly glossed over persisting regional, economic, and ethnic cleavages that held the nation apart, it paid tribute to important agents of homogenization—shrinking economic borders, escalating consumerism, expanding communication networks—that made the notion of a homogenous "public opinion" more plausible. What followed was not the abandonment of private sector privacy but a recognition that public opinion, however loosely defined, mattered. As publicity agent Ivy Lee remarked in an address before the annual convention of the American Railway Association in 1916, the days of business indifference to public sentiment were over. "The crowd is in the saddle, the people are on the job." "Publicity must be considered" he advised, ". . . as an antiseptic which shall cleanse the very source of the trouble and reveal it to the doctor, which is the public."[18]

17. Tedlow, *Keeping the Corporate Image*, p. 5.
18. Brandeis quoted ibid., p. 29; Ivy L. Lee, *Publicity for Public Service Corporations: Substance of Address before Annual Convention of American Railway Association at Atlantic City, New*

Welfare work assumed an important place in emergent corporate public relations. Heightened interest in industrial affairs, particularly the success of muckraking journalism in promoting awareness of labor exploitation, encouraged firms to broadcast their benevolence, spotlighting the "humanitarian" face of American capitalism. Welfare work publicity reflected employers' awareness that the approval of individuals outside the executive office was worth having, and that the ability to secure this approval depended in part on public perceptions of labor conditions.[19]

Not all firms with welfare programs publicized them. In some companies, the expense of welfare work did not permit the added cost of publicity. Other firms decided that their welfare work programs were too small in scale to warrant advertising. The Amoskeag Manufacturing Company, for instance, though regarded by its business peers as a leader in employee welfare, responded to a survey on welfare work by writing, "We are doing so little, we do not wish to publish or write anything on the subject." Other companies voiced concern that publicity of employee betterment policies would give rival firms a competitive advantage, disclosing information that could be used against them. But in general these firms were the exception and not the rule. Most firms with the wealth to publicize their benevolence toward employees did.[20]

At a practical level, publicity of welfare work provided a means to keep pace with the growing demand for information on welfare activities. As welfare work became increasingly recognized as a distinct movement with identifiable objectives and tangible achievements, curiosity about its firm-by-firm organization widened. Businessmen, labor

Jersey (Privately printed, 1916), pp. 5–7. Walter Lippmann also documented this changing attitude when he observed that businessmen "are talking more and more about their 'responsibilities,' their 'stewardship.' It is the swan-song of the old commercial profiteering and a dim recognition that the motives in business are undergoing a revolution." See Lippmann, *Drift and Mastery: An Attempt to Diagnose the Current Unrest* (1914; Englewood Cliffs, N.J.: Prentice-Hall, 1961), p. 33.

19. An editorial in the March 1904 edition of *Woman's Welfare*, an NCR publication (p. 1), strategically allied the NCR's labor policies with public wishes by noting, as a rationale for welfare work programs, that "public opinion is beginning to demand that working people be treated with humanity and consideration."

20. Amoskeag Manufacturing Co. to Boston Chamber of Commerce, May 29, 1913, BCCC, Case 48, Folder 332–19, BL. The Solvay Process Company of Syracuse, for instance, was particularly insistent about protecting the firm's privacy. The company president concluded a letter describing the firm's welfare efforts by asking the recipient, "Please regard all the above . . . for your confidential use and information. Naturally, we have no hesitation in giving you the general information above, but we do not care to have the same made public" (Solvay Process Co. to Boston Chamber of Commerce, November 21, 1912, BCCC, Case 48, Folder 332–19, BL).

leaders, academics, reformers, government bureaus, and politicians clamored for data documenting its growth and application. Agencies such as the American Institute of Social Service and the Welfare Department of the National Civic Federation routinely compiled welfare work statistics; the number of weekly inquiries they generated and received was voluminous. Companies eager to climb aboard the welfare work bandwagon often bypassed intermediary agencies, writing company presidents or their welfare workers directly. Anxious to dispel the bad publicity following the Ludlow Massacre, John D. Rockefeller Jr. wrote the American Button Company for advice on establishing welfare work. When welfare worker Elizabeth Briscoe of the Joseph Bancroft and Sons Company wanted to learn more about establishing mutual benefit associations, she wrote eight companies, including well-known welfare firms NCR, Heinz, and Westinghouse, asking for summaries of their experiences in this area. Responses to requests for information about welfare work demanded companies' time and attention. By publishing brochures summarizing their companies' welfare activities, businessmen reduced the expense and time required to respond to each inquiry individually. Meeting actual and anticipated demand, the United Shoe Machinery Company of Beverly sent a *carton* of welfare work booklets to libraries across the country, noting the "numerous requests from schools and libraries for data on co-operation between employers and employees."[21]

But more than convenience explains the spate of promotional literature. Advertising altruism was also a savvy political strategy. Companies took the time to respond to queries about welfare work because favorable publicity, insofar as it could improve the public image of corporate

21. Rockefeller to Henry T. Noyes, October 26, 1916, Rockefeller Family Papers (hereafter RFP), Record Group III 2C (hereafter RG III 2C), Business Interests (hereafter BI), Colorado Fuel & Iron Co. (hereafter CFIC), Box 12, Folder 98, Rockefeller Archives, North Tarrytown, N.Y. (hereafter RA); form letter from Elizabeth Briscoe, January 10, 1906, Bancroft Collection, Box 893, vol. 197, HML. Company correspondence attests to the volume of inquiries a single firm could receive in a few days. A letter from the superintendent of the Waltham Watch Co. to the president of the Ferro Machine & Foundry Co. of Cleveland notes, "In reply to your letter . . . in which you make inquiries concerning working conditions connected with our factory, let us say that we are receiving frequent letters similar to yours, which we are always glad to answer. With yours came one of similar character from a Chamber of Commerce, and on Monday we had a representative of the . . . Civic Federation, who came to give a *personal* inspection of our conditions." The unabated curiosity about its employee programs prompted the Waltham Watch Co. to publish a welfare work pamphlet, *Workers Together*, only three years after the above letter was sent. See Waltham Watch Co. to Boston Chamber of Commerce, June 10, 1916, BCCC, Case 48, Folder 332–19, BL.

capitalism, might also stave off critics and preserve a private sector welfare system.

To be sure, this omnipresent political mandate was usually shrouded in subtlety. Only the labor left—notably Socialists and Wobblies—routinely voiced alarm that, stripped of its ostensible benignity, publicized benevolence concealed an aggressive campaign to seduce the public into supporting a program that in the long run would hurt labor. On a few occasions, however, the political agenda motivating welfare work publicity was made palpably obvious. For example, when the International Harvester Company faced a federal investigation by the Bureau of Corporations for violating the Sherman Antitrust Act, the company tried to shore up its "good trust" image. The company's strategy was twofold: it hired the New York publicity agency Parker and Lee to supplement the work of its own publicity bureau, and it established new welfare programs. Ivy Lee's defense of International Harvester appeared in an article published in *Moody's Magazine*, "An Open and Above-Board 'Trust.'" The article, which made no mention of Lee's recent hiring by the firm, emphasized the corporation's redeeming qualities "in order to ascertain . . . whether or not it should receive public condemnation." After describing International Harvester's low profits, steady prices, and commitment to product improvement, Lee highlighted the company's "uncommon enlightenment and progressiveness" toward employees as final proof of its rectitude. "The feeling of conciliation and the desire for harmony between the employer and employee" that Lee described demanded that the public come to the benevolent corporation's aid. By the same token, after a *Collier's Weekly* article entitled "Making Cripples and Dodging Taxes" called attention to Harvester's irresponsibility toward injured workers, the company quickly approved proposals for a sickness, accident, and disability plan. Stanley McCormick, a member of the company's board of directors, justified the move by noting that "it is believed that by action at this time the Company gains the public opinion value of the voluntary act." And so it did. Newspapers applauded Harvester's generosity, and President Theodore Roosevelt extended his personal support.[22]

22. Ivy Lee, "An Open and Above-Board 'Trust,'" *Moody's Magazine*, July 1907, p. 163. For a discussion of Lee's employment by Harvester, see Alan Raucher, *Public Relations and Business, 1900–1920* (Baltimore: Johns Hopkins University Press, 1968), pp. 19–20. Stanley McCormick is quoted in Robert W. Ozanne, *A Century of Labor-Management Relations at McCormick and International Harvester* (Madison: University of Wisconsin Press, 1967), p. 80; Robert Asher, "The Limits of Big Business Paternalism: Relief for Injured Workers in the Years before Workmen's Compensation," in *Dying for Work: Workers' Safety and Health in*

Perhaps the single most successful effort to sway public opinion by publicizing welfare work was formulated under the direction of John D. Rockefeller Jr. (hereafter referred to as Rockefeller) after the Ludlow Massacre. The infamous massacre took place in April 1914. The previous summer, the United Mine Workers of America had begun an organization campaign in Colorado's southern camps. After operators ignored workers' repeated requests to discuss grievances, more than eight thousand miners struck on September 23, relocating from company quarters to union tents. Rockefeller, acting for his family's controlling interest in the area's largest employer, the Colorado Fuel and Iron Company, rejected strikers' demands and Secretary of Labor William Wilson's plea for arbitration. Instead, he hired hundreds of armed deputies and guardsmen to protect company interests, vowing to deal the miners a crushing blow. With both sides armed and angry, the Colorado militia was called to the scene to "restore order" in late October. On April 20 fighting broke out between members of the militia and miners at the Ludlow camp. By the end of the day ten men and one child had been killed by machine guns. The next morning two women and eleven children were found burned and smothered; hoping to avoid the crossfire, they had dug a hiding hole under a union tent that later was doused with kerosene and ignited by the militia.[23]

At the beginning of the strike Rockefeller advocated a strict policy of noninterference. When Secretary of Labor William B. Wilson urged Rockefeller to "use his influence" to end the strike in November 1913, Rockefeller replied, "So far as the Colorado Fuel & Iron Co. is concerned, the matter is entirely in the hands of the executive officers in Colorado." As he later explained to the U.S. Commission on Industrial Relations, the structure of modern corporate capitalism prevented a "hands on" management style: "The responsibility of stockholders is practically limited to the election of directors. . . . Labor conditions, so far as they are within the control of the corporation, are matters for which the officers of the corporation are primarily responsible and with which they, by reason of their experience and their first-hand acquaintance with the facts, are best qualified to deal."[24]

Twentieth-Century America, ed. David Rosner and Gerald Markowitz (Bloomington: Indiana University Press, 1989), p. 29.

23. Howard Gitelman, *Legacy of the Ludlow Massacre: A Chapter in American Industrial Relations* (Philadelphia: University of Pennsylvania Press, 1988), chap. 1.

24. William B. Wilson to Rockefeller, November 20, 1914, Strike Chronology, n.d., RG III, 2C, BI, CFIC, Box 22, Folder 203, RA; statement of John D. Rockefeller Jr. before

By the time the charred remains of workers' wives had been discovered and photographed in the Ludlow mining camps, the strike and its bloody aftermath had attracted national attention. Unfortunately for Rockefeller, critics did not deem "absentee capitalism" to be a worthy excuse for the Ludlow slaying, and they held Rockefeller accountable. Journalists, political leaders, and citizens alike were appalled by the sacrifice of innocent women and children; the sympathies of most Americans lay with the miners, who remained on strike even after the massacre ended. President Woodrow Wilson contacted Rockefeller, hoping that the business magnate would intervene to expedite a settlement. Wilson warned that "the impression of the public [is] that no one is willing to act, no one willing to yield anything, no one willing even to consider terms of accommodation." Daily reports from Colorado made the covers of major newspapers; soap-box orators urged listeners to shoot Rockefeller "like a dog"; picketers, including Upton Sinclair, marched outside the family's New York headquarters at 26 Broadway, assailing Rockefeller's conduct. Hundreds of letters arrived at the Broadway office daily. While some citizens and fellow businessmen supported Rockefeller's actions, most letters contained veiled threats and open denunciations. One individual sent Rockefeller a newspaper clipping with an illustration of a woman impaled on a bayonet, the caption "Crucified! Glorious Motherhood! Innocent Childhood!" written below. Beside the drawing of the dead woman the sender had left Rockefeller a message: "Hide your miserable head in Shame, Shame, Shame."[25]

Reversing his earlier strategy, Rockefeller now assumed direct control of the Colorado Fuel and Iron Company's labor policies and publicity. Two concerns prompted this change. The first was the need to clear the family name—the public portrayal of Rockefeller as a ruthless murderer contrasted sharply with his preferred persona as a stalwart God-fearing Baptist and former Sunday school teacher. A separate but

the U.S. Commission on Industrial Relations, January 25, 1915, RFP, BI, Personal, RG III 2Z, Rockefeller Jr., Folder 40, RA.

25. Woodrow Wilson to President of the Operators, September 5, 1914, RFP, RG III 2C, BI, CFIC, Box 23, Folder 210, RA; Ray Eldon Hiebert, *Courtier to the Crowd: The Story of Ivy Lee and the Development of Public Relations* (Ames: Iowa State University Press, 1966), p. 99; Gitelman, *Legacy of the Ludlow Massacre*, p. 20. Decades later Sinclair regretted his actions and wrote Rockefeller's grandson to make amends (W. Sohier-Bryant to Rockefeller, n.d., RFP, RG III 2C, BI, CFIC, Box 20, Folder 172, RA; anonymous letter to Rockefeller, n.d., RFP, RG III 2C, BI, CFIC, Box 20, Folder 185, RA).

related motive was Rockefeller's commitment to "save" the company from the clutches of unionism. Pressure before and after the massacre to bow to union demands came from many quarters: journalists, politicians, organized workers, even the White House. Agreeing to accept many of the union's work-related demands, Rockefeller refused to grant what it wanted most: recognition of the union as the workers' principal bargaining unit. The company's commitment to an open shop, he argued, "is a matter of principle which we . . . [can] not concede or arbitrate."[26]

In a carefully planned and executed year-long maneuver, Rockefeller succeeded in vindicating the family name and keeping the United Mine Workers of American at bay. Rockefeller's solution was welfare work; his success lay in its publicity. To help him mastermind his plan, Rockefeller hired two experts in the field: Canada's William Lyon Mackenzie King (the future prime minister) and public relations wizard Ivy Lee. Together, they planned and publicized the blueprint for what became the country's best-known company union. Its success was phenomenal: employees quickly voted for its adoption, while a public fast growing weary of industrial strife hailed it as a practical and just solution to the differences between capital and labor. By 1919, when an unprecedented number of strikes swept through American industrial establishments, the "democratic" company union became the employer's method of choice to quash labor unrest. And in the same year, when employees at the Colorado Fuel & Iron Company once again left the company's employ to strike against unfair practices and poor conditions, consistent with a growing anti-union resolve evident across the country, few members of the public bothered to comment that Rockefeller's policy to appease miners had failed.[27]

In a three-week trip to Colorado in September 1915, Rockefeller introduced his plan for "representative democracy" to miners and the press. Mindful of the scrutiny his presentation would solicit, Rockefeller gave workers and reporters a good show. Donning miners' picks and clothes, he and King talked with employees at work during the day and in their homes at night. His performance inspired exciting headlines

26. Statement of John D. Rockefeller Jr., April 29, 1914, p. 3, RFP, RG III 2C, BI, CFIC, Box 20, Folder 185, RA.

27. The Colorado Industrial Plan was not the first company union in the history of American labor. Similar employer-employee organizations existed in the cigar-making industry in the late 1870s. See David Montgomery, *The Fall of the House of Labor: The Workplace, the State, and American Labor Activism, 1865–1925* (New York: Cambridge University Press, 1989), p. 350.

back east: "Rockefeller Plies Pick in Coal Mine—Calls Men His Partners," the *New York Times* reported. The *New York Sun* turned Rockefeller's overnight stay with one miner's family into a scandalous slumber
party by sporting the following headline: "John D., Jr., Sleeps in
Miner's Nightie."[28]

In addition to the orchestrated casual mingling with workers, Rockefeller delivered a formal address to employee representatives on October 2. In his address Rockefeller articulated the principle of the
"Square Deal," a theme that would be associated with welfare work at
the Colorado Fuel &Iron Company for decades to come and one whose
exaltation of the large industrial enterprise as the basic economic unit
of modern society was strikingly reminiscent of Theodore Roosevelt's
New Nationalism. Never one to eschew histrionics, Rockefeller used
visual aids to drive home his points. Gesturing to a square table strategically placed in front of him, Rockefeller proclaimed that the corporation, like the table, consisted of four interrelated but separate
units. The corporation consisted of stockholders, directors, company
offices, and "last, but by no means least," employees. Like the table,
the corporation "would not be complete unless it had all four sides . . .
if the parties interested in a corporation are not perfectly joined together, you have a discordant and unsuccessful corporation . . . you will
notice that this table is square. And every corporation to be successful
must be on the square—absolutely a square deal for every one of the
four parties, and for every man in each of the four parties."[29] Tilting
one end of the table to force coins piled on top to fall to the ground,
Rockefeller explained that when one unit demanded more than its
share, all parties lost their collective wealth. This was why, he continued, he was willing to stay in Colorado to work out "some plan that
we all agree is the best thing for us all," for "there is just one thing
that no man in this company can ever afford to have happen again, be
he stockholder, officer, or employee, or whatever his position . . . another strike." After explaining the main features of the representation
plan to the miners, Rockefeller told them that "I propose to stay here
if it takes a year, until we have worked out among ourselves, right in

28. *New York Times*, September 22, 1915; *New York Sun*, September 23, 1915.
29. "Address of John D. Rockefeller, Jr. to the Employees, October 2, 1915," in *The
Colorado Industrial Plan* (New York, 1916), pp. 34–35. After the strike ended in December,
J. F. Welborn, company president, arranged a January election so that employees could
choose representatives for company-employee discussions. As a result, though the representation plan was adopted in October, its constitution provided for the election of
representatives at January annual meetings.

our own family, some plan that we all believe is going to prevent any more disturbances . . . [in] this great company in which we are all interested."[30]

Rockefeller was not forced to keep his promise. Between October 4 and October 25 miners in the four districts of the company voted 2,404 to 442 to adopt the representation plan. They also approved an appended agreement for the plan to go into effect immediately, subject to renewal in January 1918.[31]

The plan consisted of four sections: representation of employees; district conferences, joint committees, and joint meetings; the prevention and adjustment of industrial disputes; and social and industrial betterment. The first section outlined the logistics of representation: employees elected their representatives by ballot at an annual meeting, one representative per 150 workers. The second provided for an annual meeting between the president and all elected representatives, three yearly district meetings between employee representatives and the company president or his delegates, and four standing joint committees on industrial cooperation, safety and accidents, sanitation and health, and recreation and education. The third section outlined workers' rights, including their right to lodge grievances, to appeal against unfair treatment, to hold meetings, and to shop where they pleased. The final section committed employers to the advancement of the "industrial, social, and moral well-being of employees and their families," including the provision of camp hospitals and doctors and the establishment of an employee bulletin to keep workers apprised of welfare work programs. For miners whose hopes of worker-initiated organization had ended when the strike did, the Rockefeller plan offered more than no plan at all. By approving it, they were guaranteed the diluted spirit of collective bargaining, if not the union mechanism they would have preferred to give that spirit more potent expression.[32]

Having sold his "square deal" to employees in Colorado, Rockefeller returned to New York to sell his good faith and sincerity to the rest of the country. To assist him in this enterprise, he turned to longtime public relations expert Ivy Lee. The campaign culminated in the mass distribution in early 1916 of a ninety-five-page booklet, *The Colorado Industrial Plan*. The patently self-serving publication included the repre-

30. Ibid., pp. 47–48.
31. "Summary of Votes for and against Plan of Representation and Agreement," *Colorado Fuel & Iron Industrial Bulletin* 1 (October 1915): 29.
32. "The Industrial Constitution, Plan of Representation of Employees," in *Colorado Industrial Plan*.

sentation plan and lengthy "padding": sixty-two pages of Rockefeller's speeches and articles, each chosen to accentuate the businessman's largesse. The padding preceded the plan. Only after wading through Rockefeller's welfare work philosophy could a reader reach the climactic ending in its practical application, the representation plan itself. Rockefeller's solutions for the current industrial unrest echoed the sentiments expressed in most welfare work literature of the day. "Labor and Capital are partners"; "When men get together and talk over their differences . . . the ground for dispute vanishes." These were but a few of the book's adages. Those who read the ninety-five pages in earnest would finish fully informed of Rockefeller's new views on industrial relations. They might even believe that in his dealings with labor, Rockefeller was a kind-hearted man. *The Colorado Industrial Plan* offered dutiful readers the best propaganda modern advertising could buy.[33]

In a venture of mammoth scale, Lee sent almost 500,000 copies of *The Colorado Industrial Plan* to individuals across the country. The recipient list represented men and women from a wide range of professions, including 20, 271 labor officials, 2,100 of whom were affiliates of the United Mine Workers (Table 5). Professors, lawyers, clergymen, bank presidents, and municipal politicians across the country received copies. Lee's mass mailing ensured that constituencies well positioned to mold public opinion had access to his representation of the "truth" about Rockefeller and labor.

Lee's strategy was a success. Responses to *The Colorado Industrial Plan* were instantaneous and widespread. Moderate newspapers previously critical of Rockefeller now professed support for his generosity. From early February 1916 through the end of the year, 26 Broadway was flooded with letters, most from individuals wishing to record their support for Rockefeller and almost all of which Rockefeller responded to personally.

To clergymen, *The Colorado Industrial Plan* offered proof of Rockefeller's spiritual redemption. As one minister professed: "I followed your Bible class work in New York, and was seriously disappointed when I read the newspaper stories of your wickedness in Colorado. . . . Your compassion, in your brochure, your justice and humane regard for my fellow creatures . . . have given me great peace of mind." Employers found relief in Rockefeller's depiction of the businessman as a conscientious, charitable individual. Public acceptance of Rockefeller's plan reflected positively on all of them. The president of the Craig Ridgeway

33. Ibid.

Table 5. Distribution of *The Colorado Industrial Plan*

Recipients	Number
Government personnel	
Postmasters	66,420
Government officials and representatives	45,150
Total	111,570
Churchmen: Protestant clergy	88,995
Professional men	
Lawyers	47,656
Engineers	6,960
Total	54,616
Public utility executives	
Street railway officials	20,000
Electric light company officials	24,000
Gaslight company officials	10,000
Total	54,000
Merchants and manufacturers	
Trade Directory of U.S.	40,250
Silk Manufacturers Association	400
National Association of Kitchen Cabinet Manufacturers	125
Manufacturers of road machinery	1,100
Merchants Association of New York	2,963
National Inside Association of America	50
Total	44,888
Educators: faculty of all U.S. colleges and universities	25,000
Labor representatives	
United Mine Workers	2,100
Other union officials, delegates	18,171
Total	20,271
Finance: bank presidents	15,000
Librarians	1,506
Economists and sociologists: American Sociological Society	212
Newspaper correspondents	225
Directory of Directors of New York City	36,000
Farmers Congress	2,500
Other	117
All recipients	454,900

Source: Rockefeller Family Papers, Record Group III 2C, Business Interests, Colorado Fuel & Iron Co, Box 11, Folder 93, Rockefeller Archives, North Tarrytown, N.Y.

Steam Hydraulic Machinery Company of Coatesville, Pennsylvania, expressed approval of Rockefeller's attempt to assure the public "that our splendid business men are not a set of rascals, but are our very finest Christian men, spending their money and their time, and their lives, for the uplift of the race." Other employers, convinced of the utility of the plan, tried to introduce the partnership principle without the representation apparatus in their own factories. One labor super-intendent wrote Rockefeller that "we are forcibly impressed by your presentation of 'The Colorado Industrial Plan,' and . . . would like to distribute at our expense 10,000 copies of your booklet." At Rockefel-ler's insistence, Lee sent the requested copies free of charge.[34]

Opposition to the plan was minimal and came from predictable quar-ters. Samuel Gompers, though committed to the *idea* of a capital-labor fraternity, evidenced by his vice presidency of the National Civic Fed-eration, was nevertheless compelled to discredit any organization of workers that might supplant unionism "proper." Company unions pre-sented Gompers with a paradox: his disagreement was one of form, not principle. To distinguish his pro-union stance from his broader com-mitment to industrial harmony, Gompers became Rockefeller's most outspoken critic. Gompers denounced Rockefeller's "pseudo union" and questioned whether miners' spokesmen could have "the temerity of insistence in the rightful demands of the miners" before the rep-resentatives of the "richest man in the world." Other union represen-tatives, however, were more ambivalent. One union man wrote Rockefeller of his "hearty appreciation in your efforts to ameliorate the condition of your Colorado employees." The general president of the Indianapolis local of the United Brotherhood of Carpenters and Joiners, after extending similar praise, submitted his unsolicited can-didacy for employment in any welfare work–related post for which Rockefeller cared to hire him.[35]

Labor and political groups espousing a philosophy more critical than that of the AFL forcefully denounced the plan. The Socialist *New York Call,* for instance, discussed the plan as part of Rockefeller's "scab re-public" and expressed faith "that its establishment will intensify the efforts of organized labor to destroy it." The *Weekly People,* the Socialist Labor Party organ, devoted a cover story to Rockefeller's "benevolent feudalism," assuring party faithful that "all of W. L. Mackenzie King's

34. Augustine Jones to Rockefeller, February 21, 1916; Ridgeway to Rockefeller, March 17, 1916; Ivy Lee to Thomas J. Fay, May 16, 1916; Thomas J. Fay to Rockefeller, April 11, 1916, all in RFP, RG III 2C, BI, CFIC, Box 12, Folder 98, RA.

35. Press statement of Samuel Gompers, October 4, 1915, American Federation of Labor Papers, Office of the President, General Correspondence, Box 49, Folder 7, State Historical Society of Wisconsin, Madison; William L. Hutcheson to Rockefeller, May 5, 1916, and Arthur Smith to Rockefeller, March 22, 1916, RFP, RG III 2C, BI, CFIC, Box 12, Folder 98, RA.

'harmony' schemes . . . all of John D. Jr.'s sleeping, dining and talking with the miners, and all other schemes that can be devised by capitalism's puppets will not harmonize the interests of capital and labor." Unfortunately for these organizations, such overt references to inherent class conflict only mobilized support for Rockefeller. Conservative and progressive liberal Americans banded together to condemn what they represented as the predictable critique of the "radical fringe," marginalized individuals unable or unwilling to accept the realities of American life.[36]

Perhaps the most telling indication of the triumph of Rockefeller's public relations campaign was what transpired in the years after the plan's adoption. Despite two strikes by workers of the Colorado Fuel & Iron Company—one in 1917, another in 1919—few newspapers rallied to the strikers' aid. And in 1919, hundreds of companies used the Colorado plan as a model to establish representation plans of their own. Ironically, under the professed auspices of industrial democracy— a term first used by labor in the 1890s to call for a more equitable restructuring of industry—labor organizing efforts were deemed disloyal and systematically quashed, and a decade of company unionism was begun.[37]

Publicity and Consumption

In 1909 purchasers of Hershey chocolate bars received something in addition to candy when they unwrapped their purchase: a picture post-

36. "Rockefeller's Scab Republic," *New York Call*, October 2, 1915; "To 'Pacify' the Miners: Rockefeller Interests Fooling Workers into Accepting Scheme of Benevolent Feudalism," *Weekly People*, October 23, 1915. Ironically, probably the most vituperative attack on Rockefeller came not from a union or wage worker but from a lawyer. G. F. Cook of the Monroe, Washington, law firm of Walker & Cook wrote, "Ordinarily when one receives a copy of another's work he owes thanks to the giver. But when an ignorant, arrogant bigot whose chief aim in life is to grasp as much as possible of earth's treasures and exact tribute from his fellow man for the use thereof prepares or has prepared an apology for his cursed existence and ways, and sends it broadcast over the land, it is an insult rather than a compliment . . . Some day death will loosen your grasp and then many people will join in singing, "Praise God from whom all blessings flow" (Cook to Rockefeller, May 20, 1916, RFP, RG III 2C, BI, CIC, Box 12, Folder 27, RA).

37. On the changing meaning of the term "industrial democracy" in the late nineteenth and early twentieth centuries, see David Montgomery, "Industrial Democracy or Democracy in Industry?: The Theory and Practice of the Labor Movement, 1870–1925," and Howell John Harris, "Industrial Democracy and Liberal Capitalism, 1890–1925," both in *Industrial Democracy in America: The Ambiguous Promise*, ed. Nelson Lichtenstein and Howell John Harris (New York: Cambridge University Press, 1993), pp. 20–66.

card depicting the serene and picturesque environs of the Hershey Chocolate Factory. Enveloping the milk chocolate, the postcards portrayed "happy workers" cavorting on "velvety lawns dotted here and there by tastefully executed horticultural designs." Before ascending into a chocolate nirvana, Hershey customers were subtly reminded of the idyllic surroundings in which their confection had been created.[38]

The postcard may or may not have made for more pleasurable eating. Milton Hershey's bet was that it did. The founder of Hershey chocolates, the second largest manufacturer of chocolates in the world (Cadbury's of England, another pioneer in welfare activity, was first), believed that the more people learned of the welfare work at his factory, the more chocolate bars he would sell. For Hershey, publicity about "good" workers exercising their skills in "good" surroundings provided by a "good" employer could all add up to "good" profits. Hershey believed he personified the best of benevolence: there were no infamous strikes or debilitating conditions for *him* to hide. In fact, Milton Hershey welcomed personal inspection of factory premises. All who wanted to get a bird's-eye view of employee parks, meeting halls, recreation areas, classrooms, reading and dining rooms, and sports teams in action could. The town trolley and connecting railroad advertised weekend and holiday excursions to company grounds. Visitors were escorted by "white-clad girls" on a tour demonstrating each stage in the manufacture of Hershey products, from beans to wrapper. They could see for themselves "the pride which the workers have, not so much in the enormous output, as in the quality of their product." At the end of the tour, the company rewarded visitors for their diligence with a free sample of Hershey products—chocolate bars and chocolate kisses. By 1915 the chocolate factory had become such a popular tourist attraction that Milton Hershey opened a Visitors Bureau.[39]

Hershey tourists may have derived a twinge of satisfaction from their support of what they now knew to be a labor-friendly company. Perhaps, too, they believed, as Milton Hershey wanted them to, that superior working conditions engendered a superior product—that Hershey's workers were not alienated laborers but refined craftsmen, committed, even in a mass-production setting, to making items that would please the most discriminating palate. In either case, the choc-

38. Pamela Cassidy and Eliza Cope Harrison, *One Man's Vision: Hershey, a Model Town* (Hershey, Pa: Hershey Foods Corp., 1988), p. 15; Joseph Richard Snavely, *Milton S. Hershey, Builder* (Hershey, Pa.: Hershey Foods Corp., 1935), p. 52; idem, *The Hershey Story* (Hershey, Pa.: Hershey Foods Corp., 1950), p. 179.

39. Snavely, *Hershey Story.*

olate bar postcards imparted a message that a follow-up inspection of the Hershey premises was expected to confirm: consumers were as much the beneficiaries of welfare work as factory employees.

The incorporation of welfare work publicity into company advertising constituted an important dimension of the welfare movement. For John D. Rockefeller Jr., advertising benevolence had been, at least in the short term, a defensive strategy. After the incriminating events at Ludlow, Rockefeller promoted his industrial partnership scheme to exonerate the family name and to protect the Colorado Fuel & Iron Company from encroaching unionism. For other companies, including Hershey's, the decision to publicize welfare work was motivated by a more offensive strategy. For these firms, spotlighting "happy workers" represented not only a reaction to public demand but a way to define for consumers what those demands should be.

Seen in this light, welfare work publicity constituted a timely response to the growth of consumer capitalism and widespread apprehensions about manufacturing standards at the turn of the century. Changes in the economic landscape of late nineteenth-century America recast traditional exchanges between consumer and supplier. For most of the nineteenth century, this relationship had been characterized by localism; most goods purchased for everyday use were obtained from local craftsmen and storekeepers. The rise of a national market eroded the familiarity of this exchange, thrusting individual consumers into a direct relationship with large-scale, centrally organized corporations. The anonymity of the new arrangement altered the basis on which consumer confidence and loyalty were cultivated. In the absence of personal assurances about a product's safety and quality, the success or failure of national companies to influence purchasing behavior and inspire confidence among buyers depended increasingly on promises bestowed through mass advertising.[40]

Welfare work gave consumer-oriented firms a marketing edge. As consumer lobbying mounted at the turn of the century, so did doubts about the safety and desirability of manufactured goods, particularly packaged goods and ready-to-wear clothing. These suspicions were not unfounded, nor were they easily ignored. The public outcry that followed the 1906 publication of Upton Sinclair's *The Jungle*, a nauseating account of meat preparation in the Chicago stockyards, was merely the

40. Susan Strasser, *Satisfaction Guaranteed: The Making of the American Mass Market* (New York: Pantheon, 1989), pp. 7–19; Richard Tedlow, *New and Improved: The Story of Mass Marketing in America* (New York: Basic Books, 1990), pp. 3–19.

dramatic climax of a decades-old pure food movement that sought to expose the unsanitary conditions of food manufacture. Investigations that disclosed diseased meat in the 1880s had propelled the passage of numerous municipal and state regulations, and Congress itself had considered 190 pure-food bills between 1879 and 1906 when, finally, the Food and Drug Act and the Meat Inspection Act became law. Significantly, these legal measures failed either to restore consumer confidence fully or to silence public agitation. Muckraking reports in popular journals such as the *Ladies' Home Journal* and pure food campaigns sponsored by home economics groups and state agencies made product contamination an ongoing concern. As late as 1912, a grocers' trade journal noted that "many people are afraid of canned goods because of [the] sensational stories which are repeatedly printed about them."[41]

The purity crusade kept the subject of industrial conditions and their relationship to consumer safety in the forefront of Progressive era debate. This discussion, insofar as it linked the welfare of middle-class consumers with that of workers, paved the way for the emergence of a consumer-based movement to reform the workplace. The organization that best capitalized on and, in turn, furthered consumers' concerns along these lines was the National Consumers' League, established in 1899 as a federation of state consumer agencies. The league transmuted middle-class awareness of the dangers of workplace hazards to consumers into tangible gains for wage earners, particularly women and children. Organized consumption for the purpose of bettering workers' lives was not new to the United States. Various forms of worker cooperatives had existed since the 1830s, and union label campaigns, begun in the late nineteenth century in the hat and cigar industries, had spread to sixty-eight AFL internationals by 1908. But the NCL's arrival and florescence—in 1916 the league claimed eighty-nine associations in nineteen states and approximately 33,000 members—ultimately made the politicization of consumption more inclusive. For unlike workers' consumer campaigns, the NCL depended primarily on middle-class purchasing power to rectify industrial evils.[42]

41. Strasser, *Satisfaction Guaranteed*, pp. 256, 35.
42. Eileen Boris, *Home to Work: Motherhood and the Politics of Industrial Homework in the United States* (New York: Cambridge University Press, 1994), pp. 83–87; Frank L. McVey, "The Work and Problems of the Consumers' League," *American Journal of Sociology* 6 (May 1901); Florence Kelley, "Aims and Principles of the Consumers' League," *American Journal of Sociology* 5 (November 1899); Allis Rosenberg Wolfe, "Women, Consumerism, and the National Consumers' League in the Progressive Era, 1900–1923," *Labor History* 16

The founding and development of the NCL was emblematic of the expansion of a distinctive consumer class and a widening and recognizable rift between those who worked for wages and those who did not. The NCL acknowledged the economic chasm separating consumers and producers and promoted "ethical consumption" as the best method for mobilizing the power of consumers to assist wage earners. It also recognized the gendered composition of the consuming class. The advance of industrial capitalism at the turn of the century had furthered the externalization and commodification of traditionally female domestic labor. In particular, the growth of the canned goods industry, whose value rose from $6 million to $100 million between 1869 and 1909, and the expansion of the ready-made women's clothing industry, whose market worth increased from $12 million to over $300 million over the same period, shifted the production site of predominantly female-made products from the household to the factory or sweatshop. For middle-class women, these changes boosted consumption's share of their daily responsibilities. Although the prevailing gender system cast women's role as consumers as incidental to paid work, reform groups such as the NCL viewed women's status as purchasers in more economic and political terms. The NCL spoke to women as both consumers and female reformers whose "extrafamilial maternalism" would persuade them to turn an economic obligation into an ethical act.[43]

The league maintained that consumers' ability to "distinguish in favor of goods made in the well-ordered factory" equipped them with the know-how and financial clout to affect the organization of production. Appealing to, even exacerbating, existing consumer fears of prod-

---

(Summer 1975): 378; Walter E. Weyl, *The New Democracy* (New York: Macmillan, 1914), p. 252; Dana Frank, *Purchasing Power: Consumer Organizing, Gender, and the Seattle Labor Movement, 1919–1929* (New York: Cambridge University Press, 1994), p. 5. Workers' cooperatives had existed in the United States throughout the nineteenth century, but they had never achieved the stature of their counterparts in England, Belgium, France, and Germany. See Kathleen Blee, "Family Patterns and the Politicization of Consumption," *Sociological Spectrum* 5 (1985): 295–316.

On the history of workers and organized consumption, see Frank, *Purchasing Power*; Sean Wilentz, *Chants Democratic: New York City and the Rise of the American Working Class, 1788–1850* (New York: Oxford University Press, 1984); Ellen Furlough, *Consumer Cooperation in France: The Politics of Consumption, 1834–1930* (Ithaca: Cornell University Press, 1991); Patricia Cooper, *Once a Cigar Maker: Men, Women, and Work Culture in American Cigar Factories, 1900–1919* (Urbana: University of Illinois Press, 1987); Mary H. Blewett, *Men, Women, and Work: Class, Gender, and Protest in the New England Shoe Industry, 1780–1910* (Urbana: University of Illinois Press, 1988).

43. McVey, "Work and Problems of the Consumers' League."

uct adulteration, the league warned of the diseases and dangers in shops and factories that could be transmitted to unsuspecting consumers. As Florence Kelley, the NCL's secretary and most vocal advocate, explained, the spread of disease was not class-specific, and no consumer was immune. When purchasing clothes, Kelley warned, every woman was in danger of "buying smallpox, measles, scarlet fever, infectious sore eyes, and a dozen forms of diseases of the skin."[44]

NCL members beseeched the buying public to purchase only items sporting the NCL label. The label, the cornerstone of the league's strategy to reform production through guided consumption, guaranteed that the labeled item had been assembled in a designated "Fair House"—an establishment whose physical and sanitary conditions and treatment of workers met the league's criteria, which included equal pay for equal work, a living wage, and "humane and considerate behavior toward employees." In exchange for deference to the league's regulatory authority, consumers were promised a disease-free, pure product and the added reward of knowing that the workers who had assembled it had been properly treated.[45]

Sensitive to the lapse in consumer confidence but contesting the NCL's bid to be the leading arbiter of the safety and worth of purchased products, welfare capitalists heralded welfare work as a better guarantor of consumer satisfaction. This strategy sprang from necessity rather than choice: while some welfare establishments, including a handful of department stores, obtained the NCL's endorsement, more—indicating both the limited scope of NCL investigations and the misrepresentation of company claims—did not. Rather than dwelling on their shortcomings, however, companies challenged the need for labeling altogether, declaring the presence of welfare work at the point

44. National Consumers' League, *Reports for the Years 1914–1915–1916* (New York, 1917), p. 4; Kelley quoted in Wolfe, "Women, Consumerism, and the National Consumers' League," p. 380.

45. Kelley, "Aims and Principles of the Consumers' League," p. 300. The Consumers' League label competed directly and successfully with the older union label, in the short term for customer patronage, in the long term for the dominant definition of what constituted ethical consumption. Although its form and requirements for issue varied, the union label typically denoted goods made in pro-union, high-wage shops and encouraged buyers to consider economic fairness, union-style, when purchasing. Because it did not explicitly endorse the merits of the label-bearing product itself, however, the union label failed to attract buyers concerned more with customer satisfaction than economic justice. As one NCL spokesperson expounded, high wages were "not necessarily indicative of the fact that production is carried on under clean and healthful conditions." See Frank, *Purchasing Power*, pp. 195–251; Montgomery, *Fall of the House of Labor*, p. 278; McVey, "Work and Problems of the Consumers' League," p. 775.

of production to be, in the long run, the best predictor of consumer satisfaction. While the NCL promoted the Consumers' League label chiefly as a promise of the safety of purchased goods, welfare firms devised a more elaborate sales pitch that, though observant of concerns about purity, highlighted the interconnectedness of employee welfare and the finished item's cost and craftsmanship.

Consumer-oriented literature published by welfare firms insisted that favorable workplace conditions yielded more attentive, abler employees who generated a higher volume of products with fewer defects. Workers' heightened efficiency, in turn, reduced production costs, a benefit passed along to customers in the form of lower prices. As one company emphasized, "Waste within an organization will manifest itself in high cost in the market-place." In a company run efficiently, however, "fewer men work less hard . . . and deliver a cheaper product." Welfare work was cost-effective for companies and consumers alike.[46]

Welfare capitalists advertised their products as not only more affordable than competitors' wares but also better made. Employers tied the quality of their merchandise to the quality of their labor. Attentive to middle-class concerns about the degradation of American workers, apprehensions that often veiled xenophobic reactions to immigrant labor, they portrayed their workers as members of the wage-earning elite, better educated, Americanized, and skilled than their peers. Wage earners who had been exemplary at the time of hire had been improved by company programs. In contrast to the "common" laborer, typified by welfare employers as foreign, lazy, and careless, wage earners groomed by welfare work were portrayed as deferential and disciplined, attentive only to the task at hand. Under the ennobling influence of corporate benevolence, employees had attained bourgeois respectability, functioning as factory hands in wage status only. In spirit they had become middle-class craftsmen, a transformation that resulted in a better product for each and every consumer.

Employers' invocation of the craftsman ideal belied the realities of most wage earners' experiences, including the experiences of many working people in welfare firms. But it also encoded a vision of craft production that had tremendous marketability at the turn of the century. The commercial success of the arts and crafts movement during the Progressive era, which popularized Tiffany lamps, Rockwood pottery, and other decorative artifacts, reflected growing consumer demand for

46. Thomas Dreier, *The Story of Three Partners* (Beverly, Mass.: United Shoe Machinery Co., 1911), p. 11.

fine workmanship at a time when the advance of bureaucratized corporate capitalism and widespread deskilling threatened to degrade it. Welfare capitalists tapped into this escalating demand, deftly forging a link between ideal work conditions and the aesthetization of company goods.[47]

No firm outdid H. J. Heinz in enunciating the benefits of welfare work to consumers. Sketching in consumers' minds a link between the conditions under which products were assembled and their final market value, Henry Heinz made the Heinz label a household word. Unique in its success, the Heinz approach characterized consumer-focused welfare publicity in two important ways. First, acute anxieties about commercial food preparation in the Progressive era encouraged food companies to advertise workplace reforms more widely than did other industries. "Cleanliness," as the National Biscuit Company put it, became "an advertising virtue." Ads in middle-class women's magazines encouraged consumers to associate factory sanitation and product purity with specific brands. Hence Quaker Oats were "better [in] every way" because the "finest quality of selected, pure white oats" were processed in mills that were "models of cleanliness and purity." The Natural Food Company's Shredded Wheat was "the purest, cleanest cereal food in the world, made in the cleanest and most hygienic industrial building on the continent." Those in doubt could see for themselves: "Our plant is open to the world; over 100,000 visitors last year." Huyler's breakfast cocoa was "the purest possible," traveling "from bean to cup without adulteration."[48]

Second, like the majority of welfare work advertising, Heinz publicity targeted middle-class women. Paralleling the strategy of the NCL, welfare capitalists recognized female consumers as the preeminent purchasing group in American society. Acknowledging a long-standing sexual division of labor, manufacturers celebrated women's domestic acumen, the result of years of devotion to household labor. Now, ads urged, women should transfer their domestic skills as producers into the consumer realm. With a discriminating eye molded by experience,

47. Eileen Boris, *Art and Labor: Ruskin, Morris, and the Craftsman Ideal in America* (Philadelphia: Temple University Press, 1986), p. xi. Also see Jackson Lears, *No Place of Grace: Antimodernism and the Transformation of American Culture, 1880–1920* (New York: Pantheon, 1981), pp. 60–97.

48. U.S. Bureau of Labor Statistics, *Employers' Welfare Work*, Bulletin 123 (1913), p. 36; Quaker Oats Co. advertisement in *Ladies' Home Journal*, October 1906; Natural Food Company advertisements ibid., August and October 1906; Huyler's Cocoa advertisement ibid., July 1911.

An advertisement in the *Ladies' Home Journal*, October 1909.

women could exercise domestic authority as purchasers of goods they had previously made. Stressing the similarities between factory conditions and the clean home, between factory workers and proud housewives, welfare manufacturers urged women to buy only those products whose requirements for assembly rivaled or surpassed their own. As a 1911 ad for Campbell's tomato soup proclaimed, the "good-old fashioned housekeeper . . . knows. She is a real critic. She wants real soup—no wishy-washy imitation. And her praise is the highest kind of a compliment to Campbell's Tomato Soup." By the same token, ads urged women to consider factory hands not as debased workers but as refined, privileged domesticians, uplifted by welfare work. Here the craftsman ideal assumed an alternate, gendered incarnation: the craftsman was now the craftswoman whose dedication ensured merchandise as good as "homemade." While Pillsbury, in a telling gauge of consumer anxiety, advertised its VITOS wheat food as one that "from wheatfield to your table, is never touched by human hand," firms such as Heinz made the attributes of their labor force the cornerstone of their marketing campaigns.

The Heinz condiment company was founded in 1869, when twenty-five-year-old Heinz began selling horseradish grown on a small plot of land in Sharpsburg, Pennsylvania. By 1900 the company had relocated to Pittsburgh, was employing a year-round, primarily female labor force of 2,500, and had cornered the burgeoning food preservation market through its manufacture of diverse comestibles such as baked beans, pickles, ketchup, chutney, preserves, and tomato soup.[49]

From the beginning, Henry Heinz demonstrated his commitment to employee welfare. In 1903, when many employers still regarded welfare work as a risky innovation, Heinz had already established a wide range of betterment programs. Lectures by distinguished visitors, a well-stocked library of "instructive works" and "wholesome fiction," singing instruction, cooking and sewing classes for women, and mechanical drawing classes for men constituted the education component of Heinz welfare work. The Pittsburgh facilities were constructed to maximize employees' comfort: workers could eat their lunch in separate men's and women's dining rooms, avail themselves of modern bathrooms with tubs and showers, store personal belongings in individual lockers, and report to a factory hospital for "temporary indispositions." Finally, to give workers adequate outdoor recreation and leisure time, roof

49. H. J. Heinz Company, *The Home of the 57* (Pittsburgh, 1903), pp. 1–8. The company's summer labor force frequently included as many as 40,000 employees.

gardens with "palms and splashing fountains" and a wagonette for "occasional rides through the suburbs in pleasant weather" were maintained. At the time of Henry Heinz's death in 1919, the company credited welfare work for fifty strike-free years.[50]

As explicated in company advertising, Heinz's dedication to its employees was also dedication to its customers. Heinz recognized that "every housewife who owned a box of Mason jars was a potential competitor as well as a customer." The "Heinz ideal," the company explained, was to replicate the quality of food preparation consumers had grown up enjoying in their mothers' kitchens. Who can forget, one pamphlet queried, "visions of mother and grandmother, busy as bees in the roomy kitchen, their faces aglow with the heat of their work and their pride therein—surrounded by . . . the most tantalizing odors that ever assailed the nostrils of unappeasable youth[?]" The Heinz challenge was to "duplicate, nay, to improve upon, these time and man-honored products of countless snowy kitchens and skillful housewives, and to place them on the general market, within the reach of all who wish to taste their delights." This "fine old 'homemade' idea," of course, could be reproduced only by employees who maintained the housewife's commitment to product perfection.[51]

The Heinz company believed it provided the perfect setting and people to achieve this goal. As one pamphlet suggested, employees' attitudes and actions were indispensable to the company's desire to mass-produce condiments tastier than their homemade counterparts. In the final analysis, the power to make a tantalizingly tasty bottle of ketchup rather than a merely mediocre one resided with workers themselves: "The preparation of a food of any kind is a most delicate and sensitive operation. The result depends upon effort, purpose and the desire to do well—it seems almost to reflect the moods and the temperament of the workers. For this reason it is imperative that the Heinz operatives be willing, happy, contented workers."[52]

Welfare work, company publications reported, had generated and sustained such contentment. Henry Heinz's commitment to workers had been passed along to consumers through workers' commitment to their jobs. Employees may not have arrived at Heinz happy, but "they are helped to be such." "They are thrown in the way of advancement,"

50. H. J. Heinz Company, *A Golden Day: A Memorial and a Celebration* (Pittsburgh, 1925), p. 29; idem, *Home of the 57*, pt. 3.

51. Leroy Fairman, *The Growth of a Great Industry* (Pittsburgh: H. J. Heinz, 1910), pp. 9, 15.

52. Ibid., p. 28.

one pamphlet explained, "material, mental, and moral." Again invoking the homemade analogy, Heinz officials likened the factory to a large, interdependent family, in which every member played an important role. One pamphlet described the Heinz principle as the "mutual and united co-operation of the family," in which management, like employees, believed that the "interests, hopes, aspirations, and purposes of all are identical." To assuage consumers' worries about the human handling of food, Heinz made the company's predominantly female labor force in this industrial family look the part of the finicky kitchen matron. As Heinz put it, these were not soiled, sullen factory workers but "girls, bright-faced, comely and garbed in neat uniforms, with dainty white caps to keep their hair in order." Each female employee was required to discard street garments and don the guise of a fastidious domestician: uniforms, white caps, and manicured hands, fashioned weekly by the company's manicurist, symbolized personal cleanliness and product purity.[53]

Upholding the principle that in advertising excess is best, Heinz aggressively promoted his merchandise. Few women's magazines escaped his promotional fervor; whether advertising the "Luxury of Heinz Mince Meat" or "Heinz Sunshine and Purity," Heinz products were extolled as always the best, always the freshest, certain to be the tastiest. "Why not let HEINZ supply your home preserves?" one advertisement asked. "In the Heinz Kitchens preserving is done with equipment and experience that no single home could possess. . . . Even so small a thing as the seeding of a cherry, or the hulling of a berry, receives the *individual* attention of an experienced worker whose sole thought is, how clean—how well." The Heinz way of preserving, another stated, is done in "sunshine, fresh air, immaculate cleanliness and sanitation," by workers demonstrating "utmost care and precision." Magazine advertisements pledged that Heinz "products are made not only to conform to but actually [to] exceed the requirements of all State and National Pure Food Laws."[54]

Heinz advertised the superiority of his wares at other sites. Company exhibits at national and international expositions linked welfare work and product quality by showcasing photographs of workers. When the army of Heinz salesmen, numbering about five hundred by 1911, arrived in Pittsburgh for their annual week-long sales conference (a

53. Ibid., Strasser, *Satisfaction Guaranteed*, p. 121.
54. Heinz advertisements published in *Ladies' Home Journal*, September 1906, July 1906, May 1906, December 1905, January 1906, and April 1906.

Heinz tradition since 1889), they were escorted by the employee brass band from the train station to their hotel. At the conference, salesmen received the latest issues of *Pickles*, the employee newsletter, detailing, among other things, Heinz's welfare triumphs. The Heinz Pier at Atlantic City, built in 1899 and only one of three such enclosed edifices open year-round, attracted over fifty million visitors before a hurricane destroyed it in 1944. Promoting the entertainment value of welfare work, Heinz treated its tourists to a bedazzling display of company paraphernalia and propaganda. A lecture supplemented by stereopticon slides idealized the factory's work conditions and employees. A demonstration kitchen provided product samples. Free souvenir picture postcards of a dainty but determined pickle bottler immortalized "The Girl in the White Cap."[55]

Like other consumer-based welfare firms, the Heinz company encouraged factory visits: "The doors are wide open—always have been." Heinz promised visitors that they would leave the plant "with a comprehension of the methods employed and results obtained which word and picture can never convey." Visitors were given a guided tour, food samples, and a green plastic souvenir pickle. The popularity of the tour was monumental; a 1910 pamphlet estimated the average number of annual visitors to exceed 40,000.[56]

Images and Realities

But Heinz tourists did not glimpse from their ringside seats—indeed, were deliberately prevented from viewing—the harsh industrial realities that underlay the terms of company employment. Heinz employees not only had to work under constant public surveillance, they also endured low piece rates, seasonal overtime, and fast-paced machines. Weekly manicures and singing classes eased but did not eradicate the strains of industrial labor. For many workers, the personal costs of employment at Heinz outweighed their publicized benefits. The company's average length of employment, less than two years, paralleled that of workers at other Pittsburgh canneries.[57]

The cloaked realities of the laboring life at Heinz typified the incon-

55. Robert C. Alberts, "The Good Provider," *American Heritage* 23 (February 1972): 27–47; Strasser, *Satisfaction Guaranteed*, pp. 121–23, 180–81, 195–98.
56. Alberts, "Good Provider," pp. 17, 20.
57. Strasser, *Satisfaction Guaranteed*, p. 121.

gruities between projected images and actual employee experience at other welfare firms. In some cases, company advertisements and exhibits shamelessly romanticized working conditions, celebrating exceptions to the rule. Company ads rarely revealed, for instance, inequalities in the distribution of welfare provisions: factories where furnished rest areas were available only for office employees; companies that offered free meals but denied female machine operators the "privilege" of sitting in seats. Nor did ads mention the hypocrisy of forcing workers to drink from shared cups while boasting of sanitary conditions or speeding up employees to the point of sickness during rush seasons while bragging about the superiority of private sector health benefits. None pointed out the deceit of providing gratuitous dental examinations to employees only to make follow-up treatment, at workers' expense, compulsory.[58]

In other instances, the benevolence paraded before the public was altogether fraudulent because workers never received the advertised benefits. Such was once the case at Bloomingdale's department store in New York, where the only beneficiaries of some welfare activities appear to have been the media. One worker recalled an employee lawn party that the store had organized in Central Park for the *New York Herald*. The *Herald* published a favorable description of the celebration, noting an abundance of ice cream, lemonade, cake, and "girls in white dresses with white umbrellas open, smiling and apparently very happy"; it failed to mention that only a few employees had been permitted to take part in the festivities. Before the event, the firm had invited twenty female employees to the park. After small quantities of cake and ice cream were consumed—while clicking cameras recorded the generosity of Bloomingdale's for posterity—the women were ordered back to work. Bloomingdale's apparently used this strategy again at Thanksgiving, notifying newspapers that it was distributing free turkeys to employees. It neglected to tell reporters that turkeys were given to only a minority of workers. One employee recounted the lengths to which one had to demean oneself to qualify. "You have got to apply for it and ask for it, and say that you need it. It is given out just as a charity is handed out." Another worker recalled that he had "never received a turkey in three and a half years; and upon inquiry I have not been able to find

58. Don D. Lescohier, "Working Conditions," in John R. Commons et al., *History of Labor in the United States*, 4 vols. (1918–35; New York: Augustus M. Kelley, 1966), 3:317; U.S. Bureau of Labor Statistics, *Welfare Work for Employees in Industrial Establishments in the United States*, Bulletin 250 (1919), pp. 10–11.

anyone who has." The Bloomingdale example suggests that not every worker benefited from publicized benevolence.[59]

In the final analysis, filtered views of factory life fostered wider acceptance of industrial conditions but often only by camouflaging their coarsest features. Stripped of its embellishments, welfare work publicity advertised a product—the decency of Rockefeller, the desirability of Heinz ketchup, and, in a larger political orbit, a private ordering of industrial relations rooted in the message that private sector beneficence was all workers needed. Labor, the object of scrutiny, was accorded little say in creating the sanitized images of industrial labor flaunted before the public. Workers' views were sidelined for good reason: high worker turnover, strikes, and other indications of malcontent in welfare firms nationwide were steady reminders that workers were rarely as enchanted with welfare capitalism as the captious public. From the perspective of employers, however, this point was moot. Factory tours, the plethora of printed and pictorial accounts of industrial benevolence, and the local and national exhibits that hundreds of thousands of Americans encountered during the Progressive era spoke more, in the long run, to the uplift of employers than to the reformation of the workplace. Ironically, as companies trumpeted their ethics in a frenzied race for public approval, they demoted workers' welfare—the reason for the applause—to little more than a footnote in a larger business-centered story.

The profit motive behind welfare work publicity was as evident to businesses' staunchest critics as it was to the employers who tabulated its returns. One union leader scoffed: "The employer who installs shower baths, and then with a blare of trumpets . . . calls his goodness to the attention of the passer-by, belongs to the same class as a circus manager who exploits the tricks of his animals, not because he poses as the savior of the animal creation, but because he hopes it will induce money to flow into his coffers. We must, then, make a clear line of demarcation between the schemes of an enterprising publicity agent and genuine purposeful betterment work."[60] That line, however, proved difficult to draw. Reformers generally contemptuous of capital's treatment of labor found it hard to fault businessmen for initiating programs whose impact, though often exaggerated, helped employees

59. U.S. Senate, Commission on Industrial Relations, *Final Report and Testimony of the U.S Commission on Industrial Relations*, 64th Cong., 1st sess. (Washington, D.C.: Government Printing Office, 1916), 3:2322, 2338.

60. Annie Marion MacLean, "Trade Unionism versus Welfare Work for Women," *Popular Science Monthly*, July 1915, p. 54.

more than no programs at all. Reformers identified degrees of labor exploitation. Few could deny that cleaner, safer work conditions improved the quality of workers' lives—that Heinz employees fared better than those forced to work twelve-hour days in factories replete with disease, filth, and dangerous equipment. If welfare work ultimately advanced capital's interests, it seemed to do so first by boosting labor's.

Businessmen knew a winning combination when they had one. Aware that they had little to lose and everything to gain from appearing benevolent, employers publicized their "happy workers" with abandon.

4 /

Gender and Welfare Work

In 1904 the Ferris Brothers Company of Newark, New Jersey, employed 325 women to manufacture Ferris Good-Sense Corset Waists. These employees constituted 90 percent of the labor force, not an unusual proportion given the unwritten rule that deemed the making of women's shirtwaists, dresses, and garments "women's work." What *was* unusual about the company's arrangements was the range of services and facilities available to the women who toiled at the firm's sewing machines each day.[1]

Although the morning whistle at the Ferris Company blew at 7 A.M. sharp, female employees were allotted "a reasonable time of grace" to arrive. Workers entering the factory with wet feet were provided with free hosiery. During their shift, female employees were addressed only with the prefix "Miss"; managers and foremen were required to "regulate their conduct toward [women] by the same rules of politeness that are observed by well-bred men and women in the ordinary intercourse of life." The company encouraged its employees to take two

---

1. Winton C. Garrison, *Industrial Betterment Institutions in New Jersey Manufacturing Establishments* (Trenton: Bureau of Statistics of New Jersey, 1904), p. 52. On the sexual division of labor in the garment industry, see Susan A. Glenn, *Daughters of the Shtetel: Life and Labor in the Immigrant Generation* (Ithaca: Cornell University Press, 1990), pp. 110–17.

half-hour breaks each day, and extra time could be taken on request. Breaks could be spent in a lounge furnished with couches and blankets. For women more interested in distractive amusement, a recreation hall, complete with grand piano, "handsome easy chairs and pretty rugs," and the latest magazines, with flowers "lending an air of beauty and refinement," was available for use. A dining room served a midmorning snack and lunch; the firm employed a woman to tend to the room's table linen and cutlery. Hot tea was free and soup prepared by the company cook—mock-turtle or oxtail—cost 2 cents. There were five bathrooms, each attended by a woman, who furnished "clean towels and other requisites." If an employee became ill or disabled, she was "taken care of by the firm to the fullest extent." Workers were expected to leave the factory as comfortably as they had arrived. Should a storm arise at quitting time, "umbrellas, water-proof cloaks and rubber shoes" were available for loan.[2]

The company hoped that its benevolence toward women would earn it public acclaim. "It is the unavoidable lot of many thousands of women and young girls," it reported in a widely distributed brochure, to look for employment in factory surroundings that are "ever so uncongenial." But at Ferris Brothers "everything of a disagreeable nature has been absolutely eliminated."[3]

Programs for female employees at Ferris Brothers typified women's welfare work in the Progressive era. As a rule, employers treated women workers as the needy "other," tailoring welfare programs to their "special needs." The universality of the differences between men's and women's programs is striking. Despite variations in size of the labor force, the proportion of women employed, and even the industry involved, women wage earners across the country experienced welfare work through programs designed to protect female vulnerability and cultivate domestic proficiency.

The distinctiveness of women's programs reflected the degree to which welfare capitalists viewed both male and female workers as gendered rather than sexually generic beings. Welfare provisions encoded behavioral expectations that assigned women and men separate social and economic roles. Men's welfare work attempted to cement the male wage earner's status as breadwinner. Long and loyal labor "earned" male workers a good pension, a financial bonus, even a home, perquisites that fortified the male employee's position as family provider.

2. Garrison, *Industrial Betterment Institutions*, pp. 54–55.
3. Ibid., pp. 54–57.

Women's programs, in contrast, defined femininity through chastity, physical vulnerability, domesticity, and marriageability. Rest periods shielded women from the physical hardships of industrial labor; homemaking classes nurtured their larger social role as mothers and wives of tomorrow.

Why Welfare Work for Women?

The typical welfare beneficiary was young, native-born, and female. Although women represented a minority of wage earners in the Progressive era—about a quarter of the laboring population by 1920—more than half of all welfare beneficiaries were women. But not all women workers enjoyed equal access to company beneficence. Upholding sexual and racist stereotypes, employers declared native-born, white women wage earners the purest segment of the female labor force and thus the most deserving and needy of company protection. Welfare work flourished in industries where native-born women represented the majority of the labor force, such as department stores and telephone exchanges, but was less developed in industries with a high foreign-born population.[4]

Myriad and interconnected economic, political, and legal concerns encouraged the feminization of welfare work. One enduring economic problem confronting employers was women wage earners' higher turnover rate. Whether to secure other employment promising better conditions and higher wages or to marry (often with only a brief respite from paid labor), women were more likely to leave jobs than men. Employers who had invested time and money training women found turnover costly. Welfare work, promising happier, more loyal employees, was seen as one solution to the turnover crisis. In 1912 the Metropolitan Life Insurance Company credited the seven-year average length of employment of its female clerks to its welfare work.[5]

Another economic issue prompting the establishment of welfare

4. See Sanford Jacoby, *Employing Bureaucracy: Managers, Unions, and the Transformation of Work in American Industry, 1900–1945* (New York: Columbia University Press, 1985), p. 54; U.S. Bureau of Labor Statistics, *Welfare Work for Employees in Industrial Establishments in the United States,* Bulletin 250 (1919), pp. 34, 70; Joseph A. Hill, *Women in Gainful Occupations, 1870–1920,* Census Monograph 9 (Washington, D.C.: Government Printing Office, 1929), p. 54, table 39.

5. Metropolitan Life Insurance Company, "The Welfare Work Conducted by the Metropolitan Life Insurance Company for the Benefit of Its Employees" (paper prepared for International Congress on Hygiene and Demography, New York, 1912), p. 7.

work for women was the high degree of control exercised by women in industries in which they were concentrated. After 1900 the fastest-growing sectors of women's wage work included department stores, offices, and telegraph and telephone firms, industries in which workers had direct contact with the public. Because these companies' public was the consumer, profitability was inextricably linked to women's job performances. Employers thus had a special incentive to ensure that workers were content in their work and loyal to the company. As Susan Porter Benson's study of women workers and department stores shows, welfare work in the store had many meanings: it provided a better work environment, encouraged optimal employee performance, enhanced the firm's public image, and minimized class conflict between working-class saleswomen and middle-class buyers. All of these portended higher company profits. As one contemporary put it, "If a girl, say, reared in humble surroundings, spends some part of her day amid pictures and cheerful furniture and tasteful rugs and books and sunlight, will she not insensibly acquire a clear insight into the ideas and needs of the majority of the store's customers?" Female switchboard operators, albeit heard and not seen, possessed a similar power over customer satisfaction. When Theodore Vail, president of AT&T, promised in 1903 to provide customers with the "voice with the smile," he understood the need for his employees' cooperation. Vail inaugurated a comprehensive welfare work scheme as part of the company's commitment to better public relations.[6]

The feminization of welfare work also reflected employers' conviction that wage-earning women were better suited than men for welfare programs. Employers argued that the very physiological and emotional fragility that rendered women vulnerable to the hazards of an industrial environment made them ideal candidates for welfare work. Women's frailty held them hostage to their surroundings. But if bad conditions proved deleterious to their welfare, then surely good conditions would be *particularly* advantageous. What made women victims of industrial neglect would also make them welfare work's greatest success stories.

6. Susan Porter Benson, *Counter Cultures: Saleswomen, Managers, and Customers in American Department Stores, 1890–1940* (Urbana: University of Illinois Press), pp. 142–46; "Jordan-Marsh Ninth Floor Heralds New Era in Personnel Work," *Dry Goods Economist* 13 (March 1920): 73; National Civic Federation Welfare Department, "Better Conditions for Women Workers," *National Civic Federation Review* 4 (December 1913): 19; Theodore Vail, "Plan for Employees' Pensions, Disability Benefits and Insurance," in *Views on Public Questions: A Collection of Papers and Addresses of Theodore Newton Vail, 1907–1917* (New York, 1917), pp. 103–5. Also see Alan R. Raucher, *Public Relations and Business, 1900–1929* (Baltimore: Johns Hopkins University Press, 1968), pp. 52–53.

Employers also assumed that women's internalization of prescribed gender roles would predispose them to embrace company programs more readily than men. Women not only deserved protection, they *desired* it. Their presumed acceptance of their future roles as mothers and wives meant that they would participate fully in company programs. As one welfare work advocate promised, "Women are especially sensitive to their . . . opportunities and they will soon respond to everything done for them with a loyalty and enthusiasm that is not known where men alone are employed."[7]

Although all of these considerations help explain why women workers were privy to more benefits than men, they do not explain the gendered organization of welfare work—why women received not only more benefits but decidedly different benefits too. To understand the feminization of welfare work at a programmatic level, we must again delve into the politics of labor reform in the Progressive era, in which gender played a pivotal role. By the late nineteenth century the "woman and work question," decrying the social costs of women's wage work, was decades old. But increased female employment at the turn of the century, the profoundly urban and increasingly public environment in which work was performed, and the demographic profile of female wage earners collectively stoked the fires of discontent among reformers. This discontent, in turn, drove the passage of statutory protections for women workers, the necessity for and desirability of which welfare capitalists challenged through private sector reforms supporting women's social roles. A response to economic considerations, women's welfare work was, like welfare work generally, politically motivated.

The wide-scale entrance of women into the paid labor force at the turn of the century, the result of massive immigration, economic necessity, and new job opportunities, created a climate for reform. Between 1880 and 1920 the number of female nonagricultural workers increased almost fourfold, from 1.8 to 7.3 million. Moreover, in this same forty-year period, the proportion of women in the adult nonagricultural labor force rose from 20.5 to 24.2 percent. While this shift reflected a general increase in the adult female population, it also pointed to a greater tendency among women to enter the paid labor force. Between 1880 and 1920 nonagricultural wage-earning women as a proportion of all adult women rose from 12.8 to 21.3 percent. In just

---

7. Edward Shuey, *Factory People and Their Employers: How Their Relations Are Made Pleasant and Profitable* (New York: Lentilhon, 1900), p. 113.

forty years the likelihood that a woman would work for wages had risen from almost 1 in 8 to more than 1 in 5.[8]

This new generation of wage earners labored in employment sites newly opened to women at the turn of the century. In the nineteenth century, female paid labor was concentrated in domestic service and household manufacture. By the early twentieth century new opportunities for women in factories, department stores, telephone exchanges, and offices had diminished the importance of domestic service and household manufacture to white female employment; between 1870 and 1910, for example, the proportion of women workers employed as domestic servants decreased from 61 to 26 percent. Employers in these new settings altered employment patterns in two ways. First, by creating new employment opportunities for women, they encouraged more women to work outside the home. In addition, precisely because these workplaces were outside the home, they weakened the supervisory protections of women's wage work by placing it beyond immediate family control.[9]

The demographic profile of women workers contributed to contemporaries' anxieties. The typical female wage earner was young and single. In 1900 a majority—86.6 percent—of nonagricultural female workers were unmarried. Almost half, 46.1 percent, were under 25 years of age; 71.8 percent were younger than 35. Women workers' youth and marital status were viewed as symbols of female chastity. Concern that this virtue would be trampled by the rhythms of the urban, industrial world resounded widely in the Progressive era. The panic created by the exaggerated incidence of white slavery, for instance, reflected concerns about prostitution. But it also indexed contemporaries' fears that the general commodification of America, which had reduced work, play, and even sex to the cash nexus, was guilty of, in this case literally, raping female virtue. Seduction narratives and novels such as Theodore Dreiser's *Sister Carrie* and Upton Sinclair's *Jungle* di-

8. U.S. Bureau of the Census, Special Reports of the Bureau of the Census, *Status of Women at Work, 1900* (Washington, D.C.: Government Printing Office, 1907), pp. 162, 170; Hill, *Women in Gainful Occupations,* pp. 19, 54. Figures were calculated controlling for occupations categorized as agricultural pursuits. See also Alice Kessler-Harris, *Women Have Always Worked: An Historical Overview* (Old Westbury, N.Y.: Feminist Press, 1981), p. 80. Both men's and women's participation in the nonagricultural labor force grew between 1880 and 1920. In 1880 the number of nonagricultural workers in the United States was 9,240,368; in 1920 the number had risen to 30,247,541.

9. Mary Odem, *Delinquent Daughters: Protecting and Policing Adolescent Female Sexuality in the United States, 1885–1920* (Chapel Hill: University of North Carolina Press, 1995), pp. 21–22; Hill, *Women in Gainful Occupations,* p. 45.

rectly engaged this theme, expounding the story of female innocence overwhelmed and overpowered by modern industrial life.[10]

Young, single, and freed from their parents' social custody, the new female workers were believed to be in grave moral danger. Reformers contended that on or off the job, a woman worker's life was fraught with unforeseen perils. The enervating routine of wage labor, necessitating long hours spent performing monotonous labor, made working women, the more fragile sex, particularly susceptible to challenges to their character and resolve. As William Tolman warned, "When a girl begins work in a factory or store, the strangeness of the new life, the timidity that comes with the forming of new relationships and the unusual fatigue, frequently bring depression and discouragement." Exhaustion and emotional despair jeopardized women workers' ability to recognize the hidden dangers surrounding them: unsupervised restrooms—"necessary and yet . . . so liable to misuse"—covert overtures from unsavory male supervisors, forced friendships with older women "whose character they do not know, and with whom companionship may mean untold harm."[11]

After-work hours could be equally hazardous. Commercial amusements catering to a young, primarily mixed-sex and working-class crowd were widespread in urban centers at the turn of the century. Cafés, amusement parks, movie theaters, and dance halls gave working women unsupervised spaces in which to enjoy new social freedoms. But working women who sought friendship, fun, and romance in the world of commercialized leisure, reformers warned, endangered themselves and their virtue. Nickelodeons and amusement parks were viewed as gathering places for dishonorable men whose "evil imaginations" and "powerful and primal" instincts, as Jane Addams put it, would induce moral transgressions in unsuspecting female patrons. Public dance halls, where "improprieties are deliberately fostered," were equally suspect. Reformers denounced popular dance styles such as the one-step, spieling, and pivoting, which combined heterosexual touching with spontaneous movement, as examples of working-class propriety gone awry.[12]

10. Joanne J. Meyerowitz, *Women Adrift: Independent Wage Earners in Chicago, 1880–1930* (Chicago: University of Chicago Press, 1988); Ruth Rosen, *The Lost Sisterhood: Prostitution in America, 1900–1918* (Baltimore: Johns Hopkins University Press, 1982), chap. 3; Odem, *Delinquent Daughters*, chap. 1.

11. William H. Tolman, *Social Engineering: A Record of Things Done by American Industrialists Employing Upwards of One and One-Half Million of People* (New York: Macmillan, 1909), pp. 50–52; "Value of the Social Secretary," *Social Service,* July 10, 1904, p. 10.

12. Jane Addams, "A New Conscience and an Ancient Evil," *McClure's Magazine* 38

Reformers insisted that working women did not freely choose debaucherous thrills. Rather, in the absence of proper supervision, young working women were too naive to recognize danger. While the "desire for a good time is perfectly legitimate," cautioned William Tolman, "in the absence of wise direction, [it] finds its satisfaction in vicious surroundings, with the tendency ever downward." The danger for "factory girls," he elaborated, stemmed from the fact that "so many . . . have no idea of wholesome recreation; they want a pleasant time, but do not know how to get it. They walk the streets at night, ogling the men, picking up acquaintances who lead them to dance halls where they get their first lessons in drink; after that, the downward career is begun."[13]

Inadequate moral supervision was deemed a major cause of the supposedly widespread adulteration of female purity in turn-of-the-century America. A female worker's search for amusement could lead her down a treacherous path to a painful love affair, even prostitution. Indeed, many feared that prostitution was a routine part of the wage-earning woman's workweek. Tales of stockroom and office seduction were legion; journals printed sensationalist exposés that reinforced the image of new female workplaces as breeding grounds for sexual improprieties. Although employers insisted that such charges were spurious, few could ignore the haunting images the specter of prostitution presented: young, chaste women—today's workers, tomorrow's mothers—forever ruined by the sexual licentiousness endemic in the workplace.[14]

Concern over the female role in the family and the social costs of women's wage work loomed large in the campaign for protective labor legislation. The campaign gave the larger Progressive debate over the industrial question and the determination of government's role in its resolution a sharper, more immediate focus by channeling broad discussions of state involvement in industrial relations into a carefully circumscribed debate over the advantages of voluntary versus state welfarism for women. Many reformers believed that the intervention of the state was necessary to protect women and public morals. Employers, having everything to gain from the freedom of contract that protective

(January 1912): 340; Kathy Peiss, *Cheap Amusements: Working Women and Leisure in Turn-of-the-Century New York* (Philadelphia: Temple University Press, 1986), pp. 88–114.

13. Tolman, *Social Engineering*, p. 52.

14. Low wages were often considered as blameworthy as inadequate moral supervision for adulterating female purity. Indeed, the final report of the 1901 Industrial Commission concluded that "the low rate of wages paid to women is one of the most frequent causes of prostitution" (U.S. House of Representatives, *Report of the Industrial Commission on the Relations and Conditions of Capital and Labor Employed in Manufacturers and General Business,* 57th Cong., 1st sess. [Washington, D.C.: Government Printing Office, 1901], 19:927).

legislation abridged, viewed the bulk of legislative initiatives warily. At an important level, women's welfare work was their attempt to rally support for their antistatist position.[15]

The campaign for protective legislation received backing from disparate quarters. The National Consumers' League, the American Federation of Labor, and the Women's Trade Union League were among its most ardent supporters; asserting the centrality of gender difference, they demanded state regulation to protect working women from exploitation by masculine industrial capitalism. To be sure, many reformers, notably Florence Kelley of the National Consumers' League, pushed for legislative protections for working women *and* men. Although she operated within the confines of a maternalist discourse that declared women different from men, Kelley never lost sight of the need for larger structural change to improve the well-being of male workers as well. But Kelley and other reformers encountered an insurmountable obstacle. In a series of decisions that collectively set the course for the protective legislation campaign, the Supreme Court stymied attempts at legislative gender inclusivity.[16]

The Supreme Court was extremely important in establishing the

15. On protective labor legislation in the United States, see Ulla Wikander, Alice Kessler-Harris, and Jane Lewis, eds., *Protecting Women: Labor Legislation in Europe, the United States, and Australia, 1880–1920* (Urbana: University of Illinois Press, 1995), especially the introduction and the chapter by Kessler-Harris, "The Paradox of Motherhood: Night Work Restrictions in the United States," pp. 337–58; Kathryn Kish Sklar, *Florence Kelley and the Nation's Work: The Rise of Women's Political Culture, 1830–1900* (New Haven: Yale University Press, 1995); Eileen Boris, *Home to Work: Motherhood and the Politics of Industrial Homework in the United States* (New York: Cambridge University Press, 1994); Theda Skocpol, *Protecting Soldiers and Mothers: The Political Origins of Social Policy in the United States* (Cambridge: Harvard University Press, 1993); Linda Gordon, ed., *Women, the State, and Welfare* (Madison: University of Wisconsin Press, 1990); Susan Lehrer, *Origins of Protective Labor Legislation for Women, 1905–1925* (Albany: SUNY Press, 1987); Alice Kessler-Harris, *Out to Work: A History of Wage-Earning Women in the United States* (New York: Oxford University Press, 1982), chap. 7; Judith Baer, *The Chains of Protection: The Judicial Response to Women's Labor Legislation* (Westport, Conn.: Greenwood Press, 1978).

16. The campaign for shorter hours was never an open-and-shut case of middle-class reformers' efforts to eliminate working women's economic freedoms. Kelley, for instance, viewed protective legislation as an important step toward female *and* working-class emancipation. Her battle for laws setting maximum work hours for children and women was part of a larger push for improvements in workers' housing, health, and industrial conditions, reforms intended to lighten the load of both women and men. Kelley regretted that judicial review of the Fourteenth Amendment prevented the realization of her inclusive vision. As Vivien Hart has put it, "Kelley committed herself to the best she could get, under the circumstances." See Hart, *Bound by Our Constitution: Women, Workers, and the Minimum Wage* (Princeton: Princeton University Press, 1994), p. 100; Sklar, *Florence Kelley and the Nation's Work*; Sybil Lipshultz, "Social Feminism and Legal Discourse, 1908–1923," *Yale Journal of Law and Feminism* 2 (Fall 1989): 131–60.

boundaries of protective labor legislation during the Progressive era. Its verdicts on the constitutionality of state statutes dictated the ground rules for the advance of legislative labor reforms, rules that affected reformers, employers, and workers alike. That gender stood at the center of the Court's ruling reflected its importance to understandings of work and social welfare at the turn of the century.

The chief issue of contention was freedom of contract embedded in the Fourteenth Amendment's prohibition of state interference with an individual's pursuit of "life, liberty or property." Industrialists and entrepreneurs viewed laws regulating work hours, the backbone of the protective legislative campaign, as a violation of their Fourteenth Amendment right to enter into contracts free from state interference. Sidestepping the reality of debilitating work conditions and the universality of the wage system, employers insisted that freedom of contract placed businessmen and workers on the same footing: in determining terms of labor such as wages and hours, employers and employees came to the bargaining table as equals. Clinging to the fiction of mobility derived from an outdated vision of free labor, employers argued that workers' bargaining power came from their ability, when dissatisfied, to find employment someplace better.

Advocates of laws regulating hours more accurately depicted the harsh realities of industrial life at the turn of the century. Central to their demand was the recognition that workers' vaunted power as freely contracting individuals amounted to little more than the "right" to accept whatever substandard employment terms employers imposed. Insisting that workers' welfare had become a matter of public welfare, they argued that labor conditions were a suitable subject for state regulation.

Until 1905–6 the Supreme Court failed to provide a clear indication of the conditions under which hours laws would be upheld. In *Ritchie v. People* in 1895, the Illinois Supreme Court struck down an eight-hour law for female factory workers, finding "no reasonable ground . . . for fixing eight hours in one day as the limit which woman can work without injury to her physique, and beyond which if she works, injury will necessarily follow." Three years later, the U.S. Supreme Court's decision in *Holden v. Hardy* superseded the Illinois ruling. *Holden v. Hardy* upheld the constitutionality of a Utah ten-hour law for male workers in mines and smelters, the first mandatory hours law for men of its kind passed in the country, declaring it a reasonable restraint of freedom of contract. Shared concerns about the harmful impact of unlimited hours on state welfare and miners' health, a harm exacerbated by the peculiar dangers of mine labor, underlay the Court's decision. Justice Henry B. Brown, writing for the majority, noted:

> While this Court has held that the police power cannot be put forward as an excuse for oppressive and unjust legislation, it may be lawfully resorted to for the purpose of preserving the public health, safety or morals. . . .
>
> While the general experience of mankind may justify us in believing that men may engage in ordinary employments more than 8 hours per day without injury to their health, it does not follow that labor for the same length of time is innocuous when carried on beneath the surface of the earth, where the operator is deprived of fresh air and sunlight, and is frequently subjected to foul atmosphere and a very high temperature, or the influence of noxious gases generated by the process of refining or smelting.[17]

So framed, the Court's decision suggested that the constitutionality of other hours laws would be measured by the ability of regulated workers to withstand the physical hazards of their occupation. That ability, in turn, would be determined by the stamina necessary to complete the job as well as the social effects of unrestricted working hours on the general public.

Applying these guidelines, the Court in *Lochner v. New York* in 1905 struck down a New York law limiting the working hours of bakers to ten per day and sixty per week. Assessing the characteristics of those who worked as bakers as well as the demands of the occupation itself, the Court ruled:

> There is no contention that bakers as a class are not equal in intelligence and capacity to men in other trades or manual occupations, or that they are not able to assert their rights and care for themselves without the protecting arm of the State, interfering with their inde-

17. Ritchie v. People, 155 Ill. 98 (1895); Holden v. Hardy, 169 U.S. 366 (1898). Also see Lehrer, *Origins of Protective Labor Legislation for Women*; Elizabeth Brandeis, "Labor Legislation," in John R. Commons et al., *History of Labor in the United States*, 4 vols. (1918–35; New York: Augustus M. Kelley, 1966), 3:668–89; and Eileen Boris, "Reconstructing the 'Family': Women, Progressive Reform, and the Problem of Social Control," and Alice Kessler-Harris, "Law and a Living: The Gendered Content of 'Free Labor,' " both in *Gender, Class, Race, and Reform in the Progressive Era*, ed. Noralee Frankel and Nancy S. Dye (Lexington: University Press of Kentucky, 1991), pp. 73–109.

pendence of judgment and of action. They are in no sense wards of
the State. . . .

   We think that a law like the one before us involves neither the safety,
the morals, nor the welfare, of the public. . . . It does not affect any
other portion of the public than those who are engaged in that occupation. Clean and wholesome bread does not depend upon whether
the baker works but ten hours per day or only sixty hours a week. The
limitation of the hours of labor does not come within the police power
on that ground.[18]

In addition to striking down the New York hours law, *Lochner* did two
things. First, because it was the first time the Court had declared a
statute protecting labor unconstitutional, it furthered speculation about
the constitutionality of other hours laws. Second, it solidified a gendered interpretation of freedom of contract that presaged the Court's
subsequent affirmation of protective laws for women. Emphasizing the
ability of bakers, as men, to "care for themselves without the protecting
arm of the State," the Court underscored the "natural" ability of men
to thrive without state support. In addition, the language of the decision opened the door to a gendered determination of public welfare,
health, and morals. By asking whether the law for bakers affected "any
other portion of the public than those who are engaged in that occupation," the Court affirmed the idea of a differential impact on public
welfare that varied according to the class of workers in question. In
Lochner the Court defined the "public" consequences of bakers' work
narrowly as the tangible by-product of bakers' labor: "clean and wholesome bread." But in designating the class of workers—disaggregated
by sex and by occupation—a critical variable for determining the circumstances under which workers' welfare might become a matter of
state welfare, it suggested that other classes of workers might be held
to different standards.

   The Supreme Court's ruling in *Muller v. Oregon* sealed the justices'
gendered construction of freedom of contract. At issue was the constitutionality of Oregon's ten-hours-per-day/sixty-hours-per-week statue
for laboring women passed in 1903. The plaintiff, a Portland launderer
named Curt Muller, insisted that his right to negotiate hours of labor
with laundresses independent of the Oregon restriction was constitutionally protected. Louis Brandeis argued the case for the state with
the backing of the National Consumers' League. His 113-page brief,

18. Lochner v. New York, 198 U.S. 45 (1905).

largely prepared by his sister-in-law, the NCL activist Josephine Gold-
mark, cataloged differences between the sexes to support the claim that
women were more vulnerable to the hazards of wage work than men.
Affirming Progressives' faith in scientific evidence as the basis for public
policy, the brief included reports by factory inspectors, labor commis-
sioners, and physicians "documenting" women's inherent physical,
mental, and emotional fragility. "Women are fundamentally weaker
than men in all that makes for endurance," the brief asserted, "in
muscular strength, in nervous energy, in the powers of persistent attention and application." As a result, "overwork . . . is more disastrous to
the health of women than of men, and entails upon them more lasting
injury."[19]

Hoping to dodge *Lochner*'s shadow and persuade the Court that the
restriction of women's working hours was a valid police power measure, the brief focused on the sex of the regulated workers. It asserted
the primacy of a woman worker's social identity as prospective wife
and mother over her economic identity as a freely contracting individual, so delineating a gendered assignment of roles that distinguished
male from female workers in their relation to the public welfare and
the proper functioning of the state. Whereas in *Lochner* the public
value of male bakers' labor had been determined by a strict economic
criterion, in *Muller*, the Brandeis brief argued, the social stakes were
higher. Because the workers being regulated were women, the determination of social value must, in deference to men's and women's different public functions, focus on women's contributions to society not
as workers but as women. To the extent that unrestricted hours of
wage work jeopardized a woman's maternal and reproductive health
and thus the health of future generations, the state's regulation of
women was valid.[20]

The Supreme Court accepted the logic of separate spheres. It ruled

19. Louis D. Brandeis, *Women in Industry: Decision of the United States Supreme Court in Curt
Muller vs. State of Oregon Upholding the Constitutionality of the Oregon Ten Hour Law for Women
and Brief for the State of Oregon* (1908; New York: Arno Press, 1969), pp. 18, 57. On Muller
v. Oregon see Nancy Woloch, *Muller v. Oregon: A Brief History with Documents* (Boston:
Bedford Books/St. Martin's Press, 1996); Ronald K. L. Collins and Jennifer Friesen,
"Looking Back on *Muller v. Oregon*," *American Bar Association Journal* 69 (March 1983):
294–98, and 69 (April 1983): 472–77; Ann Corinne Hill, "Protection of Women Workers
and the Courts: A Legal Case History," *Feminist Studies* 5 (Summer 1979): 247–73; and
Nancy Erickson, "*Muller v. Oregon* Reconsidered: The Origins of a Sex-Based Doctrine of
Liberty of Contract," *Labor History* 30 (September 1989): 228–50.
20. Brandeis, *Women in Industry*, p. 113.

that a working woman "is properly placed in a class by herself, and legislation designed for her protection may be sustained, even when like legislation is not necessary for men and could not." The combined effect of *Lochner* and *Muller* was to protect the dependence of women and the contractual freedoms of men. The gendering of state protection turned back the clock of universal reforms affecting male and female workers equally, granting states free license to expand the scale and scope of regulations for women. Between 1909 and 1917 nineteen states passed statutes limiting the hours of women's work. By 1917, only nine lacked restrictions on women's hours.[21]

It was in this political and legal context that women's welfare work flourished. Welfare capitalists established women's programs to challenge the assertion—now the basis for law—that wage work violated female virtue, jeopardized women's reproductive functions, and endangered the public welfare. Employers professed agreement that the employment of women was not only a contractual relationship but also a moral obligation. Where employers stood apart from their critics was on whether businessmen, as the "offending party," had relinquished the right to remedy labor conditions for women by themselves.

Employers challenged the assumption that the evils in industry that stripped women workers of their femininity were unalterable. Instead they argued that welfare work, by improving the experience of women's wage work, transformed the factory itself into an agent of female reform. Stopping short of protective labor legislation's mandate to remove women from the marketplace, welfare work proposed a compromise in which the social costs of wage work would be offset by company protections. Elaborately decorated rest rooms, frequent rest periods, sexual segregation policies, domestic education classes, meals to fortify women's strength and other principally female benefits treated women workers as special beings with special needs, which employers claimed the private sector was well positioned to safeguard and nurture. "Many people think that when a girl enters a factory she leaves part of her womanliness behind," said a National Cash Register forewoman in 1904. "A girl can be neat in appearance and ladylike in behavior in a factory as well as in the home. . . . Today our young women are respected because they respect themselves. We have proved

---

21. Brandeis, "Labor Legislation," p. 673; Kessler-Harris, *Out to Work*, pp. 187–88.

in our factory that a woman can go into the business world and retain all her womanliness.''[22]

Women's Welfare Work in Practice

A wide array of benefits showcased employers' role as the self-appointed guardians of wage-earning women. Employers structured a woman's workday in ways designed to prevent physical and mental fatigue. They extended special rest breaks to female workers, encouraging women to spend them in restrooms and lounges embellished with the fineries of a middle-class home. The Bureau of Labor statistics' observation in 1919 that, in general, welfare firms' ''men's rooms are usually less pretentious than the ones for women'' was not an understatement. The restrooms for women employees at the John B. Stetson Company of Philadelphia, for instance, sported nothing less than ''wicker arm-chairs, reclining chairs, settees, and tables, with cretonne cushions and covers . . . , electric lamps with silk-lined shades [giving] a restful light . . . , windows . . . tastefully draped with curtains.''[23]

Many firms adopted sexual segregation policies that gendered both the organization of workplace space and the activities performed within it. Physically separating men and women workers as they worked, ate their lunches, or made their way home, employers paid tribute to the value of separate spheres in a public setting many had come to view as dangerously interactive. Institutionalized segregation thus served to buttress employers' claims of respect for canons of sexual propriety and respectability, assuring critics of the protective features of corporate custodianship. National Cash Register for example, limited opportunities for heterosocial exchange by forbidding female workers to enter men's departments and by having them start work half an hour later and quit fifteen minutes earlier than men so that they could travel to and from work on different streetcars. The Eastman Kodak Company of Rochester reported that its ''toilet rooms for men and women are separated when possible in diagonally opposite corners of the building on alternate floors.'' The Metropolitan Life In-

22. Alfred A. Thomas, *National Cash Register Factory as Seen by English Experts of the Mosely Industrial and Educational Commissions* (Dayton, 1904), p. 69.

23. U.S. Bureau of Labor Statistics; *Welfare Work for Employees*, p. 71; idem, *Employers' Welfare Work*, Bulletin 123 (1913), p. 46; John B. Stetson Co., *The Human Element in Business* (Philadelphia, 1921), p. 14.

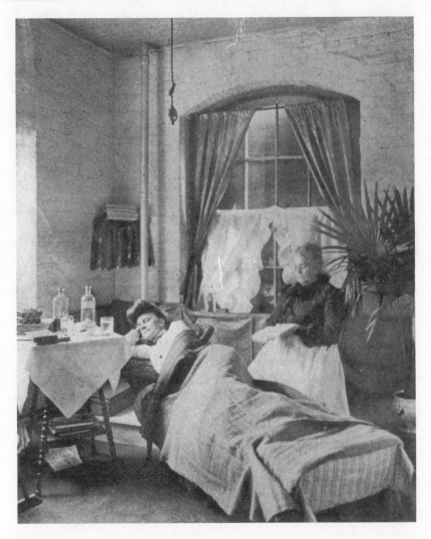

Acknowledging that women workers had special needs, welfare capitalists argued that they were able to protect and care for their female employees without state legislation that forced employers' hands. Note the rest room's decorative touches. (*Engineering Magazine* 20 [January 1901].)

Welfare programs were often sexually segregated. (*Engineering Magazine* 20 [January 1901].)

surance Company maintained two "admirably lit" employee dining rooms on the upper floors of the main building, "one floor for men and the other for women." Use of the insurance company's gymnasium rotated between male and female workers; it was reserved on Mondays, Thursdays, Fridays, and Saturdays for men and on Tuesdays and Wednesdays for women.[24]

Efforts to control leisure were also important to women's welfare work. In lieu of unsupervised entertainments, company recreation offered female workers "wholesome," chaperoned leisure. At the United Shoe Machinery Company, three hundred acres of "beautiful countryside" surrounding the factory presented women workers with a wide choice of recreational activities, including tennis, cricket, golf, and yachting. The

24. Thomas, *National Cash Register Factory as Seen by English Experts*, pp. 37, 69; Manufacturers' Association of the City of Bridgeport, *Report on Welfare Work in Bridgeport and Elsewhere* (Bridgeport: Brewer-Colgan Co., 1918), p. 19; Metropolitan Life Insurance Company, *Welfare Work Conducted by the Metropolitan Life Insurance Company for the Benefit of Its Employees* (New York, 1915); idem, *The Welfare Work of the Metropolitan Life Insurance Company for Its Employees: Reports for 1918* (New York, 1918), p. 11. On sexual segregation policies in the financial industry, see Angel Kwolek-Folland, *Engendering Business: Men and Women in the Corporate Office, 1870–1930* (Baltimore: Johns Hopkins University Press, 1994), chap. 4.

Company dance classes sought to formalize social interactions among working men and women. (*Cassier's Magazine*, September 1905.)

General Electric Company of Schenectady, New York, hosted tennis tournaments, canoeing expeditions, picnics, and corn roasts in the summer and dancing classes, parties, recitals, and glee club performances in the winter. Hoping to redefine the behavioral boundaries of the most popular commercial working-class women's entertainment, dancing, companies organized dances where female physicality and desire could be monitored and restrained. The Shredded Wheat Company, the Thomas G. Plant Company, the Gorham Manufacturing Company, International Harvester, Metropolitan Life Insurance, Filene's, and the Stetson Company were but some of the establishments providing halls for "lunch dances." At NCR, chaperoned evening dances were designed to minimize the potentially dangerous consequences of spontaneous social intercourse. Interdepartmental marriages resulting from formal courtship were encouraged—the company claimed that married men "settle down and attend to business"—but clandestine forays of the flesh were not.[25]

25. Thomas, *National Cash Register Factory as Seen by English Experts*, p. 37; Gertrude Beeks, *Welfare Work: An Address before the National Association of Wool Manufacturers* (New York, 1906), p. 20, State Historical Society of Wisconsin, Madison (hereafter SHSW); Louis A. Coolidge, *From the Boston Transcript* (n.p., 1913) p. 9; Charles M. Ripley, *Life in a Large Manufacturing Plant* (Schenectady: General Electric Co. Publication Bureau, 1919), p. 24; U.S. Bureau of Labor Statistics, *Employers' Welfare Work*, pp. 35, 40, 43, 53, 58, 62, 66; Mary

Finally, companies sponsored educational programs. More than other welfare programs for women, the substance and purpose of educational work depended largely on the ethnic and socioeconomic background of targeted workers. As a rule, educational welfare work, like welfare work generally, arose most frequently in companies with a young, native-born female labor force deemed particularly worthy of protection. But there were important exceptions to this rule. In some consumer industries, notably garments and food, both of which claimed a disproportionately large number of foreign-born and first-generation workers, concerns about product safety facilitated the establishment of welfare programs. As well, during World War I, when immigrant women were hired for factory work in unprecedented numbers, welfare work became one way employers helped them adjust to new routines and expectations. When the majority of a company's female employees were immigrants, educational welfare work converged with Americanization.[26]

Educational welfare work for immigrant women cast the company as a nursery of gendered Americanism. Company instructors and nurses taught foreign-born and second-generation women principles of family survival—how to cope with language differences, municipal regulations, and the consumer orientation of American society—while inculcating deference to codes of female respectability. Immigrant women were taught that cleanliness, thrift, moral virtue, and culinary competence mattered to their immediate family and the company, as well as to the welfare of society.

Take the case of Marja, an imaginary peasant girl featured in the D. E. Sicher Company's *Where Garments and Americans Are Made.* The New York firm, by 1917 the largest manufacturer of muslin underwear in the world, began a factory school in 1913 for its female employees to prove "that in thirty-five weeks the illiterate girl, foreign born and trained, can be transformed into a literate American woman with good

---

E. Thaon, "Report on Welfare Work, McCormick Twine Mill 1904–05," Cyrus H. McCormick Jr. Papers, Box 42, SHSW; Metropolitan Life Insurance Company, *"Welfare Work,"* p. 19; U.S. Bureau of Labor Statistics, *Welfare Work for Employees,* p. 71; "Jordan-Marsh Ninth Floor," p. 77; Committee on Industrial Welfare, *Industrial Profit Sharing and Welfare Work: A Report of the Committee on Industrial Welfare of the Cleveland Chamber of Commerce* (Cleveland: Cleveland Chamber of Commerce, 1916), p. 52.

26. The likelihood that companies would develop welfare programs for immigrant women increased when labor shortages heightened the economic bargaining power of immigrants, giving them access to jobs from which they would otherwise be excluded. This was particularly the case during World War I, when many companies needed to hire female immigrants to maintain full production.

mental equipment and social knowledge." The book, in part a fictional sketch of the company's real-life education system, follows Marja's maturation from ignorance to educated womanhood. Marja, determined to "make good in this rushing, enigmatical America," begins attending the factory school for forty-five minutes a day. Under the tutelage of dedicated instructors, she learns English "in the natural way in which a language is acquired by the growing child." As she becomes literate, Marja is taught the principles of proper womanhood. She is instructed on hygiene, etiquette, and personal cleanliness; she learns how to wash, comb, and present her hair. The fundamentals of domestic economy are also emphasized: "She soon learns thrift and in its train follows its natural handmaiden, orderliness." Marja is taught the techniques of good housewifery, "how to keep her work and home surroundings neat and tidy." At the end of her thirty-five weeks at the company school, Marja prepares "simple meals and does her buying with intelligence. . . . She is no longer the woman who put raw meat into her fireless cooker . . . and complained that it did not cook." Marja has joined the ranks of other Sicher graduates who have "bloomed out into intelligent, educated and cultivated young women."[27]

The spirit of the Sicher method, though not so entertainingly portrayed, was implemented elsewhere. The Scovill Manufacturing Company of Waterbury, Connecticut, developed welfare work for foreign-born women as a response to the feminization of the labor force during World War I. Like many companies during the war, Scovill, a manufacturer of brass goods, experienced a labor shortage when many of its employees were recruited for military service. The severity of the situation—Scovill lost 500 workers—was amplified by the scarcity of potential male replacements in the local labor market: more than 3,500 men from the Waterbury area alone were recruited for military duty. To meet heightened production quotas created by wartime government contracts, Scovill suspended its regular hiring practices which favored the employment of men. Because most government contracts with Scovill were for the manufacture of weapons, the company experienced an increased demand for light handwork (rather than machine work), such as installing and setting clocks on timed munitions fuses. Employers' stereotypes of women stimulated female employment: the supposed dexterity of women was interpreted to mean that they had a "natural" aptitude for

27. Jessie Howell McCarthy, *Where Garments and Americans Are Made* (New York: Writers' Publishing Co., 1917), pp. 3, 15, 18, 20, 21, 24, 26.

such work. As the company actively recruited women, its labor force became increasingly feminized. Between 1914 and 1918 the number of women in the company's employ rose from 750 to 4,200.[28]

Because most newcomers were foreign-born and unable to read or speak English, the company tried to expedite their adjustment to the rhythms of industrial life. As early as January 1918, hourly classes for foreign women were organized at nearby public schools, and women were encouraged to attend them between work hours. When time wasted in transportation to and from the public school and women's own reluctance to devote their evenings to classes inhibited attendance, the company decided to take charge of employee education itself. In September 1918 Scovill began classes for immigrants on company time; by March 1919 all new employees were required to sign a contract agreeing to attend classes as part of their employment.[29]

Scovill's classes gave the company an opportunity to teach English, inculcate an industrial work ethic, and promote cultural assimilation. Conversational lessons on "Why I obey orders," "How I ring the time clock," and "Why I must learn to read signs" were coupled with sex-

---

28. "Women Workers Are Wonderful," *Scovill Bulletin*, May 1919, p. 5, in Case 33, Folder "Writings from Bulletin," Scovill Manufacturing Co. Papers II (hereafter SMCP), Baker Library Archives of the Harvard Graduate School of Business; "The Scovill Manufacturing Company," *Metal Industry* (August 1923): 312–13; U.S. Employment Agency recruitment form letter of 1918 on behalf of the Scovill Co., Folder "Efforts to Secure Labor, 1917–18"; E. G. Main, 1918 Annual Report of the Industrial Service Department, Folder, "Industrial Services Department, 1917–21"; R. E. Platt to D. L. Summey, January 24, 1918; Platt to Maude E. Woodruff, June 8, 1918; and Woodruff to Platt, June 25, 1918, Folder "Efforts to Secure Labor, 1917–18," all in Box 33C, SMCP. The employment office hired recruiters and sent them throughout New England and Pennsylvania; in June 1918, the company placed a female representative in the New York office of the U.S. Employment Service. The company's labor superintendent, R. E. Platt, asked recruiters to "appeal particularly to the unmarried women and girls, and to the married women without children," but the company agreed to employ any female willing to make the trip to Waterbury and work for $14.50 a week. The only recruitment restrictions upheld were those that could be used to weed out potentially "unprofitable" workers: "exceptional cases over 50 years of age" were to be brought to the company's attention before being sent; women of "loose morals, of uncertain health, of superficial intention, [or] of bad disposition" were not to be sent at all (W. H. Monagan to J. H Goss, March 8, 1918, Box 33C, Folder "Efforts to Secure Labor, 1917–18," SMCP).

On Scovill and scientific management, see Sharon Hartman Storm, *Beyond the Typewriter: Gender, Class, and the Origins of Modern American Office Work, 1900–1930* (Urbana: University Illinois Press, 1992), pp. 35–52.

29. Payroll Department Records, Box 33C, Folder "Figures: Labor by Departments, 18–20," SMCP; memo to heads of departments, March 21, 1919; F. A. Shattuck, to L. Summey, July 3, 1918; F. A. Shattuck, Educational Report for October," November 1919; and Platt to N. F. Fogarty, March 10, 1919, all in Box 33, Folder "Educational asses, 1918–20," SMCP.

specific lessons on clothes, shopping, and family health. The company's objective was not only to make the foreign-born woman worker "learn to talk good English and read and write" but also to enable her to "conduct herself and run her house on hygienic American lines." At Scovill, as at D. E. Sicher, educational welfare work taught women English, factory discipline, and "respectable" female behavior.[30]

The majority of welfare firms, employing a different stratum of the female labor force, predictably had a different educational emphasis. Because restrictive recruiting practices resulted in a labor force made up chiefly of native-born, educated women workers, employers likened their educational welfare work to that of an elite finishing school. Challenging the view that work and home were antithetical realms, they portrayed the workplace as a training site for domestic excellence.

NCR and H. J. Heinz were two such employers. The women hired to work at NCR were an exclusive group. The firm upheld a strict hiring policy. Only single women (no widows) over 17 years of age and weighing more than 115 pounds could apply. High school graduates were preferred, as were native-born women. On the latter point the company was insistent. "Many factories . . . recruit their lower and cheaper grades of labor from a new or foreign immigration which is wholly uneducated," it asserted. "These we do not want."[31]

These educated women of proper upbringing were placed under the company's protective surveillance so they would stay that way. The company encouraged women employees to fill their after-work hours with wholesome company-supervised activities. The Woman's Century Club operated as the company's female literary organization. Members met at noon to recite poetry and discuss domestic affairs. To develop women's domestic prowess, the company created a Domestic Economy Department that sponsored cooking and sewing classes. Typical classes taught "cooking, . . . housekeeping, marketing, and the details of domestic economy." The company also organized classes for women only in hygiene, emergency nursing, and dancing. While NCR's outdoor activities were said to ensure that male workers' "surplus energy . . . could be directed into good channels," dancing gave women "grace and self-possession."[32]

According to company spokespersons and many of the factory's

30. Shattuck "Educational Report for October."

31. Thomas, *National Cash Register Factory as Seen by English Experts*, pp. 36–37; idem, *How the Factory Grew and What It Does* (Dayton: National Cash Register Company, 1905), p. 20.

32. U.S. Bureau of Labor Statistics, *The Betterment of Industrial Conditions*, Bulletin 31 (1900), pp. 1127–31; "N.C.R. Welfare Work," *Woman's Welfare*, March 1904, pp. 8–10.

40,000 yearly visitors, NCR's welfare work transformed female workers of good character into ladies of bountiful womanhood. A reporter for the *Cincinnati Chronicle* opined that "to one who had just come from tales of petty oppression, of factory girls fined for violating rules that are in conflict with nature, the sight of these young ladies sitting in a fern-embowered dining room eating their lunches, with soup and coffee furnished by the Company . . . was overpowering." In one of its many welfare work publications, NCR boasted that "nowhere in America is there another similar body of factory women . . . They are serious-minded, well-bred, well-dressed, self-respecting and profoundly respected."[33]

Women's welfare work at Heinz followed a similar course. The company had much to gain from safeguarding employers' right to hire women and countering the image of the factory as a site of female impropriety; Heinz's advertising campaign explicitly linked the superiority of its products to women workers' culinary prowess. To this end, the food factory focused all of its welfare efforts for women on what it openly admitted to be "character building." A women's library with several hundred volumes—"carefully selected" essays, "wholesome fiction," and history—was open daily; female employees were encouraged to take books home to "read and improve your minds." Factory facilities reflected the company's motto that "while it is true we can live without poetry, music and art, yet we can live broader and better lives with them." The walls of the women's dining hall, occupying the entire fifth floor of the baked beans building, were covered by more than one hundred pictures, photographs, pastels, etching, engravings, and watercolors. According to an article in *Pickles*, the employee magazine, the pictures' "beauty appeals to the aesthetic side of life, and their ethical and refining influences can not be measured." The employee auditorium, "a roomy theater of comfort and elegance," was furnished with "comfortable opera chairs, . . . its general attractiveness . . . heightened by beautiful stained glass windows, and numerous oil paintings." Here women could attend noon-hour lectures and evening entertainment organized by the company. The auditorium also featured regular performances by the women's glee club. If any or all of these efforts failed to transform the incoming Heinz female factory hand into a cultivated, domesticated woman, there was still hope: she could attend company classes in drawing, cookery, millinery, and dressmaking. The company

33. Quoted in National Cash Register Co., *Welfare Work* (Dayton, 1900), p. 36; National Cash Register Co., *A Trip through the NCR Factory,* (Dayton, 1904), p. 36.

The factory as finishing school. (*Cassier's Magazine*, September 1905.)

offered proof of the efficacy of these educational efforts. The classes, claimed one Heinz pamphlet, gave the young women "the best of tuition, not only in the art of making their own hats and clothing, but in all the accomplishments of the housewife—and the large number of marriages among them would indicate these courses are eminently successful in teaching self-help and developing the true housewifely qualities."[34]

Heinz's emphasis on the factory as a finishing school revealed some of the internal contradictions of women's welfare work. As a finishing school, what was the company finishing its women workers for? Like NCR, which refused to employ married women, Heinz viewed industrial labor as a temporary stage in a young woman's life. Both firms portrayed their women wage earners as youthful and fresh. This depiction reminded and reassured reformers that *their* female employees were not the older, exploited married women whom other companies sentenced to lives of hard labor. Single, chaste, and marriage-bound, the women on these welfare firms' payrolls were employed and then released during the heyday of their youth, free to follow domestic pursuits.

The factory-as-finishing-school motif suggested more than a place of

34. H. J. Heinz, *The Home of the 57* (Pittsburgh, 1903), pp. 15, 16, 19; *Pickles*, October 1897, p. 2; Leroy Fairman, *The Growth of a Great Industry* (Pittsburgh: H. J. Heinz, 1910), pp. 33–34.

opportunities. It also suggested a place where a woman was expected, indeed encouraged, to take advantage of these opportunities before moving on to a "higher calling" as full-time wife and mother. It was the company's duty to see that she made this journey as morally pure and more intellectually and culturally prepared than she had been when she first stepped through the company's door. At NCR, female and male employees were separated in the factory, then encouraged to attend chaperoned dances and other functions at which interdepartmental courtships were encouraged. At Heinz, good grooming, good health, and good education presumably led women to good marriages.

The irony of the factory-as-finishing-school and the worker-as-prospective-wife themes was that both contradicted the importance of what industrialists desired: a permanent, well-trained workforce. Emphasizing the transforming power of welfare work and the temporary status of women workers, welfare firms may have curtailed criticisms that big business was insensitive to the perils of industrial work to the moral, physical, and spiritual constitution of female employees. How destructive to womanhood could a factory be, the establishment of women's welfare work implicitly asked, when the workplace not only improved a woman's expertise in fulfilling female obligations to home and society but also encouraged her to leave its employment upon her betterment? But by pushing the ideology and practice of women's welfare work to an extreme, placing the woman before the worker and the school before the factory, welfare firms such as NCR also placed themselves at a competitive disadvantage. Even as it embraced the logic inherent in welfare work that happier, educated women workers meant loyalty, better production, and higher profits, NCR promoted female workers' marital desirability, only to remove them from the workplace upon marriage. The investment of money and time in creating and maintaining women's welfare work was a high price to pay for public approval.

Firms that employed married women, as Heinz did, did not try to emphasize the importance of a worker's womanhood to the point of severing her economic ties to the company: Heinz wanted its improved workers to stay. Indeed, most welfare firms tried to project an image of the factory that so closely approximated that of an unblemished middle-class home that they challenged the division of a woman's life into two incongruous domains: a demonized world of work and an idealized domestic retreat. Welfare capitalists glorified work as both a paying occupation and a preparation; the workplace itself became not a site of dirt and debauchery but a domesticated space. The United

Shoe Machinery Company's literature focused on the company's luxurious recreational setting, not its factory buildings. In this mockery of reality, women were not machine workers but ladies of leisure who went yachting or played tennis in their spare time. The "soft lazy tones" of the Curtis Publishing Company's women's restrooms suggested a world of coziness and comfort, not paper and dust. Heinz attempted to bridge the gulf between women's home and work spheres by characterizing the workplace as an extension of the home. In the Heinz scenario women were not workers in an industrial setting but domestic artisans in their natural habitat, a kitchen—but a kitchen so grand as to surpass expectation: clean, sparkling, with all the amenities of a middle-class home.

Reformers' charge that the only way to save womanhood and society was by removing women from the workplace by statute was turned on its head by welfare capitalists. Welfare work offered a vision of a new corporate order in which work became both a means for individual survival and a vehicle for societal uplift. Employers proclaimed that the combination of company provision and female participation would permit welfare work to transform working women into ladies whose etiquette, domestic skills, and behavioral propriety rivaled those of nonworking middle-class women. But, at least to themselves, employers also set limits on how far this character makeover should go. Women's welfare work was intended to give its recipients the *appearance* of being middle class, endowing women with the mannerisms but never the means to transcend their economic status. Promising to mold wage earners into the living embodiment of radiant femininity, employers never lost sight of the underlying rationale for women's programs: to offer whatever concessions were necessary to keep the poorest paid contingent of American workers on company payrolls.[35]

Masculinity and Welfare Work

Although the majority of welfare programs targeted women, employers also organized male-only programs that appealed to, even as they attempted to redefine, working-class masculinity. Business and labor leaders alike glorified the virtues of the manly, autonomous worker whose

35. Hershey Corp. *The Story of Hershey, the Chocolate Town* (Hershey, Pa., 1960), p. 42; minutes of the fifth meeting of the Conference on Welfare Work at Chicago Commons, May 1, 1906, Cyrus H. McCormick Jr. Papers, Box 40, SHSW.

virility constituted the backbone of the American character. Employers were sensitive to the possibility that welfare programs might threaten male workers' implied claim to "manly independence." They wanted male employees to view the company as an agent of self-definition, not emasculation. In establishing welfare schemes for men, employers trod cautiously, hoping to make men feel that they were not forfeiting independence by participating in company programs.

The necessity for preserving and promoting masculinity guided discussions of men's programs. One manufacturer explained the significance of men's welfare work by noting that "men want to *be* men, want to be manly . . . all they need is the opportunity." The *Brooklyn Citizen* agreed. "Employers of labor," it noted as early as 1900, "are beginning to see that . . . it pays to invest something in the manhood of their men."[36]

But whose masculinity? Conceptions of working-class masculinity were being contested and recast at the turn of the century. In previous decades the prevailing ethos had linked workplace masculinity to the dignity and self-respect that came with the ownership and execution of a time-honed skill. As Lisa Fine has argued, craftsman manliness in the nineteenth century was "bound up with the dignity [a skilled worker] derived from his work, his autonomy on the shop floor . . . his fraternal identification and mutualism with others of his trade, and his ability to earn a wage to care for his family." The introduction of new technologies and management strategies such as scientific management degraded skill and devalued what had previously been central to professions of labor manliness. The tempo of this change was uneven, and it affected pockets of workers differently at different times. But in general, technological innovations and the reorganization of work demanded new, less skill-centered understandings of what it meant to be a "manly" worker.[37]

Welfare work programs for men were developed with this crisis of

36. Samuel M. Jones, *Letters of Love and Labor* (Toledo: Franklin Printing & Engraving, 1900) p. 67; Shuey, *Factory People and Their Employers*, pp. 80, 208; lecture by Mr. Thomas of NCR, in minutes of the fifth meeting of the Conference on Welfare Work.

37. Lisa Fine, " 'Our Big Factory Family': Masculinity and Paternalism at the Reo Motor Car Company of Lansing, Michigan," *Labor History* 34 (Spring–Summer 1993): 279. Also see David Montgomery, *Workers' Control in America: Studies in the History of Work, Technology, and Labor Struggles* (New York: Cambridge University Press, 1979), pp. 13–14; Ava Baron, "An 'Other' Side of Gender Antagonism at Work: Men, Boys, and the Remasculinization of Printers' Work, 1830–1920," and Ileen A. DeVault, " 'Give the Boys a Trade': Gender and Job Choice in the 1890s," both in *Work Engendered: Toward a New History of American Labor*, ed. Ava Baron (Ithaca: Cornell University Press, 1991), pp. 47–69, 191–215.

labor masculinity in mind. Instead of making the manliness of laborers dependent on skill on the job, welfare work offered alternate paths to manliness and respectability.

The most common substitutes promoted by welfare programs were leisure and financial security. Downplaying the importance of workshop autonomy to male workers' identity, welfare capitalists endorsed sports as a suitable way to demonstrate "manly" skill. Privileging excellence in the realm of leisure over expertise on the shop floor, welfare work lionized male heroism as it was exhibited on the field or court. The explicit linkage between prowess in sports and virility was not exclusive to welfare work; indeed, it was made credible by the cultural context in which it occurred. Since the 1890s, rigorous athletics had been vaunted as a remedy for bourgeois emasculation, the regrettable but inevitable by-product of an economy in which a growing number of middle-class men—clerks, professionals, engineers, and managers—sat at their desks all day. From Theodore Roosevelt to Henry James, Americans spoke often of the "overcivilization" and "overrefinement" of American men, the "softening" of their physicality, the "weakening" of their moral fiber, and the "laxity" of their resolve. When Bernarr McFadden, proud exhibiter of his own toned muscles, issued the first issue of *Physical Culture* in 1899, he offered readers a slogan that struck at the core of the ethos of the cult of male physicality: "Weakness Is a Crime." Fears of effeminization were culturally countered in numerous ways: from the commercial success of male impotence cures, to the popularity of adventurer and detective tales, to the newfound respectability of boxing, a respectability that Elliot Gorn has shown symbolized the desire of middle-class men to use fists and wits to "smash through the fluff of bourgeois gentility." Other sports were also enlisted in the service of restoring virility. Racing, bicycling, football, and hiking enjoyed a national following. Within a cultural framework that already conceptualized sports as an antidote to the emasculation of men in a newly rationalized and bureaucratic workplace, athletic programs came to occupy an important part of male welfare work.[38]

38. Elliot J. Gorn, *The Manly Art: Bare-Knuckle Prize Fighting in America* (Ithaca: Cornell University Press, 1986), p. 247. On the crisis of masculinity, see ibid., chaps. 6 and 7; John Higham, "The Reorientation of American Culture in the 1890s," in *The Origins of Modern Consciousness*, ed. John Weiss (Detroit: Wayne State University Press, 1965); Arnaldo Testi, "The Gender of Reform Politics: Theodore Roosevelt and the Culture of Masculinity," *Journal of American History* 81 (March 1995): 1509–33; Jackson Lears, *No Place of Grace: Antimodernism and the Transformation of American Culture, 1880–1920* (New York: Pantheon, 1981); Kevin J. Mumford, " 'Lost Manhood' Found: Male Sexual Impotence and Victorian Culture in the United States," *Journal of the History of Sexuality* 3

Baseball diamonds, basketball courts, rifle ranges, gymnasiums, bowling alleys, and pools abounded in predominantly male firms in the Progressive era, inviting workers to flex their masculine might physically after the workday ended. At the United Shoe Machinery Company in Beverly, Massachusetts, tennis courts, football, baseball, cricket, and track-and-field teams, a clubhouse containing equipment—including bowling alleys, billiard and pool tables, and a shooting range where "shot-guns, rifles, revolvers of all shapes, sizes, and families" could be deployed—linked masculinity to physical prowess and corporate largesse. At the International Harvester Company, baseball teams and ten-pin clubs were popular; at the Solvay Process Company, classes in male physical culture were held in the company gymnasium. Company leagues formally encouraged athletic rivalries, making sports a vehicle for undercutting class solidarity. Normally competitions occurred within a single firm, but not always; International Harvester teams, for example, played men from other companies. Sponsored prizes helped to cement new definitions of male skill by financially rewarding male employees "talented" enough to win. Athletic champions could expect to see their pictures in the employee paper, a visual tribute to the importance of accomplishment through sports to the masculine culture companies wished to create. Photographs of the man strong, fast, and coordinated enough to catch "the winning catch" reinforced the belief that masculine achievement was more important and discernible in the world of leisure than in the world of work.[39]

Even more important than leisure to men's welfare programs was financial provision. Men's welfare work tried to redefine the requirements of a successful breadwinner. Economic independence and the ability to provide for one's family were central to welfare capitalism's masculine vision, just as they had been to traditional skill-bound conceptions of labor masculinity. But welfare capitalists gave men's bread-winning role a new twist, emphasizing that the kind of work employees performed was less important than the financial benefits they acquired

(1992); Elizabeth H. Pleck and Joseph H. Pleck, eds., *The American Man* (Englewood Cliffs: Prentice-Hall, 1980), Introduction; Joe L. Dubbert, "Progressivism and the Masculinity Crisis," in Pleck and Pleck, *American Man*, pp. 303–20; Peter N. Stearns, *Be a Man! Males in Modern Society* (New York: Holmes & Meier, 1979); E. Anthony Rotundo, "Body and Soul: Changing Ideals of American Middle-Class Manhood, 1770–1920," *Journal of Social History* 16 (Summer 1983): 23–28; David Macleod, *Building Character in the American Boy: The Boy Scouts, YMCA, and Their Forerunners, 1870–1920* (Madison: University of Wisconsin Press, 1983).

39. U.S. Bureau of Labor Statistics, *Employers' Welfare Work*, pp. 11–14, 38; Thomas Dreier, *The Story of Three Partners* (Beverly, Mass.: United Shoe Machinery Co., 1911), p. 29.

for performing it, benefits whose pecuniary orientation would support men's financial role as family providers. What workers had to do to qualify for benefits—to demonstrate manliness as breadwinners—was to exhibit stamina on the job and loyalty to the company, not craft skill or erudition. Thus, although the emblems of labor masculinity remained the same, welfare provisions radically recast the requisite traits needed to obtain them.[40]

Financial security framed the orientation of the bulk of men's programs. Pensions, profit sharing, stockholding, savings plans, and housing and loan funds were the benefits most frequently reserved exclusively for men. All celebrated the value of men's economic role as family providers. Comfort and domesticity, salient and publicized objectives of women's welfare work, were deliberately omitted from discussions of men's programs. Indeed, to counter the charge that welfare programs were emasculating, proponents of welfare work made a point of distinguishing the crude roughness of men's facilities from the domesticated spaces of women's. In contrast to women's "pretentious" and garishly decorated rest rooms, men's rooms were "very simply furnished with plain tables and chairs . . . planned with a view to having them practical and substantial rather than ornamental." Employers characterized the workingman as strong and robust, not needy or desirous of special comforts and coddling. This vision championed the individual achiever who through his own hard work, initiative, and acumen "roughed it" while climbing the ladder of economic success. Because he was a man, he needed no feminine comforts.[41]

Men's benefits supplied the material means to manly independence. Profit sharing and pensions, for instance, were set up specifically to reward company-approved behavior and long-term loyalty with financial compensation. Profit sharing enabled conscientious, steadfast men to achieve their goal of economic independence faster. Profit-sharing schemes usually functioned in one of two ways. The most popular re-

40. In 1906 the American Institute of Social Service urged employers to plaster factory walls with posters announcing that "labor is a girdle of manliness." The advice was given as part of the institute's campaign to "develop and increase the efficiency of . . . working people" through "desirable mottoes" that exercised "through the power of suggestion" an "unconscious influence upon [factory] occupants." But nothing in the institute's long list of catchy slogans mentioned skill, and the very fact that the link between work and manliness required explicit advertisement was a telling indicator of how tenuous the connection was thought to be. Letter of October 24, 1906, American Institute of Social Service Weekly Commercial Letter Service, Cyrus H. McCormick Jr. Papers, Box 41, SHSW.

41. U.S. Bureau of Labor Statistics, *Welfare Work for Employees*, p. 71.

quired workers to buy company stock and then "share profits" through regular dividends. Another provided a direct quarterly, semiannual, or annual payment of a fixed percentage of a company's surplus earnings. Each method gave a worker what he did not receive from wages alone: a financial stake in his productivity. The harder he worked and the more he produced, the greater his remuneration.

Pensions, in turn, promised long-term security. Although every company's plan was in some ways unique, most required employee contributions. The amount of the contribution was determined by taking 1 to 2 percent of an employee's salary at the time of retirement (usually occurring between ages sixty and seventy) and multiplying that amount by the total years of employment. In all cases, eligibility required a minimum length of employment, usually over twenty years. Here again, eligibility requirements were deemed an important feature in the protection of workers' manhood. Exacting requirements tested the mettle of prospective recipients. Only worthy men would be rewarded.

The structure of men's benefits asserted the connections between political voluntarism and manly self-respect, making men's welfare work as politically encumbered as women's. In the case of financial benefits, for instance, the comparison between public and private was explicit. Employers viewed the act of contribution as critical to the protection of men's self-respect. Charles Piez of the Link Belt Company, favoring sickness insurance paid for jointly by employer and employees, cautioned that a state-funded system "would shatter the fiber of the man himself." "The State ought not to go so far as to take away from a man all sense of responsibility for his own future," Piez warned. "I do not think it is good for the man." Andrew Carnegie agreed. Criticizing the possibility of government-funded pensions in 1908, Carnegie glorified the contributory model with an appeal to masculine pride. According to Carnegie, the act of contribution itself was the plan's "most salutary feature. It gives a man that feeling of independence and true manhood that he is doing for himself, and when he has contributed to his pension, and the time comes to get it, it is not another's money he is getting—it is his own. I would not sacrifice the manly, independent spirit of the American for a great deal."[42] Whereas public welfare bestowed charity upon the unfit and unable, pensions rewarded the fit

42. U.S. Senate, Commission on Industrial Relations, *Final Report and Testimony of the U.S. Commission on Industrial Relations*, 64th Cong., 1st sess. (Washington, D.C.: Government Printing Office, 1916), 4:3184; Andrew Carnegie, "Old Age Pension," in *Proceedings of the National Civic Federation Annual Meeting* (New York: National Civic Federation, 1908), p. 205, SHSW.

and hardworking. According to employers, only that which was earned was manly.

In a revealing indication of the importance of both leisure and family security to welfare work's masculine vision, welfare capitalists sometimes appealed to "masculine" athleticism in the name of "masculine" breadwinning. Such was the case at the Scovill Company, which during World War I established war gardens for its employees. A practical measure to encourage workers to grow their own food to overcome wartime scarcities, the war gardens also held larger gendered meanings. According to company literature, the gardens supplied male workers with the opportunity to make leisure the basis for their most important responsibility: providing for their families. Exhortations to garden were couched in the language of male craft autonomy, urging men to use their hands to produce an artifact of social value. "Somewhere, somehow, you can lay your hands on a little parcel of ground," the company told workers. "You can put your back muscles into the soil. You can hoe and cultivate and harvest a bunch of vegetables that won't come out of somebody else's labor." As the company also made clear, however, gardening was challenging work. Only the most skilled, strong, and hardy laborer would be manly enough to succeed. "These men who have gone in for this gardening are to be respected," the *Scovill Bulletin* noted, "that is, those who stick it out. For it is no child's play and some nights a man's muscles will ache." To chronicle visually the company's conflation of leisure, provision, and masculinity, photographs published in the *Bulletin* captured manliness in action—in the garden rather than the workplace, "drops of sweat rolling down the brow of the man with the hoe." The *Bulletin*'s photographs and stories identified those the company thought were "real" men.[43]

In sum, men's welfare work offered an alternative prescription for proving manhood. Encouraging men to be independent achievers and family providers, men's welfare programs downplayed skill in the job as an emblem of masculinity but kept the steps to achieving successful manhood inextricably tied to the workplace. Labor masculinity, company style, asserted the importance of independence—socially on the baseball field and financially at home—but made that independence contingent upon company support. This uneasy balance between independence achieved through dependence on their employer made many workers question just how "manly" beneficiaries of welfare work could be.

43. Case 33, Folder "War Gardens," SMCP.

Gender and Welfare Work Administration

When Joseph Bancroft & Sons, manufacturers of fine fabrics, established a welfare department in 1906, it hired a social secretary, Elizabeth Briscoe, to supervise the work. Like most social secretaries of her day, Briscoe entered the new field of welfare work as a single, educated, middle-class woman. Briscoe received no formal training for her new job, although her former position as factory schoolteacher had acquainted her with factory faces and routines. Hired because of her proper upbringing and demeanor, she was expected to rely on female intuition and common sense to carry out her responsibilities.[44]

Briscoe's duties kept her busy. Occupying a middle ground between management and labor, she enforced company policies even as she served as the employee advocate at monthly meetings of the Bancroft board of directors. It was Briscoe who saw employees when they were short of rent money and Briscoe who evicted them. When the company loaned workers money, Briscoe supervised repayment. Sounding more like a disappointed parent than a cheated loan officer, she advised one debt-ridden employee who quit the company without giving her advance notice: "I am quite surprised . . . that you left the employ of the Company when in debt to us. I came to your rescue when you were in financial straits, and I think . . . you would have staid [sic] here . . . until your indebtedness was paid. As I am responsible for the money loaned you, I will be at your rooming place every Saturday morning to collect the dollar which you say you will pay weekly."[45] When employees became too sick to work, Briscoe visited them to assess their condition. If an employee seemed seriously ill and if the company secretary to whom Briscoe was accountable agreed, she sent the worker to the countryside on retreat. When employees approached retirement, Briscoe attempted

44. Stuart Campbell, "Welfare Work at Joseph Bancroft and Sons Company, 1901–1912" (M.A. thesis, University of Delaware, 1968), p. 47, Joseph Bancroft & Sons Co. Papers (hereafter BP), Hagley Museum and Library (hereafter HML). Discussions of the coexistence of welfare work and scientific management at Bancroft & Sons include Daniel Nelson and Stuart Campbell, "Taylorism versus Welfare Work in American Industry: H. L. Gantt and the Bancrofts," *Business History Review* 46 (1972): 1–16; and Steven Usselman, "Scientific Management without Taylor: Management Innovation at Bancroft," in *Working Papers from the Regional Economic History Research Center: Essays in Textile History*, ed. Glenn Porter and William H. Mulligan Jr. (Greenville, Del.: Eleutherian Mills–Hagley Foundation, 1981), pp. 47–77.

45. Elizabeth Briscoe to Herbert Soull, February 1, 1917, Welfare Department Letter Book, p. 278, BP, Box 893, vol. 197, HML.

to secure them a pension by presenting their cases before the monthly board meeting.[46]

For fourteen years Briscoe worked as Joseph Bancroft & Sons' social secretary in what she described as a "modest, quiet way." As employee nurse, loan officer, counselor, and advocate, Briscoe assumed multiple roles. By her own account, the social secretary's duties required her to have an infinite reservoir of "tact, patience, good judgment, resourcefulness, firmness, good common sense, enthusiasm and a sense of humor."[47]

The social secretary represented an important new occupation in the industrial landscape of the early twentieth century. It was her job to administer welfare programs, supervise and modify employee behavior, and promote a familial spirit in the workplace. Her unusual range of tasks and her curious position in the company hierarchy—straddling the workers' and the mangers' worlds—made the social secretary unique in the history of labor management. The position's popularity increased as the welfare work movement expanded. In 1901, fewer than 10 social secretaries were employed in the United States; by 1916, more than 140 social secretaries, mostly middle-class women, were working full-time in establishments across the country. All told, more than 200 social secretaries were employed between 1900 and 1920.[48]

That most social secretaries were women reveals how the gendered structure of welfare work affected women not only as recipients but also as providers. In 1916 the Bureau of Labor Statistics reported that "one might conclude that all welfare secretaries are women," and "in the majority of cases this is true." Only in all-male firms, the minority of welfare establishments, were male social secretaries employed.[49]

46. On October 25, 1906, for instance, Briscoe wrote John Elliott, manager of an inn in Centerville, Delaware, "One of our employees, who has been suffering from bilious remittent fever and congestion of the lungs, is now convalescent, but is in a low nervous condition. Mr. John Bancroft [company secretary] has thought that a change of a couple of weeks in the country where he could have the benefit of fresh air and fresh eggs and milk, might be a good thing for him, and has suggested that I write to ask if you would be willing to take him for two weeks" (ibid., p. 59).

47. Elizabeth Briscoe to E. E. Pratt, February 12, 1910, ibid., pp. 54–56.

48. Dorothy Drake, "The Social Secretary," Social Service 3 (February 1901): 33; Anice L. Whitney, "Administration and Costs of Industrial Betterment for Employees," Monthly Review of the Bureau of Labor Statistics 6 (March 1918): 200, 205; Daniel Nelson, Managers and Workers: Origins of the New Factory System in the United States, 1880–1920 (Madison: University of Wisconsin Press, 1975), p. 111.

49. Whitney, "Administration and Costs of Industrial Betterment for Employees," pp. 200–204.

The occupation's feminization sprang in part from the gendered pattern of welfare provision. Because women were the primary welfare beneficiaries, employers deemed it natural for women to "care for their own." The same rationale that underlay the gendering of welfare programs informed the gendering of their administration. Women wage earners, naive and away from family supervision, needed protection and supervision. The presence of a female social secretary, employers claimed, would encourage women wage earners to view the workplace as a second home, complete with a surrogate mother to instruct them on social and sexual matters. Through compassionate prodding, the social secretary would persuade women to "entrust to her their home troubles and their personal affairs." Possessing the intimate details of women's lives, the social secretary could prevent her wards from being led astray. "The personal influence of a cultivated lady in a shop full of wild girls, eager for pleasure and unmindful of the danger," is beyond measure, industrial sociologist Charles Henderson opined. "Where troops of inexperienced girls are brought together," the female social secretary becomes "an angel of light."[50]

Equally important to the feminization of welfare work administration was employers' conviction that irrespective of the sexual composition of the labor force, women were better able than men to attend to workers' needs. Invoking an ideology of maternalism, employers argued that women were innate caregivers, naturally more sensitive, sympathetic, and compassionate than "go-getting male business aspirants." As the more emotive sex, women could respond to workers' personal needs in a way men could not. Their nurturing instincts and moral authority justified maternal intervention: middle-class women could "mother" employees without transgressing prescribed gender norms. "It is in such situations . . . of infinite complexity and delicacy," Charles Henderson insisted, "that we see how the personal and human factor comes in to supplement the relatively rough and clumsy provisions of . . . male management."[51]

Such maternalist thinking was not limited to the social secretary; it also supported the feminization of other middle-class occupations at

50. Tolman, Social Engineering, p. 50; Charles Henderson, Citizens in Industry (New York: D. Appleton, 1915), pp. 280–81; "Value of the Social Secretary," Social Service 10 (July 1904): 10; National Civic Federation, "Working Conditions in New York Stores," National Civic Federation Review 4 (July 15, 1913): 18.

51. Frank B. Miller and Mary Ann Coghill, "Sex and the Personnel Manager," Industrial and Labor Relations Review 18 (October 1964): 43; Henderson, Citizens in Industry, pp. 280–81; Strom, Beyond the Typewriter, pp. 109–13, 120–25.

the turn of the century. Social investigators, reformers, educators, and nurses invoked maternalist arguments about women's special sensitivities to expand female participation in middle-class employment. As a strategy for earning economic equality and professional respect, however, maternalism was a double-edged sword. On the one hand, it enabled women to subvert preexisting economic exclusions by encouraging the feminization of occupations that seemed to demand—or could be defined as needing—a "feminine touch." On the other hand, the appeal to maternalism, insofar as it highlighted differences between men and women, unwittingly encouraged the pathologizing of those distinctions: women, because they were women, made good nurses, the argument ran, but their "female monthly" prevented them from being competent surgeons. By asserting the certainty of biologically ordained differences, maternalism helped, in the long run, to legitimize economic discrimination and exclusion.[52]

The feminization of the occupation of social secretary also enabled welfare firms to promote a persona of corporate domesticity and responsibility to the public. We have already seen how familial metaphors influenced the spirit and shape of welfare work programs, encouraging workers to identify personally with the company and its management. The employment of a female social secretary, whose presence, connoting sympathy and concern, symbolically feminized the corporation it-

52. On women, maternalism, and professionalism, see Sklar, *Florence Kelley and the Nation's Work*; Strom, *Beyond the Typewriter*, Pnina G. Abir-Am and Dorinda Outram, eds., *Uneasy Careers and Intimate Lives: Women in Science, 1789–1979* (New Brunswick: Rutgers University Press, 1987); John C. Burnham, "Medical Specialists and Movements toward Social Control in the Progressive Era: Three Examples," in *Building the Organizational Society*, ed. Jerry Israel (New York: Free Press, 1972); Cynthia Fuchs Epstein, *Woman's Place: Options and Limits in Professional Careers* (Berkeley: University of California Press, 1970); Barbara J. Harris, *Beyond Her Sphere: Women and the Professions in American History* (Westport, Conn.: Greenwood Press, 1978); Regina G. Kunzel, *Fallen Women, Problem Girls: Unmarried Mothers and the Professionalization of Social Work, 1890–1945* (New Haven: Yale University Press, 1993); Judith Walzer Leavitt, *Brought to Bed: Childbearing in America, 1750 to 1950* (New York: Oxford University Press, 1986); Barbara Melosh, *The Physicians' Hand: Work Culture and Conflict in American Nursing* (Philadelphia: Temple University Press, 1982); Regina M. Morantz-Sanchez, *Sympathy and Science: Women Physicians in American Medicine* (New York: Oxford University Press, 1985); Robyn Muncy, *Creating a Female Dominion in American Reform, 1890–1935* (New York: Oxford University Press, 1991); Margaret W. Rossiter, *Women Scientists in America: Struggles and Strategies to 1940* (Baltimore: Johns Hopkins University Press, 1982); Frank Stricker, "Cookbooks and Lawbooks: The Hidden History of Career Women in Twentieth-Century America," *Journal of Social History* 10 (Fall 1976): 1–19; Daniel J. Walkowitz, "The Making of a Feminine Professional Identity: Social Workers in the 1920s," *American Historical Review* 95 (October 1990): 1051–75; Mary Roth Walsh, *"Doctors Wanted: No Women Need Apply": Sexual Barriers in the Medical Profession, 1835–1975* (New Haven: Yale University Press, 1979).

self, enabled firms to promote this image of domesticity to the public. As protective mother to a family of workers, the social secretary was to tend to the personal needs of each and every employee. At a time when muckraking literature portrayed the modern corporation as cold, aloof, and fiercely competitive, the social secretary functioned to negate masculine modernity: she was a compassionate, feminine influence in an otherwise indifferent world.[53]

Social secretaries were most likely to be hired in welfare firms that had experienced a rapid growth in the scale of production and in the size of their labor force. In this regard, the emergence of the social secretary as a salaried occupation signified employers' awareness of the growing distance between employer and employee in the modern corporation. In theory, welfare work alone addressed this estrangement. But employers could not force workers to attend company programs or to accept welfare work's harmonizing message. They needed a company cheerleader: someone who would bring welfare work to employees' attention and personify the spirit of company congeniality. When welfare programs represented little beyond erratic and periodic gestures of goodwill extended to a handful of workers, an employer or manager could assume this responsibility. But when these programs evolved into a comprehensive labor policy affecting hundreds, even thousands of workers, concentration of responsibility under a separate manager became necessary. Social secretaries became both goodwill ambassadors and administrative specialists.

The reorganization of business benevolence at Joseph Bancroft & Sons provides one example of how this transition occurred. The company was founded in 1831 when Joseph Bancroft began manufacturing cotton cloth along the banks of the Brandywine River in Delaware. From the beginning, Bancroft took a personal interest in employees' welfare. As of the first week of operation, he paid workers weekly in cash. To avoid the abuses of a company store, he provided a wagon to escort them to shops in downtown Wilmington. In 1857 he established a school for operatives' children and a library for employees and their families. After Joseph's death, his sons William and Samuel continued their father's tradition. By 1895 Bancroft employees could live in the firm's electrically lit dwellings (specially equipped with water purification filters), eat meals at cost in one of the first factory cafeterias in the country, send their children to a free kindergarten, and count on Jo-

---

53. On corporate domesticity and public relations, see Kwolek-Folland, *Engendering Business*, pp. 131–34.

seph's widow to deliver her home-baked pies in times of illness. So innovative was the company's policy toward workers that in 1895 the journal *American Carpet and Upholstery Trade* described its employees as the "happiest and most contented lot in America."[54]

During the next decade, however, much of this personalism was lost. Between 1895 and 1905 Joseph Bancroft & Sons expanded its facilities and diversified production, adding to its original product line new fabrics such as cambric, dress goods, linings, upholstery cloth, umbrella covering, and windowshades. This expansion required a larger labor force, and by 1906 the company employed 1,400 people, almost triple the number of employees on the company's 1895 payroll.[55]

The growing rift between employer and employed prompted the Bancrofts to establish a welfare department in 1906 and to place Elizabeth Briscoe at its helm. As John Bancroft, William and Samuel's cousin and the company's secretary, wrote years later:

> In the beginning, Joseph Bancroft considered the welfare of his employees . . . and the working conditions throughout the mill were the best that the time afforded. Since the numbers were small there was little need for special effort, as there was personal contact and supervision. As the plant grew, changed conditions required changed methods; so it was no condition of affairs that we established this new department,—simply the heads of the firm, with increased business, had not time to give their personal attention to the employees.[56]

The experience of the Delaware firm was not unique. At the turn of the century many companies with a history of philanthropy restructured extemporaneous gestures of benevolence into firm-wide policies administered by a salaried social secretary. Growth in firm and labor force size and the creation of a managerial bureaucracy necessitated a separate administrative apparatus devoted exclusively to "caring" for employees.[57]

54. "Sketch of Joseph Bancroft and Sons Company," Joseph Bancroft & Sons Co. Papers, Acc. 940, File 4A, HML; Campbell, "Welfare Work at Joseph Bancroft and Sons Company," pp. 11–12; "Rockford and Kentmere Kindergartens," BP, Acc. 940, Folder 14, HML; *American Carpet and Upholstery Trade*, June 1895, ibid., Box 1, File 4A.

55. Campbell, "Welfare Work at Joseph Bencraft and Sons Company," p. 37; Nelson and Campbell, "Taylorism versus Welfare Work," p. 7.

56. Quoted in Welfare Department Letter Book, pp. 89–90, BP, Box 893, vol. 197, HML.

57. Dexter S. Kimball, "Need of Special Supervision Demonstrated," in National Civic Federation, *Conference on Welfare Work* (New York: Andrew H. Kellogg, 1904), pp. 117–18.

The social secretary thus occupied an anomalous position in the welfare firm. As part of the company bureaucracy, her job was to remedy its deadening effects. In the daily administration of welfare activities, she was also expected to restore a sense of intimacy between management and labor. As the *New York Daily News* explained, the social secretary could be "the connecting link to bring the human touch between employer and employee now lost in this era of great corporations." The social secretary would take the time to cultivate a sense of personal importance and worth among employees—time the employer in a large commercial enterprise no longer had. As John Patterson explained to NCR employees assembled in 1897 to meet Lena Harvey, the company's first social secretary: "I should like to shake hands with each of you. . . . But this factory is now growing so large that I cannot meet you all personally. I wish that I could." And so he hired Harvey: "She is to be our bridge between capital and labor."[58]

Employers and other welfare work advocates argued that biology and attitude rather than formal training supplied the appropriate background for a social secretary. As the American Institute of Social Service's monthly organ *Social Service* explained, the social secretary who succeeds does so because of her "natural adaptation to such work, and not [out of] special training for it." A maternalist "instinct," sensitivity and discretion, and a keen sense of propriety were preparation enough. Knowledge of the behavioral code workers were expected to emulate was experiential, not learned from books or in classrooms, derived from a proper upbringing and the internalization of "respectable" morals, etiquette, and behavior.[59]

Social secretaries found their responsibilities complex and wide-ranging. Like welfare work itself, the job met objectives peculiar to individual employers' needs. But despite this structured variability, the occupational expectations of the social secretary maintained a uniformity across firms. A glimpse into the daily experiences of two social secretaries reveals the commonalities that gave the occupation coherence.

After working as secretary of the Chicago-based Civic Federation

58. "For the Welfare of the Workers: A New Profession for Men and Women That Lightens the Burden of the Toiler," *New York Daily News*, April 3, 1904; Lena Harvey Tracy, *How My Heart Sang: The Story of Pioneer Industrial Welfare Work* (New York: Richard R. Smith, 1950), pp. 112–13.

59. Josiah Strong, "The American Institute of Social Service," *Social Service* 6 (October 1902): 69; "Wanted: A Social Secretary," *Social Service* 2 (February 1900): 4; Tolman, *Social Engineering*, p. 52.

(precursor of the National Civic Federation), Gertrude Beeks began her long career in the industrial welfare movement by assuming in 1901 the post of social secretary at the McCormick Works, soon to become International Harvester. After hiring her, Cyrus H. McCormick, company president, outlined Beeks's assignment. "See what you can do to make the three hundred girls and five thousand men who work for us like to work for us," he urged. Although she was hired to look after the welfare of all Harvester employees—"their comfort during working hours, their care in sickness, and their pleasures"—Beeks decided to focus first on women workers, whom she believed most desired and needed her guidance. Beeks's decision prompted the *Chicago Evening Post* to nickname her the "Florence Nightingale of factory womanhood."[60]

Beeks inspected the factory premises and women's quarters and discovered "things which her feminine insight told her should be corrected." One was the presence of a single diminutive mirror in the dressing room, a room used regularly by women to change from work clothes to regular clothes. Believing that women liked knowing how they looked, Beeks persuaded company officials to outfit the room with numerous "looking glasses," an act that apparently "endeared her to all of the girls." Concerned about women's dietary habits, she asked the company to set up a lunchroom where "hot soups" and "good stews" would be sold at cost. Beeks continued her efforts to promote women's welfare by establishing a dancing area with piano, toilet rooms with hot water, towels and soap, and an amusement club, the Sisal Club, named after the fiber used by the women who made binding twine.[61]

After establishing personal rapport with women wage earners, Beeks broadened her efforts to promote men's welfare: the organization of a factory-wide ventilation system, an annual company field day, men's lockers. Soon home visits to male workers' families in times of crisis or illness such as Beeks had established with the women much earlier became a routine part of her daily work.[62]

60. Sarah Comstock, "A Woman of Achievement: Miss Gertrude Beeks," *World's Work* 26 (August 1913): 445; "The 'Social Agent,' " *Rochester Union Advertiser*, September 27, 1902; *Chicago Evening Post*, September 24, 1902.

61. Comstock, "Woman of Achievement"; John R. Commons, " 'Welfare Work' in a Great Industrial Plant," *Review of Reviews* 28 (July 1903): 80; "The Social Agent," *Rochester Union Advertiser*, September 27, 1902; *Chicago Evening Post*, September 24, 1902; Gertrude Beeks, "Report on Entertainment for the Young Women at the Mill, 13 July 1901," Nettie Fowler McCormick Papers, Box 27, Folder "Gertrude Beeks: 1901," SHSW.

62. According to her contemporary Sarah Comstock, Beeks had tremendous difficulty winning men's acceptance. The turning point allegedly occurred after a "queer little

At Macy's in New York, social secretaries were employed to tend to the welfare of a very different labor force, one that was nonindustrial and predominantly female. Still, the duties of the social secretaries roughly paralleled those of Beeks. Like Beeks, Macy's secretaries sought to gain workers' trust, befriend employees, and promote what they saw to be in the workers' "best interests." They addressed employees' problems on a personal level, treating home and work as inseparable dimensions of a worker's life.

As Macy's chief social secretary, Geneva Furman, reported to a welfare work conference, establishing and maintaining contact with individual workers was indispensable to helping resolve employees' personal crises. In one instance, Furman was asked to discover why a young female packer was fainting. After befriending the employee, Furman discovered that the nineteen-year-old was supporting her recently widowed and bedridden mother. Mother and daughter were living off the daughter's wages, a shared 15-cent restaurant meal their only source of food. The employee, eager to expedite her mother's recovery, was giving her the largest portion, arriving to work so hungry that she fainted. Furman made arrangements for the young woman to eat meals at the store: "good, hot, substantial meals and all the rich milk she could drink." The mother was furnished with tonics and medicine; the employee was promoted to a better-paying position. The social secretary supervised the young woman's improvement. In the long run, Furman's maternal ministrations were successful: the mother became stronger "and the brave little daughter [was] happier than she had ever been since [coming] to New York."[63]

On a different occasion, another of Macy's social secretaries discovered a "refined young woman . . . weeping and in a state of melancholia." After coaxing the woman into disclosing the source of her despair, the social secretary found that she had been keeping house for several years for a male friend who had promised to "reward" her efforts with marriage. One day the young woman returned home to find it stripped of her private possessions, gas, and food; only her empty trunk remained. The woman attempted suicide. According to Furman, "We gave her our sympathy, put money in her pocket and found a com-

---

incident": Beeks gave a man a rose pinned to her buttonhole after she heard him remark to another worker that he thought the rose was pretty. At that point, "the human note was struck. She had their friendship which is the first essential in welfare work" (Comstock, "Woman of Achievement," pp. 445–46).

63. National Civic Federation, *Proceedings of the Eleventh Annual Meeting of National Civic Federation* (New York, 1911), pp. 373–77.

fortable room and good food. For weeks this young woman was seen and talked with every day." The attentive bedside manners paid off: the grieving woman, freed from despair, soon became a "valued saleswoman." "She looks at life cheerfully now," claimed Furman, "[she] says she was saved from suicide's grave, and is a happy little business woman, thinking life worthwhile and making it so for herself and those about her."[64]

The jobs of Beeks and Furman were strikingly similar. Each sought to make employees better workers by understanding the totality of their experience—not only the time a woman passed performing paid labor but how she felt and behaved away from the factory: what she ate, whom she befriended, how she lived. Social secretaries recognized that a precondition for reforming workers' lives was gaining their trust. Accepting and working around the barriers that naturally separated them from wage earners—be those barriers rooted in diet, language, deportment, or culture—they sought to establish personal bonds with workers that transcended evident class differences. They encouraged workers to talk with them, to air their grievances and worries. Having won workers' confidence, social secretaries placed workers under their maternal supervision and suggested measures informed by company policy and their own sense of decorum to reform employees' spirits, minds, and morals.

Social secretaries' careful construction of familial intimacy presented workers with both possibilities and problems. On the one hand, it sought to restore to workers a sense of community overwhelmed and displaced by corporate bigness. The social secretary brought the promise of personal renewal: "The moral bond is restored; the severed nerve of communication is joined and healed; there is a better understanding, and the spirit of concord is once more felt." On the other hand, it provided social secretaries with a pretext for reforming workers' ways. When workers accepted the family metaphor, they abrogated their right to anonymity by inviting employers to intervene in their lives. Negotiating the boundaries between desired and intrusive benevolence was one of the chief issues shaping workers' responses to welfare work.[65]

64. Ibid., p. 375.
65. Henderson, *Citizens in Industry*, p. 270; "For the Welfare of the Workers."

5 /

Organized Labor Responds

The strategies and structure of business benevolence—the motives behind its advancement, how and for whom it was organized, its administration—occupy only a portion of the history of American welfare work. Also significant are the responses of workers themselves, the thoughts and deeds of the hundreds of thousands of men and women who experienced welfare work on a daily basis. A consideration of labor's role raises important questions: What did workers think about welfare programs and the employers who initiated them? Did the presence of welfare work affect labor productivity and workers' resistance in the way employers hoped? Four of the most prominent labor organizations of the Progressive period, the American Federation of Labor, the Socialist Party (SP), the Industrial Workers of the World (IWW), and the Socialist Labor Party (SLP), frequently debated the merits of welfare work. As a practice gaining popularity and an ideology gaining support, welfare work had become too important a topic for organized labor to ignore.[1]

1. This analysis does not include the Amalgamated Clothing Workers, an organization exceptional in the Progressive era not only for its success in organizing immigrant workers along industrial lines but also for its support of expanded government authority and government-backed social welfare. See Steven Fraser, "Dress Rehearsal for the New Deal: Shop-Floor Insurgents, Political Elites, and Industrial Democracy in the Amalgamated

The tactical and philosophical differences separating labor organizations resulted in bitter exchanges over the strengths and weaknesses of the welfare movement. Each group was determined to educate rank-and-file workers about welfare work in its own way; each was committed to defining the possibilities and limitations of industrial reform on its own terms. The disputes reveal some of the fundamental differences in labor leaders' assessment of private workplace reforms, differences that often mirrored rank-and-file workers' mixed feelings about welfare work.

The American Federation of Labor and Welfare Work

Leaders of the American Federation of Labor, the largest labor organization in the Progressive period, gave welfare programs a mixed review. On the one hand, they publicly endorsed welfare work through their collaboration with the National Civic Federation, of which Gompers was vice president from its founding in 1900 until his death in 1924. On the other, they repeatedly cautioned workers to stay alert to employers' ulterior motives for instituting workplace reforms, motives that often conflicted with employees' separate interests. While recognizing that many instances of private sector philanthropy immediately improved workers' experience, the AFL worried that workers would become so impressed by reforms that they would forget that their oppositional class position necessitated independent action and organization. The AFL also saw welfare work as a threat to the craft union's longtime role as a provider of benefits. Like ethnic associations, trade unions in the Progressive era cemented their popularity with working people in part by offering members a variety of protections, from sick benefits, to pensions, to burial insurance. It was imperative for the AFL's survival for workers to identify unions as a more trustworthy source of benefits than business. Welfare work, the AFL insisted, must not displace the workers' quest for self-advancement or the organization that gave that quest focus and meaning, the trade union.

The AFL's pro-welfare position commended the movement's practical reforms and the antistatist way in which it delivered them. The

---

Clothing Workers," in *Working-Class America: Essays on Labor, Community, and American Society*, ed. Michael H. Frisch and Daniel J. Walkowitz (Urbana: University of Illinois Press, 1983), pp. 212–55; idem, *Labor Will Rule: Sidney Hillman and the Rise of American Labor* (Ithaca: Cornell University Press, 1993).

organization's most forceful expression of support was the 1907 pamphlet *The Trade Unions' Attitude toward Welfare Work*, by J. S. Sullivan, president of the Central Federated Union of New York City. To the extent that welfare work supplemented union goals, Sullivan declared, it was a treasured ally in the fight for better conditions. Pragmatic necessity required the union man to concern himself with negotiating higher wages and shorter hours, the most important variables affecting work conditions. But "even after the rules of the unions . . . are in force," Sullivan asserted, "something else is needed to improve the conditions of employees." Enter welfare work. While unions focused on wages and hours, welfare work addressed broader but vital concerns such as workers' education, safety, and comfort. As Gompers himself put it, "It is clearly recognized that the first essentials to the welfare of employees are steady work, a fair wage and reasonable hours of labor; but . . . the employer has a further obligation . . . [to] take up those matters which relate to the physical and social well-being of employees." Trade unions and welfare work thus shared a complementary objective: the uplift and advance of American labor.[2]

The AFL also applauded welfare work's antistatism. AFL leaders had long opposed government regulation of male workers' wages and hours, fearing that labor laws for men would established standards inferior to those union bargaining could attain. Once the union bequeathed to government the power to negotiate wages and hourly rates, moreover, it permanently forfeited the right to bargain for these things as union men. Likening the court system to Greeks who "bore gifts and [then] attempted to entrap . . . workmen into a species of slavery," Gompers denounced government regulation on the grounds that "once a court has jurisdiction over an individual, it has the power to exercise the field and authority of that jurisdiction."[3]

When statutory enactments circumscribed the range of women's economic activity, however, AFL leaders took a different stand. "I think it is generally regarded that . . . minor women, anyway, and women, perhaps, generally, are the Wards of the Nation," Gompers explained to

2. J. W. Sullivan, *The Trade Unions' Attitude toward Welfare Work* (New York: Welfare Department of the National Civic Federation, 1907), p. 3, State Historical Society of Wisconsin (hereafter SHSW); interview with Gertrude Beeks in "Welfare Work May Conquer Great Labor Problems," *New York Times*, November 17, 1913, p. 1; Samuel Gompers to Morris Hillquit, July 21, 1911, American Federation of Labor Papers, President's Office, General Correspondence, Box 14, Folder 2, SHSW.

3. U.S. Senate, Commission on Industrial Relations, *Final Report and Testimony of the U.S. Commission on Industrial Relations*, 64th Cong., 1st sess. (Washington, D.C.: Government Printing Office, 1916), 2:1499, 1525.

rationalize state provisions for women. The AFL's view of state protections as applying specifically to women fueled its support for voluntary reforms for men. Like welfare employers, AFL leaders equated dependency on the state with emasculation. Their vision of masculinity was interwoven with workers' cultural and economic autonomy—workers' authority as men of skill to hold their own on the shop floor. Welfare work fortified the AFL's masculine vision by improving work conditions without encouraging "effeminate" dependency. Workers' manhood was safeguarded through benefits they earned as skilled breadwinners, not generic citizens in need. Moreover, workers collected the benefits without a third party intervening in matters that hitherto had been negotiated "freely" between manly workers and employers.[4]

But although AFL leaders supported welfare work in principle, they often rejected it in practice. In a 1913 editorial entitled "The Good and Bad of 'Welfare Work,'" Gompers articulated his ambivalence about the movement. Of pressing concern was the encomia welfare programs generated in the press. Gompers did not dispute that workplace reforms warranted praise, but he feared that media enthusiasm would brand reforms atypical and abnormal. Instead of opening the door to more and better improvements, the press's unbridled excitement would slow the reform impetus by legitimating the unimproved workplace as the norm. The celebratory fervor greeting welfare firms found heroism in acts of common decency. The Bureau of Labor Statistics' 1913 welfare work bulletin was a case in point. The bureau happily observed that at the International Harvester Company, "the drinking water is everywhere pure." "This astounding good deed . . . perhaps merits public commendation and notice," Gompers responded sarcastically. "Perhaps it really is a matter of great self-restraint and inhibition of vicious impulses on the part of the management to refrain from furnishing water polluted by disease, germs and dirt." The decent treatment of workers ought to be too routine a feature of em-

4. As Ann Schofield has argued, the AFL in the Progressive era asserted an ideology of gender difference, embodied in the idea of the "union maid," that accepted conventional female roles and thus reinforced a traditional sexual division of labor in the workplace and in the home. See Schofield, "Rebel Girls and Union Maids: The Woman Question in the Journals of the AFL and IWW, 1905–1920," *Feminist Studies* 9 (Summer 1983): 335–58. On the relationship between laborers' manliness and skill, see Lisa Fine, " 'Our Big Factory Family': Masculinity and Paternalism at the Reo Motor Car Company of Lansing, Michigan," *Labor History* 34 (Spring–Summer 1993): 275; David Montgomery, *Workers' Control in America: Studies in the History of Work, Technology, and Labor Struggles* (New York: Cambridge University Press, 1979), pp. 11–15.

ployment to warrant special acclaim. That such provisions were still so unusual was cause for alarm, not celebration. Gompers concluded his diatribe with a pointed plea: "Let welfare work become what it should be—conscience work."[5]

AFL leaders also expressed concern that employers sometimes used welfare work to smother workers' independence. Although "progressive" businessmen might appropriate the "vocabulary and the proposals of idealism," Gompers cautioned, nothing that "even the devil may quote scripture," welfare work frequently became an epithet for employer control. The challenge for workers was to know when the line separating good and bad welfare work had been crossed. The AFL "contends that welfare work should be developed in so far as necessary," the organization's official organ, the *American Federationist*, proclaimed, but it "does not admit that the workman is a dub and must have things done for him. . . . The best kind of American citizen, stands on his own feet."[6]

The fear of beleaguered manhood that underwrote the AFL's opposition to government reform was evident here. Again associating dependency with emasculation, the *American Federationist* expressed its determination to "stand for a policy and system that will develop real men; men of intelligence, men of courage, independence, good workmanship and responsibility, who pulsate with the discontent that makes men divine." Manly unionists would not support a paternalistic feudalism characterized by employer dominance and employee submission; as self-respecting men, they would resist efforts to transform them into effeminate toadies. In the final analysis, benevolent feudalism would fail to force a union man to relinquish his most cherished desire: to fend for himself. In the end, the only organization capable of protecting workers' dignity and manliness was the trade union itself in a solidarity forged through craft autonomy.[7]

AFL leaders urged workers to enjoy the practical fruits of welfare reforms while simultaneously cautioning them not to succumb to paternalist entrapment. But the mixed messages of their critique ultimately left it up to the rank and file to determine for themselves when

5. U.S. Bureau of Labor Statistics, *Employers' Welfare Work*, Bulletin 123 (1913), p. 15; Samuel Gompers, "The Good and Bad of Welfare Work," *American Federationist* 20 (December 1913): 1041.

6. Ibid.; Samuel Gompers, "Wages and Health," *American Federationist* 21 (August 1914): 643; "Contented Cows," *American Federationist* 30 (September 1923): 761–62.

7. "Contented Cows," pp. 760–62.

the price tag of benefits was betrayal. For other labor groups, the AFL's qualified endorsement of welfare work came to symbolize much more.

The Labor Left and Welfare Work

Unlike the American Federation of Labor, the Socialist Party, the Industrial Workers of the World, and the Socialist Labor Party found nothing beneficial in welfare work. To be sure, these groups disagreed among themselves about many labor matters. The Socialist Party, enjoying mounting political popularity since its establishment in 1901 in the merger of several socialist groups, advocated electoral politics as the best way to achieve collective ownership of industry. Although the IWW enjoyed the backing of many prominent Socialist, it pursued a different tactic. It championed the inevitability of a strike waged by "one big union," a militant union of unskilled and skilled, native-born and foreign-born, that would destroy the wage system and decentralize industry by giving the people as a whole the power to run it. The Socialist Labor Party claimed to preach a more dogmatic and revolutionary brand of socialism than that espoused by the SP. Founded in 1877, the SLP emphasized political education, party building, and industrial unionism as the best strategies for ushering in a more humane society. Notwithstanding each group's separate ideology, they stood united in their critique of welfare work and the AFL's support of it. These groups, which were less likely than the AFL to represent workers employed at welfare firms, made the AFL-NCF alliance the basis for a stirring appeal to encourage rank-and-file workers to join labor organizations that would not betray their interests by embracing capitalist handouts.

From the perspective of the labor left, the motive behind welfare work was clear. Pensions, bowling teams, and other benefactions were not, as the capitalist press insisted, outgrowths of a newly found humanitarianism. Rather, they were part of a capitalist trick to confuse workers' loyalties and dissolve class solidarity under the banner of industrial harmony. But capitalist reform did not mean a better deal for workers, as a poem published in 1913 in the radical magazine *The Masses* made clear:

> Sing a song of "Welfare,"
> A pocket full of tricks
> To soothe the weary worker

When he groans or kicks.
If he asks for shorter hours
   Or for better pay,
Little stunts of "Welfare"
Turn his thoughts away.

Sing a song of "Welfare,"
   Sound the horn and drum,
Anything to keep the mind
   Fixed on Kingdom Come.
"Welfare" loots your pocket
   While you dream and sing,
"Welfare" to your pay check
   Doesn't do a thing.

Sing a song of "Welfare,"
   Forty 'leven kinds,
Elevate your morals,
   Cultivate your minds.
Kindergartens, nurses,
   Bathtubs, books, and flowers,
Anything but better pay
   Or shorter working hours.[8]

The IWW, the SLP, and the SP were united in their condemnation of welfare schemes by their insistence that only the radical restructuring of both the ownership and operation of production could improve labor's lot. Piecemeal reforms gave workers short shrift. On the surface, welfare work might appear to make the immediate experience of being a wage earner seem more tolerable. But improvements were superficial. Welfare work masked capitalism's most egregious symptoms without eradicating the structural source of workers' woes. But educated workers would not be fooled. They would learn to recognize "capitalist treachery" for what it was and refuse to exchange short-term benefits for long-term justice. To this end, the IWW, SLP, and SP assumed the task of educating laborers, using editorials, essays, and even poems to set the record straight. A sampling of some of their favorite targets—

8. Will Heford, "Welfare Song," quoted in *Echoes of Revolt: The Masses, 1911–1917,* ed. William L. O'Neill (Chicago: Ivan R. Dee, 1989), p. 88.

employee dining facilities, pensions, and profit-sharing plans—illustrates the common strands of their critique.

Company cuisine was a primary target. According to the IWW, one man's feast was cause for another's famine. "Although "outsiders . . . write long orations about [employees'] healthy and wholesome food," the IWW reported, the reality of firms' culinary concoctions "is far from what it is represented." At the Chicago Telephone Company standard fare for female employees was beans, Campbell's soup, and boiled bologna. "Only those girls who have to eat it do so," the IWW newspaper *Solidarity* asserted. "The majority never touch it. . . . The food is poorly cooked and disgusting to the palate." Dessert—a cup of coffee or tea and an apple—afforded no relief. "The coffee and tea is so cheap and badly prepared that it is enough to give an operator a nervous malady."[9]

Workers who ignored the deficiencies of company food and "boldly" ate it, labor spokespersons reported, did so only out of economic necessity. Company food was usually subsidized and thus cheaper to buy than food elsewhere. At Chicago's Sears, Roebuck, for example, inexpensive lunches available at the employee restaurant saved workers about 70 cents a week. But as the Socialist Party observed, it was the company, not the workers, that profited most from the subsidy. Had the company not built the restaurant, Sears would have been forced to increase workers' wages almost $3 a month to compensate for the cost of lunches bought at market prices. With the company restaurant providing low-cost meals, the company could justify abnormally low wages. The company profited in two ways: first, by paying substandard wages, and second, through the accolades it received for its apparent generosity to workers.[10]

The labor left similarly denounced the "veiled peonage" of pension plans. Pensions were viewed as a "carrot," encouraging employees to tolerate a life's worth of oppression, low wages, and deplorable conditions for the illusory promise of ultimate financial security. Because eligibility for pensions required a high minimum length of employment and because pensions were not portable, workers had to ensure that

9. "Hello Girls: How the Chicago Telephone Company Sweats the Last Penny of Profit from Its Slaves at the Exchange," *Solidarity*, January 25, 1913, p. 1. For an equally blistering indictment of company food, see "Carnegie Company Bosses 'Entertain' Slaves at the Latter's Expense," *Solidarity*, July 8, 1911, p. 1.

10. Phillips Russell, "A Study in Distribution: Sears, Roebuck & Company," *International Socialist Review* 12 (January 1912): 424.

their work performance did not jeopardize their standing with the company. As a result, workers suppressed their natural instinct to resist capitalist exploitation with the hope that their passivity would be rewarded at retirement. The labor left questioned how many employees would live to the age of retirement; for most workers, the promise of a pension would be unfulfilled. As the *Weekly People* commented after the Chicago packing firm of Morris and Company established employee pensions, "It sounds grandiose to say that 20,000 will benefit by such a scheme. How many of them, though, will reach the age in which the pension becomes operative? How many of them will survive the accidents that are yearly killing and injuring thousands upon thousands of mill and railroad employees? How many of them can withstand the terrific strain imposed upon them until they reach the pensionable age?"[11]

The labor left also criticized profit sharing. To the extent that profit sharing promised workers a piece of the capitalist pie, it was the most dangerous and subversive reform measure. "Wall street has a standing joke," the IWW reported. "It says that today you don't need to club a workingman. Neither is it necessary to bayonet him, when he becomes rebellious over conditions—just hand him a sugar-coated pill, label it 'profit-sharing' and the job is done." Profit sharing gave workers a financial incentive to accept their status as wage earners. In search of an additional few cents, the employee was required to enter into partnership with the employer in which class divisions were transcended by the shared pursuit of money. But as the labor left reminded workers, "profit sharing does not free labor from competition in the labor market, from labor-displacing machinery, or efficiency systems, all of which determine original wages, destroy jobs, and render participation in profits uncertain." In the end, profit sharing, like all welfare work, was yet another capitalist trick to induce employees to work harder for nothing. Profit sharing, the IWW maintained, is "not a partnership, but an insult to the intelligence.... It is worthy of the 'Progressive,' ie. ultracapitalist intellect that evolved it. But it will not fool anyone, except those who think they are fooling others with it."[12]

11. "Veiled Peonage," *Weekly People*, January 2, 1909, p. 4; "A Capitalist Gold Brick: Old Age Pension Schemes That Benefit a Few Only," *Weekly People*, January 18, 1902, p. 1.

12. "Profit Sharing Humbug of the United States Steel Corporation," *Solidarity*, October 8, 1910, p. 4; "Profit Sharing: An Old Humbug with a New Advocate," *Solidarity*, July 19, 1913, p. 1; "Profit Sharing," *Weekly People*, October 24, 1903, p. 1; "Steel Trust

Labor leaders expressed confidence that the rank and file would not be duped by welfare capitalists' piecemeal solutions. "The Socialist can well afford to laugh to scorn such dodges of an alarmed capitalist class, knowing that no move of theirs can forestall their doom," assured the Socialist Labor Party. "For the time it may divert attention from the real issue, but for a time only." The IWW concurred. The educated efforts of labor's real friends would expose the treachery of reform capitalism. Once workers understood that "no reform advocates the abolition of capitalism which is the cause of working class misery," they would sever emotional ties with the employer class and act collectively in their best interest. The enlightened laborer would cast off the chains of philanthropic oppression, they averred. It was only a matter of time. In the long run, "dissatisfaction over wages, a long workday . . . and other necessary accompaniments even of capitalist 'philanthropy' . . . will again penetrate the skulls of workers in 'model factories' and drive them into rebellion against their masters. The worker will finally insist on 'taking care of himself.' " Then he, and not his employer, would become master of his fate.[13]

But the labor left reassured too much. The IWW, the SP, and the SLP rarely missed an opportunity to voice their confidence that welfare work was doomed. The frequency and pointedness of their assurances told a different story, one anchored not in confidence but in anxiety and doubt. Wobblies and Socialists were united not only in their opposition to welfare capitalism but in their fear that it would do precisely what they claimed it would not: make the rank and file content with a slightly improved, but structurally unmodified, capitalist system. Next to employers themselves, the group they held most accountable for planting the traitorous seeds of labor quiescence was the American Federation of Labor.

'Welfare Schemes' Work against Welfare of Employees," *Weekly People*, March 2, 1913, p. 1; "Great Profit Sharing: Magnanimous Condescension of Switch Company," *Weekly People*, August 19, 1912, p. 1; "Music to the Slaves," *Solidarity*, September 6, 1913, p. 2; "Profit Sharing: The Steel Trust Gives a Practical Demonstration of Its Meaning," *Weekly People*, October 24, 1903, p. 1; "The Law of Competition," *Solidarity*, March 22, 1913, p. 2.

13. "Profit Sharing Scheme to Fasten Chains of Slavery Forever about Workers," *Weekly People*, January 26, 1909, p. 1; *Solidarity*, May 11, 1912, p. 2; "Capitalist Philanthropy," *Solidarity*, December 17, 1910; " 'Welfare Work': Trolley and Railroad Men Receive No Benefit from Scheme," *Weekly People*, August 14, 1909, p. 2; "Trust Beneficence: Pensions, Stockholding and Other 'Benefits' for Employees Only Devices to Head off Socialism," *Weekly People*, January 17, 1903.

A Crisis of Masculinity and Representation

As qualified and contingent as the AFL's support of welfare work was, left-wing labor groups latched onto it as proof of the trade union movement's ineptitude to lead the masses. They parlayed AFL support of welfare work, evidenced most tangibly by its alliance with the NCF, into an all-out war on AFL leadership and the trade union movement. Their belligerence was informed by a vision of labor masculinity that rooted manhood in defiance and physical virility rather than the autonomy of the craftsman. According to the labor left, AFL support for welfare work and the NCF revealed not only the economic ignorance of the trade union movement but also its willingness to sacrifice labor manhood to effeminate capitalism.

Unlike the AFL, the labor left pronounced *all* welfare schemes intrinsically emasculating. Contesting the AFL's association of masculinity with craftsman solidarity, the labor left constructed labor masculinism around metaphors of strength and struggle, military metaphors that emphasized the fighting spirit of the common manual worker. The language of left-wing labor masculinity invited a comparison between the militancy of the labor left and the pacificism of trade unionism. The common worker might not be as skilled or as privileged as his AFL counterpart, but at least he was not a puppet of capitalism. His brute strength and fighting instinct would throw off the chains of capitalist oppression. In the end, the labor left asserted, this philosophy was a better claim to, and a better kind of, manhood.[14]

The labor left press couched its critique of welfare capitalism in recognizably gendered terms. "Long term 'agreements,' insurance, pensions, profit sharings and the like," the Socialist Labor Party reported in 1903, "proceed from the theory that the workingman, so long as his belly is filled, is willing to abdicate his manhood and resign himself like cattle to the safety of the arrangement." The IWW's William D. "Big Bill" Haywood concurred. Commenting in 1911 on the growing popularity of pension schemes, he observed that "pensions by govern-

14. For IWW imagery and metaphors, see Francis Schor, "Masculine Power and Virile Syndicalism: A Gendered Analysis of the IWW in Australia," *Labour History* 63 (November 1992): 83–99; Joyce L. Kornbluh, *Rebel Voices: An I.W.W. Anthology* (Ann Arbor: University of Michigan Press, 1964); also see Elizabeth Faue, *Community of Suffering and Struggle: Women, Men and the Labor Movement in Minneapolis, 1915–1945* (Chapel Hill: University of North Carolina Press, 1991), pp. 71–75.

ments create serfs. Pensions by capitalists make unwilling slaves. In either instance they must violate some manly principle."[15]

In the same spirit and language, the labor left denounced the NCF, the welfare work movement's biggest supporter, for trying to enervate militant masculinity. The Socialist Party accused the federation of trying to destroy organized labor's "independence, virility and militant enthusiasm." In turn, to distinguish NCF men from "real" workingmen, NCF leaders were discussed and discredited through feminine metaphors. Labor left leaders portrayed the quintessential capitalist as small, effeminate, and weak. Ralph Easley, founder of the NCF, was "Sissy" Easley and the organization's "little boy." Andrew Carnegie was the "little Scot." NCF luminaries were described as "parasites" who gave "spread-eagle" speeches. Like women, they were fond of "meddling." In each of these rhetorical portraits, class and gender were inextricably linked. Not only were welfare capitalists and their toadies not blood-and-toil workers, the labor left insisted; in the final analysis, they were not even men.[16]

The AFL's involvement in the NCF made it guilty by association. As the foremost representatives of the rank and file, AFL leaders had forfeited their right to honest leadership and labor manliness by siding with effeminate capitalism. The *International Socialist Review*, the "Fighting Magazine of the Working Class," emphasized the AFL's docility and submission, accusing AFL leaders of "sit[ting] supinely by" and permitting capitalists to undermine workers' self-respect. Applying military metaphors toward different ends, the IWW likened AFL support of the NCF—its apparent willingness to sacrifice labor's interests to capitalism even as it pronounced itself labor's staunchest ally—to treason:

> What would you think of a General who, when he saw his infantry being destroyed would refuse to bring the cavalry and artillery and the other divisions of the army to their assistance? . . . And when you saw your General go into the enemy's camp, wining and dining with them,

15. "Trust Beneficence," p. 3; William D. Haywood, "Against Old Age Pensions," *International Socialist Review*, November 1911, p. 281.

16. Morris Hillquit to Ralph Easley, June 16, 1911, American Federation of Labor Papers, President's Office, General Correspondence, Box 14, Folder 5, SHSW; "Carnegie-Ridden," *Weekly People*, November 25, 1911, p. 1; "The World of Labor," *International Socialist Review*, March 1902, p. 690; "The World of Labor," *International Socialist Review*, June 1902, p. 854; "The World of Labor," *International Socialist Review*, January 1902, p. 546; "The World of Labor," *International Socialist Review*, April 1902, p. 673.

what would you think? . . . This typifies the tactics of the American
Federation of Labor, which is financed and directed by the Civic Federation, an organization that *has no other purpose than to emasculate workers* [emphasis added]. . . . It is not unreasonable nor unfair to say that
the A. F. of L. does not represent the American working class.[17]

The Socialist Labor Party likewise used the manliness of labor to distinguish Socialists from trade unionists. After denouncing AFL leaders as
"the greatest spies to be found in or out of [workers'] ranks," the
Socialist Labor Party declared itself to be the only organization "that
hold[s] out to the wage-workers the hope of a better future resulting
from manly . . . action."[18]

The president of the AFL did not take such accusations lightly. Privately and publicly Gompers denounced criticisms from the left and
defended his involvement with the NCF. In a twenty-eight-page letter
to Morris Hillquit, one of the most intellectually distinguished spokespersons of the left and chair of the national committee of the Socialist
Party, Gompers explicated and justified the AFL's position. Gompers
argued that despite Socialist claims, neither he nor other AFL leaders
believed that capital and labor had identical interests. They did, however, accept the permanence of the capitalist system. NCF support gave
organized labor new opportunities for instituting reforms to improve
the lives of those forced to labor in that system. According to Gompers,
the most divisive issue separating the AFL and Socialist positions was
not whether classes had competing interests or which organization best
defended labor manliness, but the issue of expedience. How long,
Gompers asked, should workers be forced to endure the misery of their
condition? The Socialists, claimed Gompers, maintained that relief—
from unemployment, poverty, exhaustion, and dangerous work—would
follow on the heels of a Socialist victory. But they offered no reliable
timetable as to when this Socialist paradise would arrive. "If we can
wait until the Socialist Party has captured the governments of this country, Federal, State and Municipal, and has taken over all the factories,
stores, railways, banks, mines and farms, a solution will be furnished
for such problems," Gompers wrote. "[But] I gather that the leaders
of the party themselves do not expect such a state of affairs to be

17. A Ledots, "The National Civic Federation," *International Socialist Review*, March
1910, p. 809; "Two Kinds of Unionism," *Solidarity*, March 14, 1910, p. 4.
18. "Civic Federation's Principles Exposed to All Who Can and Will See," *Weekly People*,
May 23, 1903, p. 1.

brought about in our time nor in the time of our children or even in the time of our children's children." The question was whether to wait for a Socialist win that might not occur "in this and many succeeding generations" or to address workers' needs in the present. "My dear Mr. Hillquit," Gompers queried, "should the people be obliged to wait until that time for reforms, admitting—which I don't—that such a change would mean reform? . . . I think I am safe in saying that ninety-nine percent of the wage-earners of the country would decide that they would rather have their conditions improved *now.*"[19]

Gompers cited the value of existing workplace reforms as evidence of the validity of the AFL's now-or-never strategy. "I do not mean to say that there is not much still to be done," he claimed, "but the hundreds and thousands of men and women in this country who have enlisted in the warfare against economic and industrial evils, through the various reform organizations, are a guarantee that the next decade is going to see still further accomplishments." He praised the work of the Welfare Department for improving "those matters which relate to the physical and social well-being of employees." Far from having produced "cheap and trivial" reforms, the Welfare Department had tangibly improved the quality of workers' lives. Most important, the relief had been immediate. "I can hardly believe that you would want to say that men and women wage-earners should continue to work under insanitary conditions which can be and are being improved daily," Gompers told Hillquit, "until such time as the Socialist Party can bring about its collective ownership and operation of all means of production and distribution [of] land."[20]

19. Samuel Gompers to Morris Hillquit, July 21, 1911, American Federation of Labor Papers, President's Office, General Correspondence, Box 14, Folder 2, SHSW. Gompers was also forced to contend with the National Association of Manufacturers' criticisms, which were as harsh as the Socialists', though for different reasons. The NAM denounced the Civic Federation for "its close alignment with the dominating influences of labor unionism," which it understood to be atheist and anarchical. The NAM's president, John Kirby, stated in the organization's journal:

> The American Federation of Labor is engaged in an open warfare against Jesus Christ and his cause. Analyze it as you may, you can make nothing else out of it, and those who profess Christ, yet hobnob with the leaders of that wicked conspiracy and give them encouragement by eating and drinking and smoking and holding social relations with them, cannot segregate themselves from the responsibility that attaches to such affiliation. On this issue, therefore, I challenge the National Civic Federation to disprove my charges, and if my conservatism is denounced as radicalism, then my mind goes back to Los Angeles, and I take refuge in the stand of Martin Luther: 'Here I stand, I can do nothing else; God help me!' " (Ibid.)

20. Ibid. Gompers's private defense of the National Civic Federation became a matter

To convince AFL members that his position on the NCF was sound, Gompers defended the AFL/NCF alliance in the *Federationist*. Gompers denounced Socialist criticism as "concerted, deliberate, theatrical, [and] manufactured." "In order to serve up their dish of scorn and derision to the taste of the ignorant," he wrote, "the Socialist leaders have thrown into it as constituent elements bitter misrepresentation, the heat of hatred, and the ginger of opprobrious epithet." Despite Socialist claims, he countered, the NCF's aims were advantageous to organized labor. The NCF provided an arena in which capital and labor could talk out their differences, in which "employers will at last be

---

of public record when Gompers and Hillquit squared off before the U.S. Commission on Industrial Relations in May 1914. The commission's chairman, Frank Walsh, instructed Gompers and Hillquit to make a preliminary statement and then engage in mutual cross-examination. Although many issues were discussed in the exchange, one that proved particularly contentious was Gompers's position as NCF vice-president. Hillquit relied on years of legal practice to force Gompers's hand. An excerpt from the commission's transcript reveals Hillquit at his finest:

MR. HILLQUIT. You have stated before, Mr. Gompers, that you believe that there was no harmony between the interests of the employing classes and those of the workers, and that you believe that the workers must depend upon their own efforts as workers, without the interventions of intellectuals, you say, or others, to secure the improvements. Now, I am asking you, do you believe that they can secure such improvements with the intervention of capitalists of the type that you have named in the Civic Federation?

MR. GOMPERS. . . . I can only judge of the people's acts, and I know their acts have never been hostile in the Civic Federation to the interests of the working people.

MR. HILLQUIT. Then, you would not think it is perfectly proper for an official representative of the American Federation of Labor to cooperate with well-known capitalist employers for common ends?

MR. GOMPERS . . . . There is no such thing as cooperation between the leaders of the labor movement and the leaders of the National Civic Federation . . . so far as I am concerned, I can go anywhere where men assemble and where they consider the question affecting the working people . . . and if I can influence them to any act of helpfulness toward any one thing in which the working people are interested I have accomplished something. . . . I will appeal to the devil and his mother-in-law to help labor if the labor can be aided in that way.

MR. HILLQUIT. And will you cooperate?

MR. GOMPERS. Let me say this: The question comes with ill grace when Socialists are butting in everywhere. . . .

MR. HILLQUIT. Let's not try to evade the question. . . . Now Mr. Gompers, you have drawn the parallel between the National Civic Federation and the devil and his grandmother. Now, I am asking you, will you go to the extent—will you expect the devil or his grandmother to aid the American labor movement, and would you cooperate with him?

CHAIRMAN WALSH. Please proceed to some other question. (U.S. Senate, Commission on Industrial Relations, *Final Report and Testimony*, 2:1540–41)

made to listen to the demands of workers." AFL leaders, Gompers explained to readers, "have simply taken advantage of a circumstance and an opportunity to bring about some advantage to labor without in the least impairing either the efficiency or the militancy of the labor movement."[21]

Gompers upheld similar views in his private correspondence. "Let me say," he confided to John Henley, president of the New York Trades Assembly, "that no trade unionist, nor does the Civic Federation, pretend, much less declare, that the interests of workmen and capitalists are identical." Notwithstanding class differences, labor profited from frank discussions with capital. The NCF helped labor's cause by forcing employers to acknowledge that in a modern industrial age, "workmen have the right jointly to have a voice in the final settlement of the conditions under which they shall labor." In the final analysis, the opportunities facilitated by the NCF upheld the AFL's maxim to do "anything that will help to bring about improvement in the condition of the working people."[22]

Gompers's public and private defenses attest to his fear that criticisms from the labor left were costing the AFL support. Gompers came to view the federation's stand on welfare work as the organization's Achilles' heel, requiring constant justification. Until his death, Gompers continued to delineate the boundaries between acceptable and unacceptable welfare work, eager to clarify the AFL's stand and protect its credibility.

For the labor left, the debate over welfare work encapsulated fundamental differences between trade unionism and left-wing approaches to the "labor problem." The labor left made the most of these differences, emphasizing dissimilarities of strategy and objective to show the rank and file that all labor organizations were not alike. While trade unionists settled for piecemeal reforms, the labor left demanded revolution; while trade unionists cooperated with employers, the labor left conspired to reveal capitalists as traitors.

By gendering its critique of welfare capitalism, the labor left also endeavored to make an individual worker's stand in the welfare debate a measure of his manhood. Although rank-and-file women workers rejected welfare programs for the same reasons men did, no organized

21. Samuel Gompers, "Organized Labor and the National Civic Federation," *American Federationist* 18 (March 1911): 181–89.

22. Samuel Gompers to John J. Henley, March 20, 1911, American Federation of Labor Papers, President's Office, General Correspondence, Box 14, Folder 2, SHSW.

labor group defended women workers as "welfare victims" with conviction. In one sense, to do so would have been to unravel the very fabric of the gender system: if women were found to prefer self-reliance and independence to dependence and charity as much as men, then the requisite ingredients of masculinity—and therefore masculinity itself—would have been called into question. Instead of supporting less rigid gender roles that would have permitted behavioral fluidity, organized labor remained conspicuously silent about the problems welfare work posed to women who happened to be breadwinners. At the same time, the fact that welfare work was organized principally for and administered by women predisposed labor leaders to couch discussions of resistance in masculine terms. Labor masculinity was defined in *opposition* to what was correctly perceived as a feminized movement.

For both these reasons, assertions of labor masculinity framed organized labor's critique of welfare schemes. Real men would not be ensnared by effeminate schemes; it stood to follow, of course, that those who did were not real men. More than a prescribed behavioral code, the labor left's vision of masculinity served as a political rallying cry, demanding that workers prove their manhood by declaring associational loyalties.

In the final analysis, the acrimonious debates over welfare work signaled just how significant it had become to industrial relations in Progressive America. The AFL, the IWW, the SLP, and the SP recognized welfare work for what it was: one answer to the labor question in America. Its fate, they acknowledged, was inseparable from that of the larger worker movement. Against this backdrop, the frequency and intensity of their discussions are significant. Supplying a means for highlighting ideological and organizational distinctions, the debates on welfare work also provided a forum for educating the rank and file about the larger costs and consequences of private workplace reform, something on which their own survival was staked.

In the end, however, the trickle-down guidance of labor leaders was of only limited value to those on the receiving end. The plethora of advice notwithstanding, rank-and-file workers used their own moral compass to decide at what point welfare work became something owed rather than something earned.

6 /

The Rank and File

While the labor left denounced welfare programs and the American Federation of Labor questioned their authenticity, enterprises such as Heinz praised their efficacy. The very schemes the IWW insisted would fail to captivate workers' attention the Heinz company credited with improving its labor force; since the introduction of welfare work, Heinz management alleged in 1903, employees had begun to display "universal enthusiasm . . . abundant good humor, [and] a keen and earnest interest in and love for . . . work." While the IWW talked of incessant class conflict and inevitable revolution, the Heinz company spoke only of unity between employer and employed, the "mutual and united cooperation of the [Heinz] family."[1]

The credibility of such accounts is compromised by the tendentious spirit that engendered them. As one would expect, both organized labor and welfare firms portrayed welfare work in a self-serving fashion. Evidence of the failure of industrial conciliation was critically important to the IWW; if workers accepted the premise of industrial harmony,

---

1. H. J. Heinz Company, *The Home of the 57* (Pittsburgh, 1903), p. 5; idem, *The Growth of a Great Industry* (Pittsburgh, 1910), both included in H. J. Heinz Company to Boston Chamber of Commerce, April 8, 1913, Boston Chamber of Commerce Collection (hereafter BCCC), Case 48, Folder 332–19, Baker Library Archives of the Harvard Graduate School of Business (hereafter BL).

the IWW's forecast of inevitable class conflict would seem untenable. Likewise, businesses spending thousands of dollars on welfare programs wanted both to justify expenditures to shareholders and to reap the benefits of public support by pronouncing their benevolence to labor a smashing success. Each group's characterization of labor's responses to welfare work unpacked a predetermined agenda, disclosing more about the opinions of organized labor and business than about those of workers themselves.

Labor polemics and business propaganda thus leave unanswered a question critical to assessing the significance of industrial welfarism: What did the thousands of rank-and-file workers who experienced welfare work on a daily basis think about the programs their employers established? Did it alter their work performance, affect their attitude toward the company, or reduce the likelihood of strikes? Employees exhibited no single universal response to welfare work. Instead, their actions elucidate a complicated pattern of participation in, resistance to, and modification of welfare work. Even under the roof of a single company, rank-and-file workers accepted employee benefits but also struck against fundamental inequities within the workplace.

Employee Participation

The longevity of many welfare programs suggests that a significant number of employees participated in welfare work. As an efficiency measure, employers had little use for welfare work unless it "worked"; that is, unless turnover and absenteeism decreased, productivity improved, or signs of industrial strife diminished. That the welfare work movement lasted as long as it did and that its legacy persists through personnel and human resource management in the corporate world today indicate that many employers were pleased with how workers' responses to welfare programs affected output.

Employees' interest in welfare work took different forms. Some workers openly endorsed employer-sponsored programs. At NCR, fifty recipients of the company's coveted suggestion prizes signed a letter to president John Patterson praising his generosity to workers. At the Cleveland Twist Drill Company, employees unanimously signed a petition thanking the company for the numerous "comforts and conveniences" it had provided. More frequently, however, employees exhibited interest in welfare programs simply by participating in them. By joining a firm's profit-sharing or pension plan, by attending company baseball tourna-

ments or cooking classes, workers accepted welfare work at least super-
ficially by setting aside time for it in their lives.[2]

Simply stated, workers participated because they discerned some benefit in doing so. For most employees, the maxim that an employer
"cannot make wages too high or surroundings too pleasant" had a
certain irrefutable logic. All things being equal, a firm with substantial
employee benefits was more attractive than one without. Why risk life
and limb at company X when company Y down the street had installed
safety devices and rewarded a worker's efforts with a one-week paid
vacation? In times of labor scarcity, employers recognized that it was a
seller's market: the better the benefits, the more likely employers were
to attract and retain workers.

Employers acknowledged welfare work's marketability to those in
search of employment. Lena Harvey discovered early on in her career
as NCR's first social secretary the importance of perquisites to labor
recruitment. After outlining the company's welfare policy to female
wage earners at the National Working Girls' Convention in April 1897,
Harvey was surrounded by women eager to learn more about NCR's
prospects. Most of the women in Harvey's audience were employed in
firms where long hours, low wages, and harsh working conditions were
routine: one commented that a sixteen-hour day was the shortest shift
available at a local silk mill. The same worker responded to Harvey's
description of NCR welfare work by exclaiming, "It would be heaven
to work in a factory like that!" All were curious to know whether Harvey
believed that NCR's innovations would mean that "girls working elsewhere [will] get some of these advantages."[3]

The aspects of welfare work that employees construed as beneficial
varied by program and company. There were, however, some common
reasons prompting employee participation. One was the opportunity
of a paid reprieve from the drudgery of industrial labor. If the company

2. Alfred A. Thomas, *Asking for Suggestions from Employees* (Dayton: National Cash Register Co., 1904), p. 117; R. E. Phillips, "The Betterment of Working Life," *World's Work*, December 1900, p. 165, quoted in Stuart D. Brandes, *American Welfare Capitalism, 1880–1940*
(Chicago: University of Chicago Press, 1976), p. 137. Employers often quantified employee
participation in welfare programs. Sears, Roebuck & Co. found that 91% of eligible employees joined the company's pension system within the first eighteen months after its introduction. When the Bureau of Labor Statistics surveyed thirty-seven profit-sharing
establishments in 1916, nineteen—over half—reported that more than 80% of eligible employees were participating in company profit-sharing programs. See Louis A. Boettiger, *Employee Welfare Work: A Critical and Historical Study* (New York: Ronald Press, 1923), p. 178;
U.S. Bureau of Labor Statistics, *Profit Sharing in the United States*, Bulletin 208 (1917), p. 19.
3. Lena Harvey Tracy, *How My Heart Sang: The Story of Pioneer Industrial Welfare Work*
(New York: Richard R. Smith, 1950), pp. 108–9.

agreed to pay employees to do something more pleasurable than wage work, they welcomed the change of pace. At the Scovill Company, employees enjoyed daily singing breaks as a distraction from the monotony of munitions manufacture. The breaks were particularly popular because the song leader permitted workers to sing songs of *their* choice. As one elderly employee in the packing room said, "The 'Sings' are grand; if it wasn't for them I'd never hear . . . new songs." The song leader toured factory departments throughout the day; every worker was allocated a fifteen-minute recess in which to break out into a rousing chorus of "My Wild Irish Rose," "Don't Cry Frenchy Don't Cry," or "An Old Sweetheart of Mine"—songs suggested by employees and approved by management.[4]

At NCR, employees looked forward to daily recesses for calisthenics. One employee explained that "when you sit still all day, a few minutes for exercise and conversation do you good." At the Joseph Bancroft and Sons Company, female employees flocked to cooking classes, also held on company time. The classes became so popular that factory foremen eventually complained that they hampered productivity. At the Ferris Brothers Company of Newark, women workers enjoyed the company's vacation home at the seaside so much that they refused to return to work promptly. Feeling that the paid vacation impeded rather than improved factory efficiency, the company abandoned the benefit. At one department store, employees turned noon-hour dances to their advantage, deliberately overstaying the assigned time to dance their way into the afternoon shift. Here again, workers' purposeful and frequent misuse of a benefit eventually resulted in its termination.[5]

Employees also participated in welfare work programs that promised financial gain. Companies frequently provided cash incentives to cajole workers into performing a wide array of tasks, from keeping an attractive garden to designing a persuasive advertisement. At NCR, for instance, workers could augment wages with prizes won in company contests. When NCR held a contest for the best poster advertisement,

4. John H. Goss to George A. Goss, March 1, 1920; Helen Duncan to Captain Gallaudet, March 20, 1920; distributed songsheet, ca. 1920, all in Scovill Manufacturing Co. Papers, Case 33, Folder "Rest Periods—Singing, 1919–1920," BL.

5. "N.C.R. Welfare Work," *Woman's Welfare* 2 (March 1904): 7; "Factory and Home Conditions of Employees," lecture by Elizabeth Briscoe to the welfare work class at New York University held under the auspices of the National Civic Federation, April 21, 1913, National Civic Federation Papers, Box 84, New York Public Library; report of Gertrude Beeks, July 30, 1901, Nettie Fowler McCormick Papers, Box 27, State Historical Society of Wisconsin (hereafter SHSW); U.S. Bureau of Labor Statistics, *Welfare Work for Industrial Employees*, Bulletin 250 (1919), p. 71.

more than three hundred employees competed for \$75 in prizes, most entrants stacking the deck with multiple entries. Even more popular was the NCR suggestion system. Posters throughout the factory outlined the benefits of participation: "Prizes given for complaints or suggestions for any improvements in the manufacture of registers." NCR's prizes were hardly superficial; it distributed over \$3,000 annually to employees whose suggestions or complaints were adopted. Such a lucrative incentive prompted a steady stream of suggestions—2,300 in 1903 alone.[6]

Indeed, the system became so popular with employees that at least one of NCR's unions, the Adjusters' and Assemblers' local 29, came to view it as a threat to workers' control of factory production. From the union's perspective, by making manufacturing faster and often more mechanized, the promotion of efficiency techniques put the indispensability of employees' skills and jobs in jeopardy. The union reprimanded workers who submitted suggestions. One worker in the brass cabinet department complained that after he made a suggestion, "The union chewed the rag with me and treated me pretty rough. They asked me what I did it for. I told them I did it just as other men made suggestions to show how the work could be better done and money and time saved." NCR management was acutely aware of how the disapproval of fellow workers might inhibit employee participation. To protect employees from the resentment of co-workers and the wrath of a foreman who decided that a worker had shown too much initiative, the company urged employees to submit suggestions anonymously, identifying themselves by a code clear only to themselves and management. Once the anonymity of the submitter was protected, employees continued to try to claim a share of the \$3,000 reward. Cash was a welcome addition to paychecks, and the letters of acknowledgment that accompanied reward payments supplied good credentials for future employment.[7]

6. Alfred A. Thomas, *Asking for Suggestions from Employees* (Dayton: National Cash Register Co., 1904), pp. 106, 124; William Ruehrwein, *A Wonderful Factory System* (1895; Dayton: National Cash Register Co., 1897), p. 3.

7. Thomas, *Asking for Suggestions*, pp. 5, 23; Alfred A. Thomas, *National Cash Register Factory as Seen by English Experts of the Mosely Industrial and Educational Commissions* (Dayton: National Cash Register Co., 1904), p. 96. Other employers also found cash incentives to be a good way to generate employee interest. W. G. Mather, president of the Cleveland Cliffs Iron Co., found the results of the company's prizes for well-kept premises "extremely satisfactory." He told the National Civic Federation Conference on Welfare Work that in the nine or ten years since the competition had been introduced, "competitors have been numerous and the general improvement of the town has been very marked.

Employees also took advantage of welfare work when it offered them practical conveniences or small luxuries to ease the strain of strenuous labor. At the turn of the century, these included benefits many workers today can take for granted: elevators in a multistory building, rest and sick rooms to retreat to in the event of illness, a place to eat one's lunch. Employees in the late nineteenth and early twentieth centuries viewed these reforms as novel and significant improvements. At NCR, workers perceived the provision of hot lunches as a meaningful amelioration. The sentiments expressed by one bindery worker probably represented those of others. "I . . . live too far away to go home at noon," she explained simply. Although intended to protect the sexual purity of women, NCR's policy of staggering male and female work schedules afforded many female workers their first opportunity to arrive at and leave work on time. Female employees were quick to appreciate the benefits of this policy. One worker claimed that before the new schedule went into effect, "young women [stood] on the corner in the bitter cold, while the men jumped on the cars ahead of them and laughed because they had to wait." Similarly, the NCR women's clubhouse supplied affordable, accessible room and board to women, enabling them to avoid the cost of daily commutes. As one worker explained, "Before going to the club house I paid $4.50 per week for board and room, without dinners. I had a nice room, well-heated, with use of the bath room. But that was down in the city, and I was compelled to take a car going to and coming from work thus making my expenses fifty cents more. Now I have just as nice a room and just as good meals, and a far pleasanter home for only $2.75 a week." An employee in the company's lock and drill department likewise expressed gratitude for the provision of high-backed chairs and footrests. "The advantage of comfortable chairs and foot stools is one which the average employer is inclined to overlook, but which has been given much attention in this factory," she stated. "Thoughtfulness in this regard . . . is appreciated by all of us." Although NCR introduced each of these measures chiefly to boost efficiency, the strong show of em-

---

The reasons are apparent. One man has a nice looking garden, and he gets recognition in the shape of a prize, and his neighbor, who may not have thought about improving the place, is immediately stimulated to do similar work, partly for the prize and partly through his aroused desire to have his premises look as well as those of his neighbor" (testimony of W. G. Mather in National Civic Federation, *Conference on Welfare Work* [New York: Andrew H. Kellogg, 1904], p. 41).

ployee support suggests that what benefited the company and its workers often overlapped.[8]

If welfare programs offered employees practical amenities, they also provided them with small luxuries—from ballroom dancing to needlepoint classes—often too tempting to resist. This was especially true for women workers, who were more likely to be the targeted beneficiaries of social programs than men. At Joseph Bancroft and Sons Company, Elizabeth Briscoe praised the success of the company's cooking classes, where "girls [take] a great deal of interest and [then] experiment . . . at home." At the Plymouth Cordage Company, women mill workers thanked welfare worker W. E. C. Nazro for organizing a cooking class by giving him a "bouquet of pinks" at their final session. Similarly, interest in the firm's first sewing class so exceeded anticipated demand that the company was forced to keep a waiting list. Female employees at Chicago's Marshall Field department store regularly patronized the store's library where they could borrow the latest women's magazines and books. Two years after the library was established, the monthly circulation had reached 5,000. At NCR taking baths in the company toilet rooms became a routine occurrence. As one worker explained, baths are a privilege "girls do not have at home."[9]

Welfare workers, employers, and union leaders commented on women workers' enthusiasm for welfare work. The participation of NCR women wage earners in welfare programs, for instance, earned them a reputation with management for being "generally disposed, and indeed, eager to educate and improve themselves in things connected with factory work." The same penchant for participation that delighted managers alarmed others. Annie Marion Maclean, a Chicago-based union advocate, lamented that "working women as a rule accept favors more readily than men, with the result that they are more prone to betray some of the characteristics of spoiled children."[10]

These observations do not prove that women as a group were, as a

8. "N.C.R. Welfare Work," *Woman's Welfare* 2 (March 1904): 5–14; Alfred A. Thomas, *How the Factory Grew and What It Does* (Dayton: National Cash Register Co., 1904), p. 81.

9. Briscoe, "Factory and Home Conditions of Employees"; reports of W. E. C. Nazro, June 1913 and August 1922, Plymouth Cordage Co. Papers, File I, Drawer I, Industrial Relations, Folder K, BL; Marshall Field & Co. to Boston Chamber of Commerce, April 19, 1913, BCCC, Case 48, Folder 332–19, BL.

10. Briscoe, "Factory and Home Conditions of Employees"; testimony of W. E. C. Nazro, welfare worker at Plymouth Cordage Co., in National Civic Federation, *Conference on Welfare Work*, p. 14; "N.C.R. Welfare Work," p. 11; Annie Marion MacLean, "Trade Unionism versus Welfare Work for Women," *Popular Science Monthly*, July 1915, p. 52.

rule, more accepting of welfare work than men. Rather, the disproportionately large number of welfare programs for women made their participation more conspicuous. In addition, the public component of
women's welfare schemes, whereby employers advertised female programs to offset concerns about the detrimental effects of wage work on
women, invited such observations. By the same token, the gendered
organization of programs supported the supposition that women were
more easily seduced by company "frills." Women's welfare work, favoring art appreciation, piano, and dance classes over pensions, was
generally more group-based than welfare programs for men. At their
inception, then, women's benefits were more likely to be noticed; companies could proudly display the end results of a sewing class but not
the pension subscription list. Finally, because women's programs were
often socially oriented and hence ostensibly more "frivolous," they
were more open to criticism from the unions and the labor left than
men's programs. Evidence of high turnouts at dance rehearsals or piano classes translated into a denunciation of women's preference for
company "spoils" rather than an acknowledgment of the gendered
orientation of programs themselves.

Indeed, if female employees enjoyed the luxury of company baths,
male workers seem to have been just as enthusiastic about company
showers, lockers, and changing rooms. Such amenities enabled working-class men to assert their masculinity through physical appearance
so they could look as respectable leaving work as they did upon arrival.
During prolonged periods of hard physical labor, one contemporary
observed, men's outer clothing "comes in contact with dust, oil, rust,
and becomes torn, untidy and dirty. The underclothing is saturated
with sweat. It is a hardship . . . to be obliged to wear this clothing
through the streets a long distance to the home. A man loses self-
respect in such a garb and the odor is offensive in the crowded and
close street cars."[11] *Engineering Magazine* agreed, advising employers that
the best way to facilitate greater efficiency among male workers was to
provide impeccably neat surroundings. "It is a sufficient concession to
their self-respect if they can mingle with the homeward bound street
crowd in a very moderate degree of cleanliness," the journal explained.
Confirming this perception, the Cleveland Hardware Company discovered that its male employees made frequent use of newly provided sanitary conveniences. The high usage debunked the myth that "men will

11. Charles Henderson, *Citizens in Industry* (New York: D. Appleton, 1915), pp.
77-78.

not use ... facilities ... provided by the employer," the company reported.[12]

Gertrude Beeks encountered a similar response to her efforts to "clean up" male workers at the International Harvester Corporation. Shortly after assuming her duties there as social secretary, Beeks, observing that male workers seemed perpetually dirty, asked a foreman if this was because male employees "like to be grimy." "Oh," the foreman responded, "that's natural to them." To test the foreman's theory, Beeks installed a row of deep washbasins, soap, clean towels, and new lockers in the men's quarters. Despite the foreman's prediction that "they'll go dirty, same as ever," the male employees began using the new facilities to clean themselves up.[13]

Supporting programs that reinforced their pride and dignity, workers of both sexes tended to be most enthusiastic about welfare programs brought about through their own initiative. Employees distinguished between welfare work "imposed from above" and that "suggested from below." As one labor management expert counseled, welfare work should be developed only because "the expanding consciousness of the workers calls for [it]. . . . Lunch rooms or showers or pianos should not be thrown at nor 'wished on' the workers, but should be introduced after a clear need and demand for them has arisen." NCR learned through trial and error of the importance of developing only those programs workers wanted. Few male employees participated in welfare functions until company president John Patterson called a mass meeting and urged them both "to take a more active share in their own way in welfare work" and to "suggest to him what they wanted to do." Employers proposed a "wish list" of things they believed would be beneficial, including the construction of a men's dining room and an athletic field. Patterson encouraged workingmen to elect three employees from each department to a "Men's Welfare Work League," to oversee construction. Once the dining room and athletic field had been built, employees expressed their appreciation through their patronage.[14]

12. Report of Mr. Hathaway, 1912, Plymouth Cordage Co. Papers, Case 47, Folder 6, "Efficiency Studies and Time Studies," BL.

13. Edwin Shuey, *Factory People and Their Employers: How Their Relations Are Made Pleasant and Profitable* (New York: Lentilhon, 1900), p. 25; O. M. Becker, "How to Increase Factory Efficiency: Cleanliness and Comfort," *Engineering Magazine* 51 (August 1916): 664; National Civic Federation, *Proceedings of the Eleventh Annual Meeting of the National Civic Federation* (New York, 1911), p. 347; Sarah Comstock, "A Woman of Achievement: Miss Gertrude Beeks," *World's Work* 26 (August 1913): 445.

14. Arthur J. Todd, "The Organization and Promotion of Industrial Welfare through

The Ludlow Manufacturing Company also learned the hard way that it paid to solicit employees' opinions *before* launching welfare work. The company built workers' housing to comply with a design made by managers, as if "we should be willing to occupy [the houses] ourselves." It was disappointed when employees responded with indifference; few made the new buildings their homes. The firm shifted tactics to discover "just what sort of homes the *people* wanted." Hoping to boost the popularity of company housing, company officials approached workers' wives and asked them to describe the "perfect" home. Using these composites, the company drafted new plans for employee housing. The solicitation paid off: the company found interest in the new housing complex "very satisfactory."[15]

Workers also participated in welfare work because some programs extended them a say in the workplace they might not otherwise have had. Work councils, representation plans, and such may not have offered workers the degree of control over factory decisions they would have liked, but for many employees, these innovations were better than nothing. Labor learned early on of the power of big business to mobilize outside support to suppress workers' quest for economic and political independence. When workers were given a choice between an employee representation plan and a long, bitter unionization campaign that might cost them their jobs—or, in the case of the Ludlow Massacre, their lives—the representation plan often seemed the better alternative. While the labor left accused Mother Jones of selling out to capitalism when she praised the Rockfellers for their generosity to labor after passage of the Colorado Fuel and Iron Company's Industrial Representation Plan, it ignored the limited bargaining power of miners in the coal fields of Colorado that fall of 1915. With management staunchly opposed to unions, the state backing management with military force, and the federal government demanding an expedient resolution to the crisis, Jones saw the representation plan as a temporary resolution to a potentially no-win situation.

At Filene's department store in Boston, employees viewed the store's Cooperative Association as a way to advance their interests, albeit about issues and in a manner that posed little threat to management. The aim of the association, as stated in its constitution, was "to give the

Voluntary Efforts," *Annals of the American Academy of Political and Social Science* 105 (January 1923): 80; Thomas, *National Cash Register Factory as Seen by English Experts*, pp. 79–80.

15. Testimony of O. F. Humphreys in National Civic Federation, *Conference on Welfare Work*, p. 65.

members a voice in their government, [and] to create and sustain a just and equitable relation between employer and employee." Every employee had a vote; together they elected annually an executive council to represent their interests. The council was empowered to initiate, amend, and cancel employment policies. Although store authorities could veto the council's decision, a two-thirds majority vote by council members could override the veto. On one occasion, employees used this veto right to implement a new policy on work attire. The workers' executive council passed a measure permitting employees to wear white in summer and black in winter. Filene's board of managers, preferring workers to wear black year-round, vetoed the council's decision. But a two-thirds majority vote by employees overturned it, enabling Filene's workers to alternate seasonally between white and black clothing.[16]

A final indication of employees' appreciation of welfare work was their growing sense of entitlement: many not only participated in welfare programs, they came to *expect* them. As welfare work became more common in the first decade of the twentieth century, workers began to take workplace reforms for granted. As Gertrude Beeks observed in 1912, "The American workman won't get down upon his knees to thank an employer for decent surroundings, but he appreciates them none the less. . . . He is now developed to the point where he demands them. His standard, both in shops and home, is so much higher than it used to be and so much higher than standards are elsewhere, that he accepts things as a matter of course which once would have amazed us and which would still amaze the residents of foreign countries."[17] As employees who had not experienced welfare work firsthand discussed their experiences with those who had, there developed what Lizabeth Cohen has aptly termed moral capitalism: a collective understanding among *all* workers that employers owed them something beyond wages. Although employment in a firm with employee benefits remained a minority experience for American workers throughout the Progressive period, workers' awareness of it meant that most began to perceive workplace reform as less a privilege than a right.[18]

Beeks knew whereof she spoke. As social secretary at the McCormick Works, she had witnessed moral capitalism at work. Her observations enable us to chart the dynamics of workers' mounting expectations.

16. U.S. Bureau of Labor Statistics, *Employers' Welfare Work*, Bulletin 123 (1913), p. 57.

17. Gertrude Beeks quoted in "Welfare Work May Conquer Great Labor Problems," *New York Times*, November 17, 1912.

18. See Lizabeth Cohen, *Making a New Deal: Industrial Workers in Chicago, 1919–1939* (New York: Cambridge University Press, 1990), pp. 159–211.

Between 1901 and 1902, Beeks established numerous welfare measures for female employees: lunchrooms, mirrored dressing rooms, lockers, a dancing platform, even an opera club. In 1902 the McCormick Works merged with four other agricultural equipment manufacturers, including the Chicago-based Deering company, to form the International Harvester Corporation. Work conditions at the four firms remained as they had been before the merger. In 1903 female employees at the Deering plant, sensing inequitable treatment, struck for higher wages, shorter hours, and welfare work, or, as they put it, "What Miss Beeks had done at the McCormicks." In response to workers' demands, International Harvester installed a welfare work program at Deering as comprehensive as the one first established by Beeks at McCormick. Deering's female employees got the treatment they requested. Far from being passive beneficiaries of business benevolence, Deering's women workers demanded and attained desired benefits.[19]

While some workers struck for benefits, other sued. A discharged worker's use of the courts to recover pension funds resulted in the first employee benefits case in United States history. In *McNevin v. Solvay Process Company*, James McNevin unsuccessfully sued his former employer, the Solvay Process Company of Syracuse, for pension earnings accumulated during his five years of employment at the firm. The court ruled that because the plan was unilaterally and voluntarily established by the company, it was legally a gift, to which McNevin had no legal claim. According to the court, it was the employer's right and not McNevin's "to fix the terms of his bounty, and provide under what circumstances the gift shall become vested and absolute." The *McNevin* decision did not prevent other workers from using the courts to try to claim promised benefits. Although, like McNevin, they were frequently unsuccessful, workers' willingness to turn to litigation as a tool for recovery of benefits illustrates the degree to which benefits had come to be viewed by employees as something to which they were legally entitled.[20]

19. John R. Commons, " 'Welfare Work' in a Great Industrial Plant," *Review of Reviews* 28 (July 1903): 79–81; Robert Ozanne, *A Century of Labor-Management Relations at McCormick and International Harvester* (Madison: University of Wisconsin Press, 1967), pp. 44–52; Gertrude Beeks to E. A. S. Clarke, June 27, 1903, McC MSS 1C, Box 24, SHSW; C. W. Price to G. F. Steele, April 10, 1905, Box 41, and Mary E. Thain to Harold F. McCormick, October 2, 1915, Box 42, both in Cyrus H. McCormick Jr. Papers, SHSW.

20. McNevin v. Solvay Process Co., 53 N.Y.S. 99 (1898). Many courts, moreover, did not uphold the gift rule established in McNevin. Some found it more useful to treat financial benefit plans according to the principle of contract law, thereby providing workers with a better legal claim to promised benefits. This decision was reached in 1912 in

Labor's culture of entitlement often irked employers. At the Helburn Thompson Company in Salem, Massachusetts, for instance, management instituted a one-week paid vacation for workers who had served a year with the tannage company as a way to retain workers during periods of labor scarcity. From the company's perspective, the results were disastrous. "The attitude of the employees," claimed one company spokesman, "was that they were conferring a favor upon the firm by working here, and that [welfare work] was no more than we should do." Angered by workers' reactions, the company abandoned the benefit.[21]

If workers felt justified in demanding that welfare benefits accompany employment, they were just as capable of expressing discontent when welfare programs to which they had grown accustomed were removed. In periods of economic instability, businessmen viewed welfare work as a dispensable luxury rather than a necessity. During the business recession of 1920–21, this perspective became practice. Across the country, individual programs were terminated and entire welfare programs shut down. One contemporary, reporting on the collapse of welfare work, noted that "factory newspapers have been discontinued, factory hospitals closed, bonuses have been omitted during the holiday season, and a number of other activities created for the safety and contentment of employees dispensed with. All of this has resulted in hard feeling, secretly nursed by many employees." These feelings, however, were not always secretly hidden. When the Waltham Watch Company reduced company expenditures in 1921 by terminating welfare programs, the result was "great dissatisfaction." Across the country, welfare employers earned the reputation among workers of being fair-weather friends—during hard times they regarded employee welfare "as the least important thing of all, while in 'fair weather' . . . [workers] have been given to believe that their welfare was the very thing about which the company was solicitous."[22]

The abandonment of welfare programs and the inadequacy of legally

---

another landmark benefits case, Zwolanek v. Baker Manufacturing Co., 137 N.W. 769 (1912). Even when analogized to the principles of contract law, however, plans still forced employees to abide by terms unilaterally imposed by employers. See Jay Conison, *Employee Benefit Plans* (St. Paul: West, 1993), p. 59.

21. Helburn Thompson Co., to R. L. Tweedy, Manufacturers' Research Association, September 26, 1923, Manufacturers' Research Association Papers, Case 2, BL.

22. U.S. Bureau of Labor Statistics, *Employers' Welfare Work*, p. 39; Charles W. Moore, *Timing a Century: History of the Waltham Watch Company* (Cambridge: Harvard University Press, 1945), p. 183, quoted in Brandes, *American Welfare Capitalism*, p. 136; Verne Edwin Burnett, "Peculiarities of Welfare Work," *Industrial Management*, June 1921, p. 439.

enforceable claims to promised benefits forced labor to learn a painful lesson about the fickleness of welfare work. What an employer provided voluntarily he could also take away. Companies whose welfare programs lasted only as long as a favorable business environment were given a "black eye" by labor when the economy improved. One contemporary observed that after production resumed in late 1921 and workers regained some of their negotiating power, "employees . . . seem[ed to have been] . . . using roller skates in running away from manufacturers who took advantage of them."[23]

In blacklisting these firms, employees probably accepted employment at companies without welfare benefits. But the mere fact that workers were angry enough to punish employers who withheld benefits demonstrates how much welfare work had become an integral part of workers' understanding of what constituted fairness in the workplace.

Rejection and Resistance

As employers sometimes forgot, there was a difference between workers' participation in welfare work and their unwavering devotion to the company. A worker could reap the benefits of a particular welfare scheme without sacrificing his or her independence. At one level, employees in welfare firms acted according to a seemingly straightforward principle: when they believed they had something to gain from welfare work, they took advantage of it; when they suspected they had something to lose, they reconsidered. But favorable or not, workers' responses were embedded in a broader, more complex web of obligations and responsibilities in the workplace. Employees did not categorize each program as a priori good or bad; a profit-sharing program that reduced labor turnover in one company could incite a strike in another; in some instances it did both. Workers defined their own moral economy, an understanding of what was just in the workplace given the circumstances of the moment. When the threshold separating fair from unfair was crossed, they responded accordingly. For some companies, reduced labor turnover, absentee rates, and good publicity were, indeed, by-products of industrial welfare work. No welfare scheme, however, could guarantee labor's unconditional loyalty or support.

Although workers' responses to perceived inequities varied, four things in particular dissatisfied them: suspicion of employers' motives;

23. Burnett, "Peculiarities of Welfare Work," p. 439.

dislike of charity; the impermanence of welfare benefits; and labor's desire to decide for itself where funds for employee welfare were best spent.

Workers recognized that few employers established welfare work altruistically. They knew that employers expected something from them in return for reforms. Welfare work, in short, although freely provided, had a price. As one contemporary explained, "The thought that something is received for nothing is incongruous with the thought that work is done for wages. . . . Sooner or later [welfare activities] are construed as a palliative for low wages, long hours, or bad working conditions, or as anti-union practices of the employer."[24]

The realization that welfare work entailed a trade-off—picnics and pensions in lieu of something else—fostered resentment. As one industrial consultant observed, "There is no man more sensitive to atmosphere and impression than the working man; . . . undoubtedly, with good reason, he is more suspicious where his employer is concerned than with any other human being. He is glad to have facilities . . . and better conditions to work under . . . but he is bound to resent any amelioration if there has lodged in his mind the least suspicion that these improvements are merely a means to an end, a bait put forth by the employer to gain some additional advantage."[25]

Workers suspicious of the "hidden motives" behind welfare programs were often reluctant to participate in them. The employment manager at the C. Howard Hunt Pen Company in New Jersey complained that the greatest obstacle in implementing welfare work was employee distrust: "They do not as a rule seem to take it in good faith and feel that we are doing it to benefit ourselves." The Michigan Stove Company found that its welfare work was not appreciated because "employees . . . conclude that we are doing it for a selfish purpose." At the Gorham Manufacturing Company, employees viewed the erection of a company clubhouse warily. "We couldn't seem to convince them that the company did not have some ulterior motive," the welfare worker complained. As one worker himself put it in a letter to the *Outlook* in 1908,

> As a general proposition, unless there was some kind of compulsion, comparatively few average workingmen would have anything to do

24. Boettiger, *Employee Welfare Work*, p. 17.
25. Giselle D'Unger, "The Spirit of Neighborliness in a Great Corporation," *World Today* 17 (December 1909): 1285.

with a plan which seemed to have back of it the spirit of patronage or paternalism. Somehow, it seems to the fellows that when a firm is too good about such things they must have something up their sleeves, and sooner or later it will come out. It's too much like a "con" game you know. Maybe we're wrong, but we have been taken so often that most of us are mighty suspicious of anything that seems like a special favor, out of which the boss isn't going to make more than we will get out of it. Therefore, when a particular scheme is presented by the office, it seems a natural thing to be "ag'in" it on general principles.[26]

In a similar vein, one welfare worker told a conference of colleagues about a male employee who refused to drink company-provided coffee. He asked the worker if he liked coffee. "Of course I do," the man responded, but "if I drink a cup or two of coffee my employer thinks I will do seventeen cents' worth of work more than if I didn't drink it, and the company gets the benefit, and I don't propose that they will get ahead of me that way."[27]

Related to workers' suspicions of employers' motives was a rejection of business charity. To be sure, not all workers viewed welfare schemes as gifts; many came to see welfare benefits as what they had produced— and hence were owed—by their hard labors. At the same time, accepting benefits that were routinely labeled "gratuitous" made some workers feel morally indebted to the company. Acceptance also implied an admission on workers' part that they depended on an employer's handouts to get by. Such dependency was anathema to employees who wanted to protect their economic and cultural autonomy as workers, even if doing so meant forsaking welfare benefits. At the Siegel-Cooper department store in New York City, only the creative maneuverings of the social secretary, Isabelle Nye, could convince female clerks to accept a company-paid vacation. "The young women had an idea they were receiving charity," she explained. "They would rather do almost anything else, even to the extent of going without a vacation, than pass it there and receive charity." To combat this feeling, Nye discarded the traditional notices advising clerks that they were eligible for a vacation after a year's service and replaced them with formal invitations, stating, "The Siegel-Cooper Company requests the pleasure of your company

26. L. A. Hawkes to Boston Chamber of Commerce, April 7, 1913, and George H. Barbour to Boston Chamber of Commerce, April 8, 1913, BCCC, Case 48, Folder 332–19, BL; "Letters from a Workingman," *Outlook* 88 (March 1908): 553–54.

27. Testimony of John F. P. Lawton and C. C. Michener in National Civic Federation, *Conference on Welfare Work*, pp. 63, 95.

at their cottage at Long Branch for the week beginning [date of week] as their guest." By treating workers as formally invited guests of the company, rather than as dependents, Nye removed some of the cultural obstacles to participation. As Nye discovered, it was the *presentation* of the benefit, rather than the benefit itself, that had held workers back.[28]

At the National Cash Register Company, a perplexed John Patterson asked welfare worker Lena Harvey to find out why women workers refused to patronize the new women's lunchroom. The company had invested a considerable sum on the room's construction: the tables were set with white damask cloths, silver, and china; the room's columns were twined with artificial grapevines and flowers; a piano and upholstered seats were provided for workers' entertainment and comfort. When Harvey questioned the women, their initial replies were "models of polite evasion." " 'I like to ride my new bicycle at noon,' said one. 'My mother's cooking is good enough for me,' said another." When Harvey persisted in her questioning, the real reason for women's disinterest surfaced. After one worker confessed that she thought "Mr. Patterson gives us enough without furnishing us with free lunches," the others "agreed in chorus." Harvey informed Patterson that the mystery of the lunchroom had been solved. "They don't use it because they don't want charity," she reported to the president. "Not one of them wants you to give them their luncheon free." The next day Patterson posted notices in each of the four women's departments in the factory: "Women's Dining Room, 5 cents." Before the week was over, the sixty-four tables in the dining room were occupied to capacity.[29]

To remove the charitable underpinnings of benefits, workers often insisted on financially contributing to them. Across the country, welfare firms experienced a common phenomenon: given the chance, workers would rather pay for benefits than receive them "free." Earned perquisites—paid for by workers or offered contractually in exchange for employment—were tolerable, and the terms of exchange were specified in advance. Under these circumstances, accepting welfare benefits meant that workers were merely getting their due, receiving what was rightfully theirs. At the Samuel L. Moore and Sons Company in New Jersey, for example, the firm's 295 male employees insisted on contributing ten cents a month for medical benefits. Although the hospital had been set up so that company could treat workmen "for free," workers insisted on paying a monthly fee so "that if, through accident

28. Testimony of Isabelle Nye, ibid., p. 106.
29. Tracy, *How My Heart Sang*, pp. 143–45.

or sickness, they become inmates, they may not be regarded as charity patients.'' By the same token, it was only after the Plymouth Cordage Company levied a one-cent rental fee for towels and swimsuits at the company's bathhouses that male and female workers used them.[30]

Closely tied to workers' quest for economic independence was their desire to protect their personal dignity and cultural autonomy from company control. Dependence on employers' charity and feelings of personal debt frequently went hand in hand; although business benevolence might provide desirable amenities, the concomitant feeling of diminished self-worth could prove too great a trade-off. In one factory, an employer who made regular visits to injured employees discovered a young male worker injured from a fall. Upon learning that the man had called in a ''quack doctor,'' the employer decided to carry the worker to his automobile, drive him to a hospital, and pay the man's medical bill. Expecting some appreciation in return, the employer was disheartened to learn that the employee, after returning to work for three days, had found work elsewhere. ''That's ingratitude,'' the employer complained. An investigation revealed that after returning to work, the employee was teased repeatedly by co-workers about his ''drag with the 'old man.' '' The incessant kidding about ''aid from the boss'' became so embarrassing for the young man that he left.[31]

In deciding which aspects of industrial welfarism were an affront to their self-respect, many workers expressed particular anger at welfare workers who tried to control their private lives. Indeed, workers may have resented welfare workers more than they did their employers; the employer was usually too busy to intervene in workers' personal lives, but it was the welfare worker's job to intrude. Workers observed welfare workers suspiciously and sought their advice and assistance with trepidation. Emphasizing female bonds that transcended class divisions, welfare workers seemed to have had the most success befriending women workers. But even female employees were likely to view welfare workers warily. When Gertrude Beeks first arrived at International Harvester, women workers suspected that she was a missionary: ''She was not one of them, they did not know her purpose, and they did not want her.'' At the Siegel-Cooper Company in New York City, the newly appointed social secretary Isabelle Nye encountered similar disdain. ''I found that

---

30. Bureau of Statistics of New Jersey, *Industrial Betterment Institutions in New Jersey Manufacturing Establishments* (Trenton, 1904), p. 80; report of Gertrude Beeks, July 30, 1901, in Nettie Fowler McCormick Papers, Box 27, SHSW.

31. Burnett, ''Peculiarities of Welfare Work,'' p. 439.

I was regarded with suspicion and doubt in the beginning," Nye recalled. "I had to feel my way tactfully."[32]

If women workers often came to accept the presence, if not the advice, of welfare workers, male employees routinely resisted both. Male workers immersed in a labor culture that celebrated "manly" self-respect and independence found the idea of being coddled and nurtured by a motherly female welfare worker repugnant. The self-reliant worker did not need outside help, and he certainly did not need a woman—the icon of dependency—to prop him up. For female welfare workers in predominantly male firms, interaction with employees was particularly difficult. Elizabeth Briscoe recalled an incident that underscored the determination of male employees to assert masculine pride in the face of maternal ministrations. After a foreman at the Joseph Bancroft and Sons Company began to suspect drunkenness as the cause of a worker's chronic absenteeism, he sent Briscoe to "check up on the worker." According to Briscoe, the ensuing confrontation was "humiliating and mortifying" for the man, who was "just as mad as he [could] be with the foreman for sending a woman after him."[33]

Both male and female workers resisted efforts to modify working-class behavior by imposing employers' values. At one Maine firm, the social secretary, nicknamed Sanitary Jane by employees, routinely conducted cleanliness inspections. At one point, thirty angry female workers banded together, told Sanitary Jane that they were just as clean as she, and advised her that they would no longer remove their shoes and stockings to submit to her physical examinations. At the National Tube Company, the playground supervisor sent an employee's unclean child home to clean her face and hands. The young child returned unwashed with a message from her mother telling the supervisor to "Go to——." When another company sent representatives to survey workers' homes to assess their need for food and clothing, resentful employees barred the representatives from the front doors. International Harvester's efforts to reform hygiene practices met with similar opposition. A company nurse visiting employees' homes reported that she had to "cajole and threaten" workers before they would adopt her suggestions. Simi-

32. J. C. Davis, "Welfare Work—Pseudo, or Real," *Industrial Management* 59 (January 1920): 48; testimony of Hilda Svenson in U.S. Senate, Commission on Industrial Relations, *Final Report and Testimony of the U.S. Commission on Industrial Relations* (Washington, D.C.: Government Printing office, 1916), 3:2316; Comstock, "Woman of Achievement," p. 445; testimony of Isabelle Nye in National Civic Federation, *Conference on Welfare Work*, p. 106.

33. Briscoe, "Factory and Home Conditions of Employees."

larly, the Plymouth Cordage Company attributed employees' unwillingness to patronize the company library to the room's "too fine" surroundings, which created an "unnatural atmosphere" that made workmen "embarrassed." The Ludlow Manufacturing Company encountered the same problem in its employee library. The trustees eventually concluded that while "some of our philanthropists seem to think that the whole race is going to be saved and regenerated by books . . . it would be easy to prove by the mouths of as many thousands of factory workers as you choose . . . that they don't want to be regenerated that way, and that whatever they want they don't want books, or if they do, they will gladly provide their own. They all know quite well that in these days books are cheaper than anything else on earth, except advice, and that they can give quite as well as take."[34] Not all welfare work was interpreted by employees as a threat to their cultural independence. But programs that assumed "the aspect of . . . meddlesome intrusion into the workman's home life and private affairs" were construed as an egregious "abridgement of personal liberties." Workers wanted their private lives kept private.[35]

Employees also expressed discontent about the impermanence of welfare programs, and they addressed two related concerns. The first was the temporary nature and at times arbitrariness of welfare work: a benefit an employer was not compelled to provide by law could be removed at any time. The second was workers' recognition of the consequences of their own precarious state of employment: should a worker be laid off, his term as welfare "beneficiary" quickly terminated. Employees who participated in welfare programs had to contend with both their own dispensability and that of the programs.

Employees in welfare firms realized and resented the discretionary character of welfare work. Why depend on pensions and profit-sharing dividends when the longevity of such schemes was unknown? Welfare work changed the rules and prerogatives of the wage relationship. Employees who accepted the freedom of contract implicit in wage labor were required in the welfare firm to compromise the limited bargaining

34. Brandes, *American Welfare Capitalism*, pp. 138–39; Burnett, "Peculiarities of Welfare Work," p. 440; testimony of Mary Goss in *Proceedings of the Eleventh Annual Meeting*, p. 341, SHSW; report of H. K. Hathaway, Plymouth Cordage Co. Papers, File I, Drawer I, Folder G, "Efficiency Studies and Time Studies," BL; Alaska Refrigerator Co. to Boston Chamber of Commerce, April 10, 1913, BCCC, Case 48, Folder 332–19, BL; testimony of J. E. Stevens in National Civic Federation, *Conference on Welfare Work*, p. 67.

35. Charles E. Fouhy, "Welfare Work and Industrial Stability," *Industrial Management* 58 (November 1919): 413.

power embedded in wage labor—the freedom to leave at any time for any reason—for employers' promises of rewards for loyal and continuous work. The provision of welfare benefits was neither contractually defined nor legally enforceable. It required workers' faith.

Labor soon realized that welfare work lasted only as long as employers thought they were benefiting from it. There were many reasons why employers abandoned welfare programs, most of which lay outside employees' immediate control. In a weak economy, welfare work was often the first expense a company cut. Workers resentful of "fair-weather welfare" expressed their displeasure whenever possible by blacklisting employers who practiced it. Often, however, workers' limited leverage in a poor economy—the same economic conditions that prompted employers to cut welfare programs in the first place—forced them to accept whatever employment they could find.[36]

It was one thing to deal with the termination of a welfare program and another matter to be promised something that never materialized. In some companies, workers discovered that company welfarism as described on paper and as it was actually practiced were quite different. Employers eager to cultivate public support went to great lengths to publicize their welfare work. But that did not mean that every worker reaped the rewards of advertised benevolence. Employers alone determined eligibility criteria. Mere employment in a welfare firm did not entitle one to welfare work; often the most needy employees were excluded. Employers who calculated pensions, profit sharing, and vacations based on an employee's length of employment ensured that unskilled laborers—the least affluent stratum of the labor force and, in employers' eyes, the most easily replaced—were the least likely to qualify. The terms of profit-sharing programs in one printing establishment, for example, were so stringent that only printers and journeymen—the firm's labor aristocracy—were eligible. The restrictions engendered so much hard feeling among those excluded that the company abandoned the program in its entirety after two years.[37]

While complaining about the arbitrary and discretionary character of welfare work, employees also resented that their status as wage workers, and hence welfare work beneficiaries, was in constant jeopardy. Employers not only had the authority to determine who got what benefits, for how long, and when, but they also had the power to terminate

36. Burnett, "Peculiarities of Welfare Work," p. 439.

37. Boettiger, *Employee Welfare Work*, pp. 171–72; U.S. Bureau of Labor Statistics, *Profit Sharing in the United States*, p. 167.

a worker's employment. Aware of their dispensability, workers often viewed welfare work as a benefit to be enjoyed in the present but not to be counted on in the future. Department store workers joked about the much-vaunted Christmas bonus clerks received for extra hours worked during the hectic holiday season. According to employers, stores were acting benevolently in a manner appropriate for the holiday spirit. But for many clerks department store work was a seasonal endeavor; the bonus they received was accompanied, ironically, by a termination notice. Although the store might rehire the worker at a busier time, the intervening hiatus removed her eligibility for welfare programs. As one woman complained, "So many times on Christmas Eve a girl is discharged and reemployed after the first of January, and the girls feel . . . that this is just to do away with their vacation. . . . In some of the stores they are discharged the night before the holiday and taken on the day after the holiday, so they are not paid for the holiday."[38]

Workers recognized that the uncertainty of their employment affected their access to welfare benefits. One could not enjoy welfare benefits when unemployed. Indeed, employees' fear of unemployment could outweigh their appreciation of welfare work. *Industrial Management* cautioned, "A man who . . . fears the loss of his position, is working under a high nervous tension . . . despite any conveniences which . . . have been supplied for his welfare." Of course, employers interpreted workers' reservations as ingratitude. Employers who suspected that employees were not appreciative enough of welfare programs often terminated those programs. Hence a peculiar cycle was established: workers' lack of enthusiasm about benefits that could be withdrawn at any moment helped ensure the impermanence of the very programs they desired.[39]

Workers who exhibited ingratitude learned still more poignantly about the link between their behavior and the longevity of welfare work. Welfare firms were not immune to strikes, work stoppages, or other manifestations of industrial strife. But employees who engaged in such acts of protest often found that welfare programs were promptly terminated—either to punish workers or to reflect management's conviction that welfare work had not eased industrial tensions as expected. In a 1916 investigation, the Bureau of Labor Statistics found that at

38. Testimony of Hilda Svenson in U.S. Senate, Commission on Industrial Relations, *Final Report and Testimony*, 3:2317.

39. G. Sumner Small, "How to Develop Executive Ability through Personality: What the 'Big Boss' Can Do for Morale," *Industrial Management* 61 (February 1921): 115–18.

least five firms out of eighty-six surveyed discontinued profit-sharing plans because employees struck. Such instances only proved to workers how little faith they should have in the permanency of welfare work. As one contemporary observed, welfare work has been "built upon the sands and [has] all too frequently . . . [been] washed away by the first wave of discontent among workers. After the first strike, the returning workman [finds] the doors of his dining-room, library, and club rooms closed to him."[40]

Workers were also quick to scrutinize the relationship between welfare work and wages, alert to the possibility that employers used welfare programs to rationalize paying low wages. Laborers knew that welfare programs financed by companies' retained earnings had not materialized miraculously; rather, they themselves had produced them. One welfare worker observed that "any welfare work of which the employees feel may come from their pockets is always . . . condemned." One employer complained, "Suppose we gave them turkeys. You would hear them muttering 'We must have made a good deal of money for the firm . . . or their consciences wouldn't have pricked them to give us this sop.' "[41]

Many employees wanted money that was applied to welfare work redirected to wages. Workers at the Plymouth Cordage Company sent a letter to the company's management describing its profit-sharing scheme as "a very stupid idea. . . . [We] are not asking for such as you call it a Bonus . . . [but] for a better condition in wages and . . . hours." At Procter and Gamble, the annual profit-sharing dividend was met by "employee grumbles." "They could not see why the dividend should be called a dividend and not simply an increase in pay," management complained. "The company took money out of one pocket and called it pay, they said; then took money out of the other pocket and called it dividends. Why not call it all wages?"[42]

Welfare programs might hold the promise of interesting leisure and long-term financial opportunities, but cash had a fixed value that could be put to immediate use. The financial value of welfare benefits such

40. U.S. Bureau of Labor Statistics, *Profit Sharing in the United States*, p. 167. The survey included 60 operating firms and 26 firms that had terminated profit sharing. See Otto P. Geier, "Health of the Working Force," *Industrial Management* 54 (October 1917): 15.

41. Testimony of Henry P. Kendall of the Plimpton Press Co. in National Civic Federation, *Proceedings of the Eleventh Annual Meeting*, p. 371; Fullerton L. Waldo, "What Employers Say of Profit-Sharing," *World's Work* 5 (December 1902): 2853.

42. Plymouth Cordage Co. letter quoted in Brandes, *American Welfare Capitalism*, p. 138; Janet Ruth Rankin, "Profit Sharing for Savings," *World's Work* 28 (July 1914): 317.

as bowling alleys and picnics was intangible. Gertrude Beeks discovered that steelworkers' ambivalence toward profit sharing in one company stemmed not only from their suspicions that such schemes deflated wages but also from a desire for "a plan which would enable them to know exactly what they might depend upon with which to meet expenses . . . [instead of] a plan . . . of a speculative nature." At another firm, management explained workers' disinterest in a newly launched profit-sharing program as the result of employees' tendency to view anticipated financial earnings as "rather a long way off."[43]

Employees also suspected that acceptance of welfare work put them at a disadvantage when the time came to renegotiate wages. Participation in welfare programs, workers feared, would unintentionally convey their tacit approval of *all* the firm's labor policies, thereby undercutting their bargaining power. As one contemporary explained, welfare work diminished the worker's ability to feel "justified in demanding an increase."[44]

Employees forcefully articulated their preference for higher wages over welfare work. After one New Jersey welfare firm refused to grant a wage increase, several hundred employees suspended work. Company officials pointed to their pension fund, sick benefits, and "other attractions" as incentives for resuming employment. Employees promptly dismissed these lures as "abstract things," demanding "more money, not welfare work." When a clothing company callously cut wages the same day it opened a new employee cafeteria, not a single employee could be coaxed into entering it. Workers unhappy with wages in welfare firms also expressed their dissatisfaction by quitting. A labor relations specialist noted an abundance of cases in which employees had "left ideal working conditions to accept positions with other concerns at a cent or two more an hour where there were . . . absolutely no social or welfare activities, and they were just as well satisfied until some other employer offered them a few more cents."[45]

Workers' preferences for wages over welfare work reflected their conviction that they, and not their employers, were best qualified to determine how funds devoted to their welfare—funds workers themselves had generated—ought to be spent. Higher wages would give workers

43. Interview with Gertrude Beeks in "Welfare Work May Conquer Great Labor Problems," *New York Times*, November 17, 1912; U.S. Bureau of Labor Statistics, *Profit Sharing in the United States*, p. 26.

44. Henderson, *Citizens in Industry*, p. 130.

45. Fouhy, "Welfare Work and Industrial Stability," p. 413; Davis, "Welfare Work—Pseudo or Real," p. 48.

the freedom both to determine which programs were of value and to control the nature and extent of their personal "improvement." Certainly there were some welfare programs employees were eager to eliminate. At a New York department store, for instance, a female clerk who had won a prize playing "roof games" at the store's Christmas party responded to her victory by immediately asking if she could exchange the prize for a " 'practical' pair of shoes." Higher wages endowed workers with the financial means to acquire benefits they desired while freeing them from subsidizing those they did not, such as prizes for roof games. As one employee noted, "Men can buy turkeys several times a year, if they care to do so, with . . . [an] increase in wages."[46]

As a final measure of resistance, workers in welfare firms struck. Dissatisfaction with wages, hours, work conditions, and other grievances induced workers to protest the terms of their employment, notwithstanding the presence of welfare work. Employers who hoped welfare work would deter labor unrest were usually disappointed. Dozens of welfare companies experienced debilitating strikes between 1900 and 1920; National Cash Register, International Harvester, Plymouth Cordage Company, and Scovill, all prominent welfare firms, were but a few. Gertrude Beeks explained the coexistence of strikes and welfare work by observing: "It's like a hungry man to whom a handsome suit of clothes is given. Good clothes won't make him comfortable unless he also is provided with a plate of ham and eggs."[47]

Because of the media attention it received and the effect it had on other employers, the 1901 strike at NCR was probably the most important of those that occurred at welfare firms. By 1900, NCR had established itself as the leader in welfare work in the United States. Businessmen, government representatives, and even labor officials praised the company's generosity. Only six years before the strike began, William Ruehrwein, Ohio labor statistics commissioner, had credited welfare work with the "permanent era of good feeling between employer and employee" at the Dayton firm. The Dayton Trades and Labor Assembly was equally enthusiastic, expressing "hearty commendation of the course pursued at the National Cash Register Company . . . to make their employees independent, skillful workmen and intelligent citizens."[48]

46. Henderson, *Citizens in Industry*; U.S. Senate, Commission on Industrial Relations, *Final Report and Testimony*, 3:2405.

47. Interview with Gertrude Beeks in "Welfare Work May Conquer Great Labor Problems," p. 8.

48. Ruehrwein, *Wonderful Factory System*, pp. 1, 8.

But company welfare work did not prevent a two-month strike. At issue in the dispute was the dismissal of four union men for alleged incompetence and insubordination. The discharged employees claimed that they had been fired because of their union affiliation and demanded reinstatement. When the company's president, John Patterson, refused, the unionized molders and metal polishers backed up the men's claims and struck. The ensuing work stoppages throughout the foundry and polishing departments prompted Patterson to retaliate: on May 3 he locked out all 2,300 production employees. Not until July 2 did the dispute end, on Patterson's terms.[49]

Although the strike was not about welfare work, the NCR experience—labor strife in the model factory—persuaded many people that welfare work could not guarantee labor docility. The labor left, assessing what had happened at NCR, delighted in the knowledge that welfare work had not dampened employees' fighting spirit. But for employers who had hoped that welfare work would palliate workers' resistance, the NCR strike was discomfiting. As one employer reported, NCR "did almost everything that human ingenuity could devise for the benefit of its people, but in spite of this . . . they went on strike for the most unwarranted reasons and treated their employers as if they were their personal enemies. There is practically no larger employer of labor but who is aware of the circumstances of the case."[50]

At NCR, Patterson expressed disappointment that the strike had occurred. He acknowledged that a welfare program for employees was "a waste unless it brings good will and cooperation on the part of the employee." This did not mean he thought that industrial welfarism had failed altogether, however, because Patterson, like most of his colleagues, had never viewed welfare work as simply an anti-union measure. Indeed, a year before the highly publicized strike erupted, the company maintained contracts with more than twenty unions, making it one of the most organized firms in Ohio. After the strike, Patterson

49. The strike is best explained in Daniel Nelson, "The New Factory System and the Unions: The National Cash Register Company Dispute of 1901," *Business History Review* 36 (Winter 1963): 369–91; and Judith Sealander, *Grand Plans: Business Progressivism and Social Change in Ohio's Miami Valley, 1890–1929* (Lexington: University Press of Kentucky, 1988), pp. 29–31.

50. Bureau of Statistics of New Jersey, *Industrial Betterment Institutions*, pp. 44–45. Radical labor groups portrayed the strike as labor's opposition to the tyranny of welfare work. The May 11, 1901, issue of the *Weekly People*, for instance, characterized the dispute as follows: "The workers, it is believed, have seen through the fraudulent character of these plans, and have, consequently, become dissatisfied. The company, it is claimed, finding that the spell of its illusion was broken, thereupon ordered the lockout."

continued to give welfare work his full support. In 1904, assessing the long-term consequences of the strike, he reported that "our welfare work is going on more than ever."[51]

Although the 1901 strike did not eliminate welfare activities at NCR —the company remained a key player in the welfare work movement throughout the Progressive era—it revealed to Patterson some of the limitations workers saw in welfare programs. Patterson restructured NCR's welfare policy accordingly. Lena Harvey, the Baptist deaconess social secretary, was replaced by a less "meddlesome" male welfare director. Many of the community programs Harvey had initiated to make the company a permanent fixture in workers' leisure time were terminated. Other programs such as health care were expanded, offered not as charity but as a benefit "purchased" by workers through monthly dues. As Judith Sealander has argued, in the strike's aftermath welfare programs at NCR became "more narrowly focused." Emphasizing individual perquisites over group uplift and purchased benefits over gratuitous handouts, NCR's new form of welfare work was remarkably attentive to the concerns and criticisms asserted by rank-and-file workers.[52]

NCR's 1901 realignment augured the sweeping changes to the organization of labor benefits that occurred after World War I. That NCR should have pointed the way at such an early stage was only fitting. Patterson, one of the first to place faith and funds in employee welfare, was able to identify some of the shortcomings of welfare work early on. For businessmen who had waited longer to explore the promises and possibilities of welfare work, disillusionment came later.

51. Testimony of John Patterson in National Civic Federation, *Conference on Welfare Work*, pp. 119–20; Nelson, "New Factory System and the Unions," pp. 170, 176.

52. Nelson, "New Factory System and the Unions," p. 176; Sealander, *Grand Plans*, pp. 31–33.

7/

Benefits for Breadwinners

Employees' responses to two decades of welfare work—their patterns of participation and resistance—had a profound impact on the evolution of private sector welfare in the United States. Employers were not oblivious to workers' behavior and actions; they learned from costly mistakes which benefits workers liked and which they did not. In the 1920s they incorporated this knowledge, derived from observing patterns of workers' participation and resistance, into emergent structures of labor management.

The perquisites workers were most likely to receive in the 1920s were contractually defined and individualized. To many workers, welfare implied charity. Employee benefits, however, represented fair compensation; stripped of the veneer of charity and reduced to the cash nexus, benefits were earned, not bestowed gratuitously. In the 1920s, workers were less likely to receive the ostensible freebies of days gone by: the "free" lunches, picnics, and excursions that had made employees feel morally indebted to employers and, by workers' accounting, were of questionable worth. Instead, employers opted to give workers more life insurance, stockholding options, and retirement packages—benefits with an identifiable value. Frills like employee libraries and company-financed clubhouses became less frequent as employers yielded to workers the freedom to manage their leisure free of company control.

The terms of pecuniary benefits were, furthermore, carefully enumerated in employee handbooks. In the 1920s, judges ruled that these enumerations were contractual promises of compensation. In the postwar business world, the worker's claim to benefits no longer rested on the caprice of the employer. Relegated to contract, the provision of benefits gave laborers more than hopes and expectations. It gave them legally enforceable rights.[1]

That employees helped shape the reconfiguration of welfare work in the 1920s does not imply that workers got everything they wanted. The 1919 strike wave and the Red Scare that followed renewed and intensified anti-labor violence. In their wake, industrial relations took a decidedly conservative turn. The 1920s ushered in labor's "lean years": years of yellow-dog contracts and anti-labor injunctions, years that saw a dramatic drop in union membership even as company unions spread far and wide.[2]

In this chillier political climate, the labor question, a prominent issue in the Progressive era, gradually receded from national headlines. The retreat sprang not only from the changed political mood but also from the conviction that employers in the Progressive era had demonstrated both the viability and desirability of a private sector welfare system. The visibility of private welfare programs, augmented by employers' shrewd publicity campaigns, seemed to demonstrate employers' sensitivity to the needs of labor. For many, in short, the employee welfare question had been asked and answered. Never again would it be asked by so many disparate groups and individuals with the same seriousness of purpose and breadth of vision. The private sector safety net erected in the Progressive era would become the cornerstone of the employee welfare system long after the term "welfare work" had faded from employers' vocabulary.

The Impact of World War I

World War I transformed American welfare work. On the one hand, the exigencies of a wartime economy accelerated existing trends in

1. On the history of fringe benefit regulation, see Darien McWhirter, *Your Rights at Work* (New York: Wiley, 1989), chap. 2. On workplace contractualism, see David Brody, "Workplace Contractualism in Comparative Perspective," in *Industrial Democracy in America: The Ambiguous Promise*, ed. Nelson Lichtenstein and Howell John Harris (Cambridge: Cambridge University Press, 1993), pp. 176–205.

2. The term comes from Irving Bernstein, *The Lean Years: A History of the American Worker, 1920–1933* (Boston: Houghton Mifflin, 1960).

employee management. On the other, as burgeoning interest in labor management aligned welfare work more closely to the scientific realm, it ushered in new patterns of industrial relations that persisted in the postwar world.

Employers' most pressing problem during the war was an acute labor scarcity created by the intersection of two competing developments: greater demand for manufacturing output and a curtailment in the supply of traditional industrial workers. Demand for military supplies skyrocketed after the war began in 1914. American firms scrambled first to meet the Allies' requests and then to power their own war machine. Even before the United States entered the war in 1917, hundreds of companies converted their production to wartime manufacturing to fill the Allies' orders for food, raw materials, and manufactured goods. Between 1913 and 1917 manufacturing output increased by almost 40 percent.[3]

Efforts to meet foreign and domestic needs were hampered by the dwindling supply of industrial workers. The heavy influx of immigrants in the Progressive period had contributed to a steady labor surplus. But after the outbreak of war, the flow of immigrants to the United States slowed, curbing immigration rates from roughly 1 million a year before 1914 to under 200,000 in 1915 and 31,000 in 1918. Wartime conscription further contracted the labor pool. By the end of the war, more than 24 million men between the ages of 18 and 45 had registered for the draft and more than 2.8 million had been inducted. These trends pushed the unemployment rate to under 2.4 percent by 1918, its lowest level since the 1880s.[4]

Employers compensated for the tight labor market by hiring women, African Americans, and Mexican Americans for occupations previously denied to these groups. Drawing thousands of women out of domestic service, textile manufacture, and sweatshops and into the iron, steel, metal, and chemical industries, the war boosted the proportion of women in the manufacturing labor force from 6 to almost 14 percent between 1914 and 1918. The war also created new opportunities for African Americans. Between 200,000 and 300,000 southern blacks in search of industrial labor and a better way of life migrated to northern

3. American Social History Project, *Who Built America? Working People and the Nation's Economy, Politics, Culture, and Society*, vol. 2 (New York: Pantheon, 1992), p. 227.

4. Ibid., p. 227; Maurine Greenwald, *Women, War, and Work: The Impact of World War I on Women Workers* (Ithaca: Cornell University Press, 1990), p. 15; Sanford Jacoby, *Employing Bureaucracy: Managers, Unions, and the Transformation of Work in American Industry, 1900–1945* (New York: Columbia University Press, 1985), p. 133.

cities during the war. The proportion of blacks in the manufacturing labor force jumped 40 percent between 1910 and 1920, with the most significant increases occurring during the war. Mexican Americans also kept the wartime machine running; exempt from the draft and immigration restrictions, thousands of new immigrants found employment in steel and mining. All told, the number of factory workers increased from 6.5 million in 1914 to 8.4 million in 1919.[5]

Despite these additions, labor scarcity persisted, giving employees a degree of leverage they readily used. Between 1916 and 1920 a wave of labor unrest rocked the country as more than a million workers each year went on strike. Neither Samuel Gompers's no-strike pledge of 1917, promising labor cooperation in exchange for government recognition of unions, nor the creation of the National War Labor Board in April 1918 to settle industrial disputes, stopped the outpouring of protest; throughout the five-year period the ratio of strikers to workers remained higher than it had ever been in American history. Turnover, too, reached epidemic proportions as more and more workers took advantage of the benefits of a seller's market, leaving less desirable jobs for better-paid, more appealing employment. Labor productivity rates plummeted in critical sectors of the economy, especially machinery and metals, as absenteeism, tardiness, and unemployment rates soared.[6]

Labor shortages, turnover, a rapidly expanding labor force, the demand for increased industrial output, and the need for employer-employee cooperation all focused attention on the inadequacies of existing labor management strategies. Hundreds of efficiency and labor motivation studies conducted by efficiency experts, industrial engineers, government personnel, and even welfare workers revealed the need for a new approach to labor management, one that would merge attention to the human needs of workers with the rigor and impartiality of management science. As the dialogue on labor management broadened, welfare work and scientific management received renewed scru-

5. Daniel Nelson, *Managers and Workers: Origins of the New Factory System in the United States* (Madison: University of Wisconsin Press, 1975), p. 142; Jacoby, *Employing Bureaucracy*, pp. 133–34; Greenwald, *Women, War, and Work*, p. 21; Foster Rhea Dulles and Melvin Dubofsky, *Labor in America*, 4th ed. (Arlington Heights, Ill.: Harlan Davidson, 1984), pp. 219–20; American Social History Project, *Who Built America?* pp. 240–43.

6. American Social History Project, *Who Built America?* pp. 226–27; Jacoby, *Employing Bureaucracy*, pp. 135–36; Committee on Recent Economic Changes of the President's Conference on Unemployment, *Recent Economic Changes in the United States*, vol. 2 (New York: McGraw-Hill, 1929), p. 517. For a discussion of labor leverage in Seattle during World War I, see Dana Frank, *Purchasing Power: Consumer Organizing, Gender, and the Seattle Labor Movement, 1919–1929* (New York: Cambridge University Press, 1994), pp. 22–25.

tiny. Contemporaries identified flaws in both strategies. Welfare work, many argued, needed to be recast impartially, to evolve, as one commentator put it, from an "unscientific mixing of purely charitable gratuities" to the distribution of a codified set of labor incentives. Scientific management, in turn, required humanization. In addition to examining "the best method of handling materials and equipment in relation to workers," it needed to appreciate better "the principles which underlie correct methods of handling men."[7]

To combine the best of both strategies and to eliminate the weaknesses of each, contemporaries proposed a hybridized approach to labor relations—personnel management. The purpose of personnel management was to combine welfare work, scientific management, and other employment activities in a single bureau headed by a team of professional labor managers. The appeal of personnel management lay in the promise that the coordination and integration of industrial affairs would boost labor efficiency. Personnel management would eliminate subjective employment decisions that aggravated workers, prompting them to leave or to perform wasteful "part-time" work. It would standardize every stage in an employee's tenure: application, employment, evaluation and study, health and safety, welfare. To curb the power of the foreman, one example of arbitrarily wielded authority, an impartial personnel manager, "a man . . . with skill, with judgment, with vision, with trained powers," would assume control of hiring, firing, and promotion. Because psychological and trade tests would determine employment suitability, science, not favoritism, would inform the personnel manager's "careful selection of workers" and "the scientific fitting of them to their jobs." The standardization and separation of jobs would encourage the specification of occupational distinctions, enabling each employee to know where responsibilities "stop and where they begin."[8]

7. Robert Williams Dunn, *The Americanization of Labor* (1927; New York: AMS Press, 1977), p. 194; Henry Eilbirt, "The Development of Personnel Management in the United States," *Business History Review* 33 (Autumn 1959): 350–59; Daniel Nelson, " 'A Newly Appreciated Art': The Development of Personnel Work at Leeds & Northrup, 1915–1923," *Business History Review* 44 (Winter 1970): 520–21; U.S. Bureau of Labor Statistics, "Personnel and Employment Problems," *Monthly Review of the Bureau of Labor Statistics* 3 (August 1916): 23; Meyer Bloomfield and Joseph H. Willits, "Personnel and Employment Problems in Industrial Management," *Annals of the American Academy of Political and Social Science* 65 (May 1916): viii.

8. Bloomfield and Willits, "Personnel and Employment Problems," pp. vii–viii; Ernest Fox Nichols, "The Employment Manager," address to the Chamber of Commerce of the United States of America, Washington, D.C., February 8, 1916, in *Annals of the American Academy of Political and Social Science* 65 (May 1916): 4–5; U.S. Bureau of Labor Statistics,

Personnel management was also designed to subsume welfare activities, a sphere of industrial relations efficiency experts criticized but still thought integral to labor stability. Concerned that "through lack of tact and judgment, welfare work in some quarters has been permitted to be interpreted by employees themselves as . . . altruism and charity," personnel advocates encouraged the standardization of welfare programs. Under the aegis of personnel management, employee benefits would be distributed only to those who wished to claim them and who had met eligibility requirements. Standardization would boost welfare work's efficacy by eliminating its arbitrariness—its "disproportionate emphases and accidents and fluctuating interests," its tendency toward "frills . . . [and] personal whims of benevolence." Standardization, in short, would transform employee welfare from an act of sentiment into a "serious project of human engineering."[9]

The wartime policy of the federal government put theory into practice. To encourage labor's cooperation in the manufacture of war products, government agencies improved wage rates and working conditions in government contract firms. By the fall of 1917, the eight-hour day, union wage rates, and standardized safety and sanitation measures had become standard fare for employees involved with military production. The government urged the installation of personnel departments in factories manufacturing munitions, war supplies, and ships to enforce standards. To expand the pool of personnel managers who could head such departments, the War Industries Board set up a six-week crash course on personnel methods, first offered at the University of Rochester. By the end of the war, more than a dozen universities, including Harvard, Columbia, Carnegie Tech, and Northwestern, were sponsoring similar training.[10]

As many as two hundred personnel departments were established during the war. Though not exclusive to big businesses, personnel de-

---

"Personnel and Employment Problems," p. 22. On the merger of scientific management and welfare work techniques, see Sharon Hartman Strom, *Beyond the Typewriter: Gender, Class, and the Origins of Modern American Office Work, 1900–1930* (Urbana: University of Illinois Press, 1992), pp. 125–29.

9. Committee on Recent Economic Changes, *Recent Economic Changes*, p. 518; Robert Clothier, "The Employment Work of the Curtis Publishing Company," paper presented at the Philadelphia Association for the Discussion of Employment Problems, April 1916, in *Annals of the American Academy of Political and Social Science* 65 (May 1916): 103. Also see David Montgomery, *The Fall of the House of Labor: The Workplace, the State, and American Labor Activism, 1865–1925* (New York: Cambridge University Press, 1987).

10. Eilbirt, "Development of Personnel Management," p. 353; Jacoby, *Employing Bureaucracy*, pp. 141–45.

partments tended to be located in large establishments. The proportion of companies employing over 250 workers with personnel departments increased from about 5 to 25 percent between 1915 and 1920. Predictably, welfare firms led the way. Typically large in scale and already attentive to the ties between factory efficiency and employee welfare, welfare firms were predisposed to favor personnel innovation. In many welfare firms, personnel departments were established as offshoots of expanded welfare departments. The organization of personnel functions varied largely according to firm size. In smaller firms, a single department administered personnel activities. In larger companies, the major personnel functions were broken down into separate branches, each reporting to a larger administrative unit.[11]

Although personnel work did not displace welfare work, it changed it significantly, especially in the administrative realm. As individual welfare departments disappeared, the position of social secretary was gradually eliminated. In its place emerged the personnel manager, a college-trained male whose specialized training was thought to equip him with the skills necessary to oversee employees. The occupation of personnel manager was largely a wartime development. Although a community of personnel managers had existed before 1914—enough to form the first employment managers' association in Boston in 1912—their membership grew rapidly as the war progressed. By 1917 ten cities had personnel associations; by 1920, fifty did. In 1918, the National Association of Employment Managers was established. More than five thousand persons attended the 1920 meeting.[12]

Although the war marked the apex of the professionalization of welfare work, the impulse to professionalize preceded it. Ironically, social secretaries were partly responsible for initiating this trend. Professionalization was not simply a process that happened to social secretaries; many actively encouraged it. Hoping to heighten their credibility by conveying an earnest, scientific intent, participants at the first national meeting of social secretaries in 1904 agreed to change their occupation's title from social secretary to "welfare secretary" or "welfare worker." As Gertrude Beeks later recalled: "Scientific welfare workers ... objected to the use of the term 'Social Secretary.' ... The term was regarded as misleading and too narrow to include the scope and re-

11. Jacoby, *Employing Bureaucracy*, pp. 137, 147; Nelson, *Managers and Workers*, p. 153; Don D. Lescohier, "Working Conditions," in John R. Commons et al., *History of Labor in the United States*, 4 vols. (1918–35; New York: Augustus M. Kelley, 1966), 3:320.

12. Nelson, *Managers and Workers*, p. 154; Eilbirt, "Development of Personnel Management," p. 353; Jacoby, *Employing Bureaucracy*, pp. 138–39.

sponsibilities of the position.'' Only five years after its appearance as a new occupation, the social secretary, in name if not in function, was already becoming a thing of the past.[13]

The name change was matched by welfare workers' resolve to make continuing education a part of welfare work practice. Beginning with its 1904 meeting of social secretaries, the NCF Welfare Department hosted regular conferences featuring speeches by prominent welfare workers who relayed tried-and-true techniques—''guarding against accidents,'' ''a complete factory plan''—to promote occupational success. Independent agencies also held welfare conferences. The Chicago Institute of Social Science sponsored a twelve-week evening conference in the spring of 1907 on welfare work in shops and stores. Chaired by Professor Graham Taylor, a founder of the American Economic Association, it included weekly discussions on welfare work among women, the qualifications, status, and problems of the welfare manager, and housing conditions and neighborhood improvement.[14]

These gatherings, as well as the regular publications of the NCF's Welfare Department and the American Institute of Social Service, introduced new criteria for measuring occupational success. The circulation of a set of core ideas—a ''what's what guide to effective welfare work''—suggested that welfare workers' definition of professional achievement increasingly encompassed more than the right attitude and a dose of common sense. Competency now necessitated acquiring standardized knowledge.

By the end of the decade, welfare workers had begun to place special emphasis on the value of classroom training as the best way to obtain this knowledge. In 1909 Yale University offered the first course on industrial service work; four years later, the omnipresent Gertrude Beeks taught the second at the New York University School of Commerce. Beeks's course description in the university bulletin reveals the degree to which occupational success had become associated with professional training. The bulletin was careful to describe welfare work as a ''phase of business activity . . . not to be confused with philanthropic and social service performed gratuitously.'' ''The profession of welfare manager

13. National Civic Federation, *Conference on Welfare Work* (New York: Andrew H. Kellogg, 1904), p. viii; National Civic Federation, *Proceedings of the Eleventh Annual Meeting of the National Civic Federation* (New York, 1911), p. 314.
14. National Civic Federation, *Proceedings of the Eleventh Annual Meeting of the National Civic Federation*, pp. xix, xx; circular of the Chicago Institute of Social Science, Spring Quarter Courses, 1907, Cyrus H. McCormick Jr. Papers, Social Science, Spring Quarter Courses, 1907 Box 40, State Historical Society of Wisconsin (hereafter SHSW).

will appeal strongly to many generous hearted persons," Beeks warned, "but its successful practice demands careful preparation." The course was designed to train students in both the theoretical and practical dimensions of welfare work. Lectures by Beeks, "prominent welfare workers, practical business men, and scientists, as well as by experts in specialized fields of welfare activity" would occupy most of the students' time. As Beeks's description illustrates, welfare workers were endeavoring to present their occupation as one that required not only intuition and compassion but rigorous formal training.[15]

By World War I, then, welfare workers themselves had taken significant steps to cement their identity as experts. But in endorsing so completely the merits of *scientific* welfare work, the personnel movement pushed professionalization to new heights. One of the most important results of the turn to science was the defeminization of welfare administration. Before the personnel boom, the majority of social secretaries and welfare workers had been women. Prevailing stereotypes had encouraged the occupation's feminization. Women's "natural" reserves of compassion and sympathy ostensibly suited them for a job that achieved its objectives through moral authority and personal persuasion. Personnel management turned this perception on its head. Eager to extirpate welfare work's sympathetic side in the name of objective science, personnel advocates denounced emotion, sentiment, and partiality, culturally designated "female" attributes, as obstacles to expertise. Personnel managers were to make decisions based on college training, not intuition; they were to be ruled by the head, not the heart. Unlike their predecessors, operating, as one commentator condescendingly put it, in a "less discriminating period," personnel managers were not dispensing charity, "women's" work, but administering standardized benefits. Casting masculine traits of objectivity and impartiality as indispensable to professional labor management, personnel management advocates ensured that the masculinization of welfare work administration would be emblematic of scientific rigor.

Thus the maternal argument that had served women well in gaining access to welfare work administration now supplied the rationale for pushing them out. By the end of the war, the majority of personnel managers were college-educated men. Many belonged to local personnel associations whose masculine culture, combining professional con-

15. Stuart D. Brandes, *American Welfare Capitalism, 1880–1940* (Chicago: University of Chicago Press, 1976), p. 3; *Commerce Bulletin* (New York School of Commerce) 8 (January 24, 1913): 2, in National Civic Federation Papers, New York Public Library.

cerns with social interaction, encouraged female exclusion. Women who managed to keep their jobs during the transition typically found themselves in support rather than supervisory roles; they were assistants to personnel managers, not managers in their own right. Differential salaries institutionalized female personnel workers' secondary status. In 1921, salaries for male personnel managers typically ranged from $2,000 to $5,000; men with exceptional experience could earn as much as $25,000. For women, the financial outlook was bleaker. In 1921, the median salary for women in personnel work was $1,846.[16]

The incorporation of welfare work into personnel work was characterized by more than administrative retooling. As the science of personnel management took hold, the very spirit of welfare work—its promise to restore personalism within the workplace—was abandoned. Evolving perceptions of labor underlay this transformation. In the early 1900s, the gospel of welfare work preached that the labor force was made up of heterogeneous human beings, each with personal characteristics and traits that, in the hands of a sympathetic social secretary, could be nurtured, moderated, and sculpted. Each worker, the ideology of welfare work assumed, possessed a unique set of attributes, the human qualities that separated human from machine. The path to profits lay in knowing how to mobilize these traits for efficient purposes.

By the 1920s the prevailing wisdom suggested that if all laborers were not alike, they could at least be divided into like-minded groups united by a single, all-encompassing variable such as ethnicity or skill, an aggregate classification rendering their behavior predictable according to immutable laws of labor. The dangers of such stereotyping were not lost on personnel managers, some of whom worried that personality standardization would strain individualism to its breaking point by accepting, as one put it, a "theory of predestination which would largely limit the opportunities for proving individual worth." One personnel manager remarked in 1916: "It is useless to expect that great businesses can be conducted without a great mass of prescribed routines designed for the greatest good in the majority of cases. But it is true that the necessary struggle for uniformity and system has involved the limitation of individualism to standardized types to an extent that raises . . . serious questions."[17]

16. Strom, *Beyond the Typewriter*, pp. 148–54.
17. Ernest Hopkins, "A Functionalized Employment Department as a Factory in Industrial Efficiency," *Annals of the American Academy of Political and Social Science* 65 (May 1916): 70.

By the early 1920s, however, few personnel managers were openly struggling with the consequences of employee standardization. To do so would have been to call into question the ideological framework within which they asserted, and claimed the prerogatives of, their professional identity. The triumph of personnel management sealed the hegemony of a scientific approach to labor, an approach predicted on group predictability. The change in terminology from welfare work to personnel management signaled this transition. Whereas the "welfare" in welfare work had suggested attention to workers' individual well-being, personnel work evinced a seriousness of purpose, qualitatively more distanced, formal, and objective than its predecessor. Thus, as it had since the early years of the welfare work movement, language indexed the shifting moods of labor management.

"What's in a Name?": The Problem with Welfare

"The poet who said, 'What's in a name,' " observed Otto P. Geier, director of the Employees' Service Department at the Cincinnati Milling Machine Company in 1919, "lived before the day when welfare came into disrepute as 'hell-fare.' " Geier's comment characterized the opinion of most welfare capitalists and personnel workers in the post-war era that if welfare work programs were to continue, they needed to be renamed and recast. By the end of the decade, they had done both.[18]

Interpretations of the word "welfare" had always been important to the welfare work movement. The NCF carefully evaluated the connotations of other terms before settling on "welfare work" as the best descriptor of the movement's goals. Welfare, Gertrude Beeks and others had argued, did not imply charity, which the Welfare Department linked disparagingly and exclusively to government provision. Distinguishing between benefits workers "earned" as gainfully employed citizens (welfare) and the "handouts" the indigent received from the state (charity) had been critical to the welfare capitalist campaign. Repeatedly, employers and welfare work organizations had equated public assistance with charity to sell the virtues of private reform; they had trumpeted the merits of welfare work by lavishing as much praise on what it did not do—destroy the independent spirit of American work-

---

18. Otto P. Geier, "Human Relations from the Standpoint of the Industrial Physician," *Industrial Management* 57 (June 1919): 503.

ers—as on what it did. Shared understandings of the different meanings of charity and welfare had been a prerequisite for the movement's success.[19]

But those understandings had changed. Or rather, they had never been as universally endorsed as welfare capitalists had hoped. From the beginning, labor leaders had refused to accept welfare capitalists' assertion of a fundamental distinction between public and private welfare. In their eyes, provisions that promoted labor dependency, irrespective of their source, were injurious to workers' well-being. The rank and file had likewise judged welfare work more on the basis of what it had delivered than on its rhetorical trappings. Although welfare capitalist ideologues had worked hard to sell the welfare label, workers themselves had viewed welfare work through the lens of practical experience. By the 1920s, these experiences had yielded mixed reviews. In two decades, welfare work had developed a checkered past that language alone could not erase.

With such an uneven history behind the welfare label, it was hardly surprising that welfare employers and industrial relations consultants eventually denounced it. As early as World War I, labor specialists were urging employers to attach the more neutral title of "service work" to company programs. "Welfare work," vocational consultant Daniel Bloomfield warned in his 1920 employee service manual, "will always be associated with paternalism and its abuses." Whether applied to the private or the public sector, welfare had come to signify charity, dependence, and emasculation. The label, if not the benefits, would have to go.[20]

In the 1920s Bloomfield's observation became the majority view among managers. In a 1923 article fittingly titled "Shall We Say Farewell to 'Welfare'?" the labor expert Maxwell Droke characterized the "problem with welfare" in the postwar era. For Droke, the problem lay in the twin realms of semantics and practice, in what welfare had come to symbolize and what it delivered in practice. The two, of course, were integrally yoked: the term "welfare work" had fallen into disrepute precisely because company offerings were substantively meager and ideologically encumbered. According to Droke, workplace benefits were packaged in a patronizing ideology that denied employees their dignity and self-respect; by telling workers, "You *must* be interested in

19. For a discussion of the origins of the term "welfare work," see Chapter 1.

20. Daniel Bloomfield, *Labor Maintenance: A Practical Handbook of Employees' Service Work* (New York: Ronald Press, 1920), p. 19.

this nice library of good moral books we have provided," employers had tried to "force the interests of workmen along unnatural lines." Workers were resentful. As Droke put it, "The workman of today sees straight, and *thinks* straight. You can't put anything like that over on him. . . . Working people [do not] take any stock in the 'uplift' welfare department. Why should they? They are independent, self-reliant American citizens who quite properly resent the so-called services so patronizingly rendered in the name of sweet charity."[21] Droke suggested that welfare work be reformed. As a starting point, it needed a new name. But it also needed a change of heart, a reorientation to anchor workplace benefits in impartial principles rather than sentimental aspirations.[22]

Other labor analysts agreed. Collectively, they called for a dramatic transformation of welfare work. They demanded fewer paternalistic and more self-help programs; they dismissed social group activities in favor of individualized benefits. They criticized programs that seemed to carry charitable overtones and called instead for financial perquisites that buttressed workers' financial security as breadwinners.[23]

Throughout this discussion, commentators' criticisms depicted the disgruntled welfare work recipient as male. Engaging organized labor's gendered critique of welfare work, industrial relations experts expressed sensitivity to the manhood/dependency debate. They agreed that the worst features of welfare work affronted American manhood. Feminizing the evils of welfare programs—their implication of dependence, reliance on charity, intrusive attempts at moral reform and social activities (what one commentator called "hurrah-stuff" welfare work)— they called for the masculinization of welfare work. As the industrial relations counselor Charles Lippincott explained in his critique of welfare work, Progressive era plans

---

21. Maxwell Droke, "Shall We Say Farewell to 'Welfare?' " *Industrial Management* 66 (October 1923): 206.

22. Ibid.

23. One industrial analyst observed that "welfare work" had "been thrown into the discard, since it is recognized that the term . . . savors of charity." Another shrewdly remarked that when the Founding Fathers had ordained the Constitution "to promote the general Welfare," they did not liken welfare to paternalism, uplift, or charity. Regrettably, workers' experiences with welfare work had altered the word's original meaning. If the spirit of welfare work were to continue, it needed both a new name and a "change of heart." See "Jordan-Marsh Ninth Floor Heralds New Era in Personnel Work," *Dry Goods Economist* 13 (March 1920): 76; Bert Hall, "What Is Wrong with 'Welfare?' " *Industrial Management* 67 (June 1924): 355.

had various ramifications, but were of one general character. All of them involved some form of paternalism and a more or less veiled bestowal of gratuities. . . . [Workingmen] did not want welfare work with its paternalism. They did not want what was justly due to them without interference, however well intentioned, with the conduct of their own affairs. They were right. This is the only ground that self-respecting, self-reliant men can stand upon. It is a healthy, independent American attitude, that should be encouraged in the interest of good citizenship, good workmanship and good morals. The sacrifice of independent manhood is too high a price to pay for any material benefit however great.[24]

Like his colleagues, Lippincott proposed not an end to welfare work but a dramatic change in its scope and substance. He called for the abolition of gratuitous reforms, which he termed "something for nothing" measures that "destroy self respect and break down moral fibre." He proposed that employers provide only financial benefits with a "sound economic" basis: paid vacations, pensions, stock purchase schemes, and insurance plans, "plans by which employees [are] given an opportunity to increase their income." By treating the workman as a breadwinner, the company would "reach the motives that determine character and make manhood."[25]

This was not the first time, of course, that advocates of private workplace reform appealed to labor's masculinity to advance their cause. From the movement's inception, welfare work's proponents had made manliness a key issue in championing the preferability of a private system of workplace reform over legislated alternatives. But organized labor groups had repeatedly challenged the veracity of this claim. While contesting among themselves divergent visions of manhood, each had portrayed welfare work as a threat to, if not an outright assault on, labor's masculinity. The frequency and potency of organized labor's critique forced employers and personnel managers to confront the issue of masculinity head-on. Significantly, their responses defended both the importance of being one's own man and the integrity of workplace benefits. Personnel experts conceded that through misguided acts and motives, welfare work had strayed from its original course and suc-

24. Charles A. Lippincott, "Promoting Employee Team Work and Welfare without Paternalism," *Industrial Management* 71 (March 1926): 147.
25. Ibid., pp. 147–48.

cumbed to emasculating tendencies. The purging of gratuitous comforts and the expansion of individualized financial benefits, they
reckoned, would put welfare work back on a masculine track. In the
final analysis, employee benefits would make better breadwinners and,
by extension, better men.

The Masculinization of Benefits

Employers heeded the call to reform. The restructuring of private welfare provisions in the 1920s was complex and far from linear. Some
firms abandoned programs, others established them for the first time,
still others accepted the high-minded management advice and gradually phased out benefits not recognizably quasi-pecuniary. Notwithstanding this unevenness, however, a pattern had emerged by the time
of the Great Depression. By the late 1920s private sector welfare was
most likely to encompass financial benefits furnished to breadwinning
men. A sketch of the scope and character of private sector provision
illustrates the forces behind this change and their larger gendered
meanings.

In the 1920s the number of wage-earning benefit holders increased
rapidly. By 1929, approximately one in seven industrial workers participated in some employee benefit program, compared to only one in
twelve in 1908. As they had in the Progressive era, workers employed
in large firms had better access to benefit programs. In 1929 roughly
20 percent of firms employing over 250 workers had instituted a benefit plan, compared to only 10 to 15 percent of all industrial establishments. Remarkably, however, welfare firms in the late 1920s invested
no more per worker on benefit provisions than they had a decade earlier. Between 1918 and 1929, employers spent an average of 2 percent
of annual payroll costs on welfare expenditures. Although more workers were participating in welfare programs in the 1920s, this expansion
did not occur at companies' expense.[26]

Several changes explain this apparent discrepancy. First, although
the 1920s witnessed an increase in the number of benefit holders, the
variety of programs decreased. Employers in the Progressive era had

26. Jacoby, *Employing Bureaucracy* pp. 189, 196–99; Lescohier, "Working Conditions,"
p. 320; Anice L. Whitney, "Administration and Costs of Industrial Betterment for Employees," *Monthly Review of the Bureau of Labor Statistics* 6 (March 1918): 199; Robert W.
Dunn, *The Americanization of Labor* (1927; New York: AMS Press, 1977), pp. 196–97; H. M.
Gitelman, "Welfare Capitalism Reconsidered," *Labor History* 33 (Winter 1992): 23.

typically favored a cafeteria approach to welfare provision—a veritable buffet of benefits that enabled individual employers both to identify the best ways to induce labor efficiency and to publicize the comforts and cleanliness of industrial life. In the 1920s, when labor's rejection of certain benefits was discernible, a labor surplus was reducing the importance of recruitment and retention incentives, and the political need to portray the workplace as an industrial utopia had greatly diminished, welfare experimentation ended. Employers narrowed benefit choices. Welfare provision came to be dominated by a handful of benefits: stock purchase plans, life insurance, pensions, paid vacations, health and accident insurance, savings plans, and length-of-service bonuses. Second, in keeping with the denunciation of paternalism and the return to a self-help ethos, employee benefits in the 1920s were increasingly contributory, requiring workers to share their costs. Rather than depending on "emasculating" gratuities, workers were expected to pay their own way.

The most popular employee benefit in the 1920s was group insurance. Although the first employee insurance policy was written in 1911, group insurance was predominantly a 1920s phenomenon. In 1912 sales of employee group insurance amounted to $13,172,198; by 1919, $425,574,000; and by the end of 1925, the value of insurance had skyrocketed to roughly $5 billion: in thirteen years the amount invested in insurance had gone up almost 400 times. By October 1928, 5.8 million employees were covered by $7.5 billion of group insurance.[27]

Group insurance was almost always life insurance, a benefit that financially protected the dependents of deceased employees by insuring the lives of the living. Like other 1920s benefits, life insurance affirmed the breadwinner's role as a family provider, someone financially able to provide for dependents. By enrolling in company life insurance, the wage earner assumed financial responsibility for his family by insuring their economic security and livelihood after his death. Most policy holders were men, and most policies were established in male-dominated industries: automobiles and airplanes, electrical supplies, foundries and machine shops, rubber goods, and railroads. Moreover, the minority of

27. U.S. Bureau of Labor Statistics, *Health and Recreation Activities in Industrial Establishments, 1926*, Bulletin 458 (1928), pp. 65–68; Abraham Epstein, "Industrial Welfare Movement Sapping American Trade Unions," *Current History* 24 (July 1926): 518–19; David Brody, "The Rise and Decline of Welfare Capitalism," in *Change and Continuity in Twentieth-Century America: The 1920s*, ed. John Braeman et al. (Columbus: Ohio State University Press, 1968), pp. 147–78. Irving Bernstein, *The Lean Years: A History of the American Worker, 1920–1933* (Boston: Houghton Mifflin, 1960), p. 181.

women who did hold life insurance plans frequently confronted blatant discrimination through payment differentials structured according to the sex of the policyholder; dependents of female subscribers generally received less in annuities than did those of male subscribers. In 1928, for example, the Procter & Gamble plan entitled dependents of male employees to $1,000 in annuities and dependents of female employees to only $500. Using one of the traditional rationalizations of gendered wage differentials, life insurance policies designated the contributions of the male wage earner primary to the economic survival of the family, those of the woman secondary and supplemental. By denying women the means to care independently for dependents, life insurance plans ensured that financial provision became linked exclusively to masculinity. Women wage earners lost out in yet another way. Because life insurance polices had no cash surrender value and terminated when an employee quit or lost her or his job, women wage earners, whose turnover rates were higher than men's, were less likely than men to meet continuous service requirements.[28]

Life insurance was masculinized through other means as well. As the 1920s progressed, insurance plans became increasingly contributory, financed jointly by employer and employed. The National Industrial Conference Board (NICB), organized in May 1916 as a clearinghouse of information on industrial development, found that the proportion of contributory insurance plans jumped from 6.7 percent in 1919 to an astonishing 68 percent in 1925. Contributory plans provided employers with a no-lose proposition. They relieved employers of some of the financial burdens of providing private welfare and at the same time refashioned benefits in a more masculine mold by encouraging workers to manage their own welfare. Promoting self-reliance and financial provision, the contributory model underscored the interconnectedness of masculinity, breadwinning, and "earned" benefits.[29]

The chief characteristics of employee life insurance—its widespread diffusion, the increased use of the contributory model, and employers' conscious casting of employee welfare as pecuniary benefits for men— became the dominant model for benefit provision in the 1920s. Like life insurance, industrial pension plans pledged financial security to the long-term worker. Between 1920 and 1927 the number of such plans roughly doubled, covering close to four million workers by the decade's

28. U.S. Bureau of Labor Statistics, *Health and Recreation Activities*, pp. 66–67; Bernstein, *Lean Years*, p. 181.

29. Committee on Recent Economic Changes, *Recent Economic Changes*, p. 526.

end. Most pension holders and recipients were men. A 1926 NICB report found that although women represented 25 percent of employees in companies providing pensions, they made up only 6 percent of pension recipients.[30]

The development of employee stock ownership followed a similar trajectory. After the business recession of 1920–21, the number of employee stockholders quickly multiplied. By 1926, approximately 1.5 million industrial workers—about 10 percent of all stockholders in the country—owned an estimated six million shares of stock, valued between $700,000 and $800,000, in the companies that employed them. Stock purchasing options were almost fully employee-financed, paid for in installments by wage deductions. Employers' financial burden in issuing stock to workers was limited to purchase incentives: extra dividend payments or the subsidy of the sale of shares at below-market rates. Ownership of stocks reverted back to the company upon termination of employment.[31]

So great was the appeal of employee stockholding in the 1920s that in many firms, including Procter & Gamble, Eastman Kodak, and International Harvester, employees made up a majority of company stockholders by the late 1920s. The democratization of stockholding did not give workers a significantly larger share in corporate ownership, however. At Eastman Kodak, for example, workers represented 57.6 percent of company stockholders in 1926, but the value of their shares amounted to only 8.44 percent of total outstanding stock. At Procter & Gamble, workers constituted 55.8 percent of stockholders, but the value of their shares totaled only 11.61 percent of the value of outstanding stock. The situation was the same at other companies.[32]

If employee stockholding did not provide workers with great riches and power, it nevertheless reaffirmed the possibilities of a masculinist American dream. In this regard, it was consistent with the outlook anchoring the provision of other workplace incentives. Like other private sector benefits, employee stockholding targeted mainly men. It appealed explicitly to male workers' economic aspirations, their respon-

30. Ibid., pp. 526–27; Dunn, *Americanization of Labor*, pp. 181–82; Epstein, "Industrial Welfare Movement," p. 519. Bernstein, *Lean Years*, pp. 181–82; National Industrial Conference Board, "Surveys of the Industrial Relations Department, February 1926," Conference Board Series V, Box 8, Folder "Industrial Relations, 1919–1930," p. 4, Hagley Museum and Library, Wilmington, Del.

31. Committee on Recent Economic Changes, *Recent Economic Changes*, p. 528; Dunn, *Americanization of Labor*, pp. 146–55.

32. Dunn, *Americanization of Labor*, p. 153.

sibilities as breadwinners. It pledged financial success achieved through workers' own efforts: in the case of stockholding, not only did workers purchase their tickets to higher profits with their own money, they also influenced the stock's performance, and hence the size of their dividends, through fast and efficient work.

Collectively these portraits of the provision of individual benefits highlight the dominant changes to employee welfare in the 1920s. Benefit programs in the 1920s differed in several respects from those of the Progressive era. Whereas welfare schemes in the Progressive period had balanced social, educational, and athletic programs with financial incentives, provisions in the 1920s favored the latter: quasi-pecuniary benefits, professionally administered, that breadwinners "earned." The sexual composition of benefit holders changed as well. In the Progressive era, women wage earners had constituted the majority of company welfare recipients. By the end of the 1920s, welfare benefits had become almost exclusively a male preserve. In the course of a decade, private welfare provision had evolved from social gratuities administered by and for women to financial benefits administered by and for men.

Epilogue

Changes to the substance and scope of private sector employee benefits in the 1920s tell a tale of discontinuity, of patterns of industrial relations that shifted dramatically over time. Though an important tale, it is not the final chapter in the history of employee welfare. The reorientation of employee benefits in the 1920s occurred within a larger framework of continuity characterized by the continued importance of employers to workplace provision. What linked the welfare work movement of the Progressive era to the 1920s, indeed, what links it to working conditions and the welfare state today, was the vital role of employers as welfare providers.

In the Progressive era wage earners in the United States had to rely on employers rather than the government for social and financial security. In times of sickness, retirement, and financial duress, employers, not government agencies, provided a safety net, fragile, small, and porous though it was. To a degree often overlooked, the same pattern prevails today. To be sure, benefit options have changed markedly since the turn of the century. Most striking, since the 1930s the federal government has claimed responsibility for guaranteeing, if not actually paying for, basic provisions. Nevertheless, since the Progressive era, American wage earners have continued to receive most of their welfare benefits from employers, not the state.

The prevalence of private benefits and the paucity of public provisions were interconnected developments. In the 1920s veteran advocates of statutory reforms who had seen their pleas for state provisions go largely unanswered commented frequently on the connection. From their perspective, the popularity of the private model in the Progressive era had doomed proposed public alternatives. The social welfare expert Abraham Epstein attributed the privatization of workers' welfare in the 1920s to the political victory of welfare capitalism. It was no accident, he reflected in 1926, that "the most extensive development of the major features of . . . 'welfare work' parallel[ed] the period of agitation for protective labor laws." Progressive era employers, anxious "to anticipate or avoid governmental regulation and legislation," had made voluntarism so attractive a model of reform that the drive for legislated change had been successfully repelled. In the final analysis, welfare capitalism's triumph had foretold welfare statism's defeat.[1]

Advocates of state protections refuted the voluntarist argument that the source of provision for workers—government or industry—mattered less than provision itself. The privatization of employee benefits in the 1920s, they argued, victimized *all* American workers. The first problem, they insisted, was coverage. Notwithstanding the attention garnered by the diffusion of employee benefits in the 1920s, welfare firms continued to account for only a minority of business establishments, welfare beneficiaries only a minority of workers. Government laws might have protected a greater proportion of workers. Related to the issue of access was workers' legal claims to benefits. Whereas company plans were discretionary, permitting employers to shrink benefits, abandon programs, and even fire workers shortly before they were scheduled to collect promised payments, state entitlements would have made benefits a permanent, or at least less easily revoked, feature of industrial relations. Finally, notwithstanding talk of welfare capitalists' magnanimity, state assistance, had it been institutionalized through law, could have been more generous than private sector provisions. In 1927 Robert Dunn reported that employers contributed five times more to state social insurance schemes in Europe than in the United States. Was it too late, he wondered, to make American employers pay up?[2]

1. Abraham Epstein, "Industrial Welfare Movement Sapping American Trade Unions," *Current History* 24 (July 1926): 517.
2. Robert Dunn, *The Americanization of Labor* (1927; New York: AMS Press, 1977), p. 268.

The shortcomings of the private welfare model, lamented by critics in the 1920s, were not eradicated in the 1930s, despite the construction of a welfare state. Historians who have viewed the New Deal as welfare capitalism's last gasp have argued that the creation of a welfare state in the 1930s corrected many of these shortcomings by eliminating the private system of employee welfare that produced them. To date, labor historians have favored a welfare-capitalism-displaced-by-welfare-statism interpretation of the New Deal. David Brody's argument that welfare capitalism and the "paternalistic course of American industrial relations might well have continued but for the Great Depression" suggests that, in the long run, it did not. The Depression and the New Deal, Brody argues, made the 1930s a post–welfare capitalist age. Stuart Brandes has likewise emphasized a permanent shift in the 1930s from a bipartite to a tripartite industrial relations system, a transition he attributes to the gradual eclipse of welfare capitalism in the 1920s and the coming of the New Deal. More recently, Lizabeth Cohen has depicted the failure of welfare capitalism during the Depression as a necessary precondition for New Deal support, one that transferred workers' loyalties from employers to the state.[3]

These interpretations exaggerate the degree to which welfare statism replaced welfare capitalism. To be sure, the Depression hit welfare programs and the wider economy hard. Work-sharing programs, favored by most welfare firms in the initial stages of the Depression, were usually followed by massive dismissals. Jobless workers not only stopped collecting immediate benefits, they lost their claim to future payments. In firm after firm, benefits shrank or were simply abandoned, as in the case of the Ford Motor Company, which eliminated its legendary profit-sharing plan in 1931. But even in the midst of the economic slump, many firms continued to finance employee benefit programs. A 1935 National Industrial Conference Board survey of 233 companies found, for instance, that only seven firms had terminated pension plans, only two had dropped group life insurance, and only one had dissolved its mutual benefit association. On balance, the Depression pushed private employee benefits in some firms into a state of dormancy but not obliv-

---

3. David Brody, "The Rise and Decline of Welfare Capitalism," in *Change and Continuity in Twentieth-Century America: The 1920s*, ed. John Braeman et al. (Columbus: Ohio State University Press, 1968), pp. 147–78; Stuart D. Brandes, *American Welfare Capitalism, 1880–1940* (Chicago: University of Chicago Press, 1976), pp. 142–48; Lizabeth Cohen, *Making a New Deal: Industrial Workers in Chicago, 1919–1939* (New York: Cambridge University Press, 1990), p. 160.

ion. The welfare state that followed supplemented rather than supplanted welfare capitalism.[4]

The terms of the major labor-related New Deal legislation—the Social Security Act, the Fair Labor Standards Act, and the National Labor Relations Act—are well known. In the short term, organizations such as the Public Works Administration and the Works Progress Administration created jobs for millions of Americans. In the long run, the New Deal permanently altered the structure of labor relations by protecting industrial workers' right to unionize, regulating their hours of work, and establishing a minimum wage. These regulations not only had an immediate impact on workers, they permanently altered the path of American industrial relations. They did not, however, usher in a comprehensive welfare state for workers. The major work entitlements created by the Social Security Act, pensions and unemployment insurance, were few and woefully inadequate. Denounced by the National Association of Manufacturers, the National Chamber of Commerce, the National Industrial Conference Board, and virtually every other major business organization in the country as unbridled socialism, social security actually operated within the strict confines of the private enterprise system. Shaped by the history of employee welfare in the Progressive era and the 1920s, it celebrated the language of male independence, validated the man's role as provider, and affirmed the male industrial worker as the backbone of the modern economy. To a large extent, social security reproduced the biases and shortcomings of the private sector model.

Unemployment insurance made a clear distinction between social insurance and public assistance. Funded by a payroll tax on employers, it offered temporary relief in times of involuntary joblessness. Employees in agriculture, domestic service, and small firms were not covered. State regulations specified the weekly compensation ceiling, typically around half of the worker's former wages, and a maximum period of compensation, usually ten weeks. To be eligible, workers had to demonstrate their availability for work. Unemployment insurance compensated only "deserving" industrial breadwinners, the vast majority of whom were male and had a strong employment history.[5]

4. H. F. Brown, "Industrial Relations Activities Survive a Critical Test," *Personnel Journal* 13, no. 5 (1935): 258–62.

5. Sanford M. Jacoby, "Employers and the Welfare State: The Role of Marion B. Folsom," *Journal of American History* 80 (September 1993): 528, 540–44; Mimi Abramovitz, *Regulating the Lives of Women: Social Welfare Policy from Colonial Times to the Present* (Boston: South End Press, 1988), pp. 289–95.

Pensions were a fiscally conservative measure, financed by a 1 percent regressive payroll tax levied jointly on employers and workers. Like many private welfare plans, old-age insurance was contributory, requiring workers to shoulder financial responsibility for their own benefits, to "pay their own way." Strict eligibility requirements excluded roughly half of all workers, particularly women and persons of color employed in nonindustrial settings. Those fortunate enough to be covered by the plan, moreover, could not count on long-term financial security. Workers forced to move from covered to uncovered work forfeited their eligibility. In addition, Congress established a monthly payment ceiling, initially set at $85. Because retirement payments were tied directly to wages, poorer workers received the smallest pensions. The majority of industrial workers initially received no more than $20 a month.[6]

The meagerness and limited scope of government welfare, conditioned by the business assumptions and practices of the previous thirty years, enabled employers to continue to play an important role in the provision of benefits. After the Social Security Act went into effect, employers stepped in to supplement the inadequate provisions of public pensions. Between 1936 and 1939 more private pension plans were established than disbanded. Congress further encouraged welfare privatization by exempting expenditures on employee benefits from payroll taxes in 1939. In effect, this exemption made welfare capitalism a state-supported policy.[7]

World War II gave the drive for private benefits an added boost. The War Labor Board (WLB) froze wages but exempted health and pension plans from wage controls. Facing widespread labor shortages, employers used this exemption to make benefits the basis for recruiting and retaining workers. Organized labor, for its part, finally hopped onto the benefits bandwagon. Unable to demand higher wages, the AFL and Congress of Industrial Organizations (CIO) found in the WLB's benefits exemption a new arena for negotiating contracts. Unsuccessful in their efforts to expand government provisions to workers through legislative action, union leaders focused instead on improvements achieved through collective bargaining. Historically a bread-and-butter union federation that had viewed welfare work warily, the AFL now found itself in the curious position of insisting on the necessity of bread, butter, and benefits.[8]

6. Abramovitz, *Regulating the Lives of Women*, pp. 248–51.
7. Jacoby, "Employers and the Welfare State," p. 546.
8. My argument here follows that of Jacoby, ibid., p. 547. Steven Fraser has demon-

But it was the CIO, not the AFL, that was chiefly responsible for ushering in what economists have called the postwar "fringe benefits revolution." Concentrated in huge mass-production industries, the CIO was better positioned than the AFL, divided into craft units dealing individually with tens of thousands of employers, to effect widespread change through negotiation. The rapid growth of unionization, peaking at a high of 40 percent of the labor force in 1946, gave mass-production unions, which registered the majority of membership gains, unprecedented leverage. With stable cost-of-living rates weakening unions' argument for wage increases and government welfare covering what union leaders considered only "basic minimums," bargaining for benefits made sound economic sense. As Walter Reuther of the United Auto Workers (UAW) explained to UAW executive board members in 1949, wages were "still a problem and still fall short of what the worker needs." But stable living costs "enable us to turn our attention to other urgent matters that inflationary pressures have hitherto forced into the background."[9]

In lieu of higher wages, unions successfully fought for and secured employee benefits. In 1946 John L. Lewis negotiated his first welfare fund and in 1948 won a contract for 400,000 miners that included a $100-million-a-year fund for pensions (at a time when the average individual old-age pension was under $25) and millions more for hospitalization, death benefits, and the retraining of injured miners. Lewis's unprecedented victory encouraged other union leaders to follow suit. In 1948 the National Labor Relations Board (NLRB) gave unions' newfound benefits strategy a green light. In *Inland Steel Co. v. NLRB*, the NLRB declared benefit plans to be in the same category as wages or "other conditions of employment" and thus made them a mandatory subject of collective bargaining. By 1957 75 percent of major labor agreements provided for increases in fringe benefits, predominantly pensions, vacation pay, life insurance, and health care.[10]

---

strated the Amalgamated Clothing Workers of America's support of state provision of distributive reforms such as social security that predated the New Deal. See Fraser, "Dress Rehearsal for the New Deal: Shop-Floor Insurgents, Political Elites, and Industrial Democracy in the Amalgamated Clothing Workers," in *Working-Class America: Essays on Labor, Community, and American Society*, ed. Michael H. Frish and Daniel J. Walkowitz (Urbana: University of Illinois Press, 1983): 212–52.

9. Juliet Schor, *The Overworked American: The Unexpected Decline of Leisure* (New York: Basic Books, 1992), p. 66; "Welfare Is the Big Issue," *New Republic* 7 (March 1949): 11–13; American Social History Project, *Who Built America? Working People and the Nation's Economy, Politics, Culture, and Society*, vol. 2 (New York: Pantheon, 1992), p. 506.

10. "Welfare Is the Big Issue," pp. 11–12; Jacoby, "Employers and the Welfare State,"

But it was more than structural obstacles to wage bargaining that made unions the driving force behind the postwar benefits boom. As George Lipsitz has shown in his study of labor in the 1940s, the benefits boom was part of a deal struck between organized labor and big business that occurred against the backdrop of an energized union movement and the consolidation of corporate capitalism. Emboldened, frustrated, and willing to act, organized labor in the postwar years offered a cogent critique of corporate capitalism, itself a much stronger entity in the wake of economic expansion and unprecedented government military spending during the war, which with taxpayers' dollars had strengthened the already prodigious grip of big business over the economy. Demanding full employment and opposing workplace encroachments ranging from technological regimentation to managers' growing bureaucratic authority, workers transformed mass demonstrations and strikes into an all-out assault on "corporate liberal presumptions about the congruence between the national interest and the interests of the big corporations." Refusing to bargain about the fundamental issue of management control in the workplace, corporate leaders offered, as they alone were financially empowered to do, huge benefits to union members to win their support. In accepting this deal, organized labor got something in return. The pension plans that became a fixture of union contracts in the late 1940s and 1950s satisfied workers' need for security, gave union leaders a say in fund management and economic decision making, and tied workers' loyalty to the company *and* the union. Ironically, because payments to pension funds were invested in the high-yielding stocks of large corporations, such "concessions" to organized labor served to cement the hegemony of corporate capitalism. Generous fringe benefits also helped to purchase organize labor's political accommodation to corporate liberalism by undercutting concerns about the inadequacies of social security provisions.[11]

Although union members were the principal beneficiaries of these agreements, union contracts also encouraged the establishment and growth of benefits in nonunion establishments. To be sure, workers in heavily unionized industries generally fared better; in 1954, for instance, oil refiners paid 56 cents an hour per worker for fringe benefits,

---

p. 551; Jay Conison, *Employee Benefit Plans* (St. Paul: West, 1993), p. 44; "Fringes Moving Up with Wages," *U.S. News & World Report*, October 25, 1957, p. 125.

11. See George Lipsitz, *Rainbow at Midnight: Labor and Culture in the 1940s* (Urbana: University of Illinois Press, 1994), pp. 57–61, 167–69, 229–48.

hotel proprietors only 20. But in general, union and nonunion workers increasingly found themselves on the receiving end of more and better benefits. Beginning in 1947, increases in fringe benefits surpassed wage increases, between 1947 and 1953 by a third. By 1954 employers total expenditures on fringes were estimated to be $22.9 billion, compared with less than $500 million spent on comparable benefits in 1929. The astronomical rise in these expenditures attests to the persisting importance of private sector welfare in the post–New Deal order.[12]

Indeed, private employee benefits not only coexisted with public provisions in postwar America, they surpassed them in both number and financial weight. By 1956 American employers were spending on private benefits roughly double what they spent on public programs— social security, workers' compensation, and state unemployment insurance.[13]

In succeeding decades, welfare privatization became even more expansive. Today the welfare of American workers is tended to chiefly by employers. The most popular employee benefits resemble those of the 1920s: contractual and individualized, they provide financial security to long-term breadwinners. But one important feature distinguishes the provision of workplace benefits then and now: the proportion of wage earners who receive them. In the late 1960s, access to private benefits became a majority experience. By 1970 most full-time wage earners had employer-provided life insurance and medical coverage. In the continued absence of statutory provisions, the privatization of employee welfare has made employers the chief guarantors of workers' security. Today an even higher proportion of full-time workers is covered by employer-provided health plans and life insurance. Most get paid time off for holidays and vacations. People who work in firms that employ more than 100 workers receive even more benefits; the Bureau of Labor Statistics found that the majority of employees in medium and large establishments received pensions and dental insurance in 1993. Only a minority of those who worked in small firms received those benefits (Table 6).[14]

12. "A Lot of Pay Is in the 'Fringe,'" *U.S. News & World Report*, October 22, 1954, pp. 97–98; "For 'Welfare Benefits'—11.7 Billion Dollars a Year," ibid., September 13, 1957, p. 106; "How 'Fringes' Are Boosting Labor Costs," ibid., September 14, 1964, p. 81.

13. Jacoby, "Employers and the Welfare State," p. 577; "For 'Welfare Benefits'—11.7 Billion Dollars a Year"; "What Workers Are Getting on Top of Big Pay Raises," *U.S. News & World Report*, January 18, 1971, pp. 56–57.

14. U.S. Department of Commerce, Bureau of the Census, *Historical Statistics of the United States: Colonial Times to 1970*, pt. 1 (Washington, D.C.: Government Printing Office,

Table 6. Benefits provided to full-time employees by private establishments, 1992–93, by size of firm (percent)

Benefit program	Small firms, 1992[a]	Medium and large firms, 1993[b]
Paid leave		
Holidays	82%	91%
Vacations	88	97
Personal leave	12	21
Lunch period	9	9
Rest time	49	68
Funeral leave	50	83
Jury duty leave	58	90
Military leave	21	53
Sick leave	53	65
Maternity leave	2	3
Paternity leave	1	1
Insurance		
Sickness and accident	26	44
Long-term disability	23	41
Medical	71	82
Dental	33	62
Life	64	91
Retirement benefits[c]	45	78
Child care	2	7

[a]Fewer than 100 employees.
[b]At least 100 employees.
[c]Defined benefit and defined contribution plans.
Sources: U.S. Bureau of Labor Statistics, *Employee Benefits in Small Private Establishments, 1992*, Bulletin 2441 (1994), pp. 5–6; U.S. Bureau of Labor Statistics, *Employee Benefits in Medium and Large Private Establishments, 1993*, Bulletin 2456 (1994), pp. 8, 10.

American employers continue to spend considerably more on fringe benefits than they do on legally required provisions such as social security and unemployment insurance. In 1996, discretionary benefits accounted for 67.6 percent of total spending on benefits by employers in the private sector (Table 7).[15]

The unchallenged strength of the private model has kept American workers in a precarious position. Most of the concerns raised by critics

---

1976), p. 344; U.S. Bureau of Labor Statistics, *Employee Benefits in Small Private Establishments, 1992*, Bulletin 2441 (1994), pp. 5–6; U.S. Bureau of Labor Statistics, *Employee Benefits in Medium and Large Private Establishments, 1993*, Bulletin 2456 (1994), pp. 8–10.

15. William J. Wiatrowski, "Factors Affecting Retirement Income," *Monthly Labor Review* 116 (March 1993): 25–35.

Table 7. Costs to private employers for legally required and discretionary employee benefits per hour worked, 1996, by type of firm

Type of firm	Legally required benefits[a]		Discretionary benefits[b]		All benefits	
	Amount	Percent	Amount	Percent	Amount	Percent
Goods producer[c]	$2.08	30.2%	$4.81	69.8%	$6.89	100%
Service provider[d]	1.44	33.7	2.83	66.3	4.27	100
Manufacturer	1.86	27.1	5.00	72.9	6.86	100
Nonmanufacturing firm	1.53	34.3	2.93	65.7	4.46	100
Average, all private firms	1.59	32.4	3.32	67.6	4.91	100

[a]Social security, federal and state unemployment insurance, workers' compensation.
[b]Paid leave, supplemental pay, life and health insurance, retirement benefits, savings.
[c]Mining, construction, manufacturing.
[d]Transportation, communications, public utilities, wholesale trade, retail trade, finance, insurance, real estate, services.
Source: U.S. Bureau of Labor Statistics, *Compensation and Working Conditions* 1 (December 1996): 60 (reporting survey of March 1996).

of welfare capitalism in the 1910s and 1920s are still valid. There are new worries as well.

The provision of fringe benefits remains discretionary. Federal and state laws require employers to make payments on employees' behalf for social security, workers' compensation, and unemployment insurance, but they do not compel employers to furnish fringe benefits. Thus, although federal and state laws regulate the way benefits are financed and administered, the regulations themselves do not ensure coverage, nor do they protect workers from the termination of benefits. Indeed, in 1976, two years after Congress passed the Employee Retirement Income Security Act to regulate private pensions and welfare funds, more than 34,000 firms had dismantled such plans.[16]

Benefit eligibility and payment criteria continue to be set by companies, so that employers decide who gets what under what terms. One restriction that has frequently been structured into the administration of benefits is a high minimum-service requirement, obligating employees to work for a company for a predetermined length of time before they become eligible for benefits. Paid vacations, personal leave, sick leave, and retirement income are all popular workplace benefits that typically carry this requirement. Minimum-service requirements make it possible for employees to work their entire adult lives in firms with private pension plans without collecting employer contributions upon

16. Robert Ellis Smith, *Workrights* (New York: E. P. Dutton, 1983), p. 193.

retirement because decisions (made out of choice or necessity) to leave work or switch jobs prevented them from meeting vesting requirements. Although some workers, notably teachers and professors, are fortunate enough to be protected by multiemployer pension plans that make employers' contributions portable among educational institutions, 90 percent of workers have no such option.[17]

These restrictions, which on paper apply to all workers equally, in fact do not affect them equally. Service requirements exact a particularly hard toll on women workers, who are more likely than men to enter the paid labor force for the first time in their forties or fifties. Women wage earners are also most likely to interrupt their employment, thereby losing service requirement credits, to care for families; because fewer than 10 percent of employers subsidize child care costs and parenting is still chiefly identified with mothering, staying at home often becomes a necessity. Women, moreover, constitute the majority— 68 percent—of the part-time labor force, a status that disqualifies many of them from most benefit programs.[18]

Coverage is also affected by other factors. Employees in large companies generally get more and better benefits. Union status is also important. In 1993, 90 percent of unionized workers employed in medium and large establishments but only 79 percent of their nonunion counterparts received medical benefits. When the distribution of benefits to workers employed in establishments of all sized is analyzed, the correlation between union status and the receipt of benefits is even more pronounced. Industry is also a good predictor of coverage. In 1996, employers spent on discretionary benefits to service workers 38 percent of what they spent on blue-collar workers and only 37 percent of what they spent on white-collar workers. These variations, combined with the continued segregation of the labor force by race, ethnicity, and sex, ensure that women and minorities are the groups least likely to receive employment benefits.[19]

17. Ibid, pp. 193–96; "Labor Month in Review," *Monthly Labor Review* 116 (January 1993): 2.
18. Smith, *Workrights*, p. 194; Schor, *The Overworked American*, p. 145; "Labor Month in Review," p. 2; part-time labor force statistics calculated from U.S. Bureau of Labor Statistics, *Employment and Earnings* 43 (December 1996): 19; for disparities in benefits received by full-time and part-time workers, see U.S. Bureau of Labor Statistics, *Compensation and Working Conditions* 1 (December 1996): 74.
19. U.S. Bureau of Labor Statistics, *Employee Benefits in Medium and Large Private Establishments, 1993*, p. 165; U.S. Bureau of Labor Statistics, *Employee Benefits Survey: A BLS Reader*, Bulletin 2459 (1993), pp. 16–24, 33–36; U.S. Bureau of Labor Statistics, *Compensation and Working Conditions* 1 (December 1996): 61–62.

As a benefit counselor observed in 1988, what we think of today as the welfare state has been constructed not on the backbone of government subsidies but "through corporate America in the delivery of social-benefit programs to the working middle class." Workers' dependence on a private sector safety net has made the United States unique among industrial nations. At the turn of the century, when Western European nations were incorporating company policies into the public system, the United States stuck with the status quo. In the 1930s New Deal measures reconfigured the welfare landscape, but not enough to eradicate workers' need for supplemental provisions. Over time, America's private welfare safety net has grown, taking the place of what other countries provide to their workers by law.[20]

Today the safety of this private welfare net is under siege. In the wake of corporate downsizing, thousands of full-time jobs have shifted from large corporations to smaller, upstart firms unable or unwilling to foot the benefits bill. As the manufacturing segment of the labor force continues to shrink, pink slips terminate both jobs and benefits. The fastest-growing sector of the economy, the service sector, typically offers low-paying and part-time jobs with few or no benefits.

The economic restructuring of the late 1980s and early 1990s has brought the weaknesses of America's private welfare system into bold relief. To cut costs, employers have transferred an ever-increasing portion of benefit expenses to employees. Employers' contributions to defined benefit pension plans have slipped from $61 billion in 1978 to $18.9 billion in 1990; in contrast, the number of defined contribution plans, in which workers contribute the majority—and sometimes all—of retirement savings, has mushroomed. To reign in health costs, currently rising more than twice as fast as inflation, employers are insisting that workers pay more expenses out of pocket: higher deductibles, higher copayments, more direct costs. Paradoxically, employees ravaged by the spiraling costs of benefits are the lucky ones: 43 million Americans have no health insurance, even though more than half of the uninsured work full-time.[21]

The benefits crisis is particularly disturbing because of the choices employers have for remedying it. The private welfare model is premised on the right of employers to terminate and modify the terms of benefit

20. "Benefits Shock: How to Protect Yourself from Cuts in Health Care and Other Benefits," *U.S. News & World Report*, March 28, 1988, p. 58.
21. "Retirement's Worried Face," *New York Times*, July 20, 1995, pp. 1–5; "Benefits Shock," pp. 58–59; "Uninsured Working, Not Getting Care," *UAW Washington Report*, November 29, 1996, p. 1.

provision unilaterally. Ironically, in ceding this right to employers, legislators have allowed business interests, not workers' interests, to dictate the scope and character of employee welfare.

The liabilities of the private sector system were not inevitable because the model from which they sprang was never foreordained. The private welfare system was historically constructed, not predetermined by a mythic, immutable "American way." In much the same way that corporations today aggressively advertise the virtues of private health insurance to ward off more universal protections, many employers at the turn of the century used welfare capitalism to keep welfare statism in check. Their success in the Progressive era, affirmed in succeeding decades and modified but not supplanted by public provisions, has made employers the chief custodians of employee welfare. A precarious relationship for the millions of workers who must depend on their employers for financial, retirement, and health security, it is one of the legacies of welfare capitalism.

Index